Accelerated GWT

Building Enterprise Google Web Toolkit Applications

Vipul Gupta

Apress®

Accelerated GWT: Building Enterprise Google Web Toolkit Applications

Copyright © 2008 by Vipul Gupta

ISBN-13 (pbk): 978-1-59059-975-4

ISBN-10 (pbk): 1-59059-975-6

ISBN-13 (electronic): 978-1-4302-0616-3

ISBN-10 (electronic): 1-4302-0616-0

Printed and bound in the United States of America 9 8 7 6 5 4 3 2 1

Trademarked names may appear in this book. Rather than use a trademark symbol with every occurrence of a trademarked name, we use the names only in an editorial fashion and to the benefit of the trademark owner, with no intention of infringement of the trademark.

Lead Editor: Clay Andres
Technical Reviewer: Eric Briley
Editorial Board: Clay Andres, Steve Anglin, Ewan Buckingham, Tony Campbell, Gary Cornell,
    Jonathan Gennick, Matthew Moodie, Joseph Ottinger, Jeffrey Pepper, Frank Pohlmann,
    Ben Renow-Clarke, Dominic Shakeshaft, Matt Wade, Tom Welsh
Senior Project Manager: Tracy Brown Collins
Copy Editor: Kim Wimpsett
Associate Production Director: Kari Brooks-Copony
Production Editor: Ellie Fountain
Compositor: Molly Sharp
Proofreader: Liz Welch
Indexer: Beth Palmer
Artist: Kinetic Publishing Services, LLC
Cover Designer: Kurt Krames
Manufacturing Director: Tom Debolski

Distributed to the book trade worldwide by Springer-Verlag New York, Inc., 233 Spring Street, 6th Floor, New York, NY 10013. Phone 1-800-SPRINGER, fax 201-348-4505, e-mail orders-ny@springer-sbm.com, or visit http://www.springeronline.com.

For information on translations, please contact Apress directly at 2855 Telegraph Avenue, Suite 600, Berkeley, CA 94705. Phone 510-549-5930, fax 510-549-5939, e-mail info@apress.com, or visit http://www.apress.com.

Apress and friends of ED books may be purchased in bulk for academic, corporate, or promotional use. eBook versions and licenses are also available for most titles. For more information, reference our Special Bulk Sales–eBook Licensing web page at http://www.apress.com/info/bulksales.

The source code for this book is available to readers at http://www.apress.com.

To my parents, for always being supportive and loving

Contents at a Glance

About the Author xv

Acknowledgments xvii

Introduction xix

PART 1 ■ ■ ■ Getting Started with GWT

■CHAPTER 1   GWT Basics and a First Application 3

■CHAPTER 2   GWT Architecture and Internal Features 27

PART 2 ■ ■ ■ UI Programming and Client-Server Communication

■CHAPTER 3   UI Programming: Basic Widgets 59

■CHAPTER 4   Communication: RPC 89

■CHAPTER 5   UI Programming: Handling Events and Using Advanced Widgets . . . 105

■CHAPTER 6   Communication: Advanced Techniques 135

PART 3 ■ ■ ■ Making Applications Ready for the Real World

■CHAPTER 7   Testing GWT Applications 171

■CHAPTER 8   Internationalizing Your Applications: A Modern-Day Reality 201

■CHAPTER 9   Some Important, Not-to-Be-Missed Techniques 233

■CHAPTER 10   Peeking Into the Upcoming GWT 1.5 Release 265

■INDEX 283

Contents

About the Author xv

Acknowledgments xvii

Introduction xix

PART 1 ■ ■ ■ Getting Started with GWT

■CHAPTER 1   GWT Basics and a First Application 3

Setting Up Your GWT Environment 4

Hosted Mode vs. Web Mode 4

    Web Mode 4

    Hosted Mode 5

What Are All Those GWT Files For? 6

Creating Your First GWT Application 6

    Tools for Creating a Project 6

    Running the Application Using Generated Scripts 9

Working with Modules in GWT 11

    Structure of a Module File 11

Creating the Host HTML File 15

Steps to Create a GWT Application 16

Creating Another Application Step-by-Step 17

    Creating the Basic Project Structure 17

    Adding the Module File 17

    Creating the Entry-Point Class 18

    Creating the Host HTML File 21

    Running the Application in Hosted Mode 22

Summary 25

■CHAPTER 2   GWT Architecture and Internal Features 27

Understanding the Components That Make Up the GWT Framework . . . 27

    Development Tools Explained 27

    Class Libraries Explained 28

What Version of the Java Language Does the GWT Support? 31

The Same Origin Policy and Its Implications on GWT 33

    Same Origin Policy Explained 33

    What Are the Implications of the Same Origin Policy on GWT? ... 34

Deferred Binding 34

Understanding Generator, Related Classes, and Code Generation

    Using Generators 36

    Example of Using Generator to Autogenerate Code for Your

        Applications 39

    Building the Generator-Based Application 40

GWT: Startup/Bootstrap Process 52

Summary 55

■CHAPTER 3   **UI Programming: Basic Widgets** 59

GUI Building with Fundamental Widgets 59

    Hierarchy of Base Classes Explained 60

    How Do You Use the Widgets Provided by GWT? 65

Understanding Layouts Using Panels 70

    Starting with a RootPanel 72

    Aligning Widgets Using a CellPanel 72

    What Is an HTMLTable Panel? 76

    What Is a FlowPanel? 78

Creating Complex Widgets Using Composites 79

    Developing a Sample Application Using Composites 80

Summary 86

■CHAPTER 4   **Communication: RPC** 89

Understanding RPC 89

How to Use RPC in GWT 90

    Creating Service Interface (Also Called the Synchronous Interface) ... 90

    Creating the Asynchronous Interface 91

    Understanding the AsyncCallback Interface 91

    Making an Actual Remote Procedure Call 92

Your First Complete RPC Example 93

RPC in GWT: Behind the Scenes 100

Summary 103

■CHAPTER 5   **UI Programming: Handling Events and Using Advanced Widgets** 105

Handling Events Generated by Widgets 105
    Handling Events Using Listeners 107
    Handling Events Using Adapter Classes 108
Styling Applications Using CSS 110
    How Do Nested CSS Classes Apply to GWT Widgets? 111
    Including Style Sheets in Your GWT Application 112
Using the TabBar Widget 114
Using the TabPanel Widget 116
Optimizing Applications Using ImageBundle 119
    Understanding AbstractImagePrototype 120
    Sample Application Demonstrating the Use of ImageBundle 121
    How Does an ImageBundle Work? 129
Building Classic HTML Forms Using FormPanel 130
    The HasName Interface (in the com.google.gwt.user.client.ui
        Package) 131
    Sample Application Demonstrating the Use of FormPanel 131
Summary 134

■CHAPTER 6   **Communication: Advanced Techniques** 135

What Is Serialization? 135
    Examining the Different Type of Objects That Can Be Used in
        Communication 136
    Making User-Defined Serializable Classes 136
Designing an RPC Application 136
    Creating the Domain Objects Used for Communication 138
    Handling UI Events 139
    Defining the Service and Asynchronous Interfaces 140
    Creating the Callback Classes 141
    Creating the Controller Class 142
    Writing the Server-Side Implementation 144
    Mapping the Server-Side Path in the Module's XML File 144
    Running the Application 145
Serializing Collection Classes 146
    Understanding Collection Classes Using a Comprehensive
        Example 147
    Creating the Entry-Point Class 151
    Example of Using HashMap 161

Creating Custom Field Serializers 162
    Understanding the SerializationStreamWriter Interface 162
    Understanding the SerializationStreamReader Interface 163
Communicating with Server Using HTTP Requests 166
Summary 168

PART 3 ■ ■ ■ Making Applications Ready for the Real World

■CHAPTER 7   **Testing GWT Applications** 171

Understanding the junitCreator Utility 172
    Creating Sample Tests Using the junitCreator Utility 172
Writing GWT-Based Unit Tests 174
    Examining the GWTTestCase Class 175
    Creating Tests Without Using the junitCreator Utility 178
    Running the Tests 179
    Points to Remember While Creating a JUnit-Based GWT
        Test Case 184
Testing Asynchronous Calls 185
    Testing by Using a Timer Object 185
    Testing by Using a Mock Callback Object 187
Using the Benchmark Utility and Writing Tests for Gathering
    Benchmark Results 189
    Examining the Benchmark Class 190
    Examining the IntRange Class 191
    Sample Application for Benchmarking 192
Summary 199

■CHAPTER 8   **Internationalizing Your Applications:**
               A Modern-Day Reality 201

What Is Internationalization? 201
    Localization 202
    Things to Remember While Developing an Internationalized
        Application 202
Understanding Character Encodings 203
    Important Character Sets 203
    Character Encoding and Web Applications 204

GWT's Internationalization Support 204
        The I18N Module 204
Internationalization Techniques Available in GWT 205
        Static String Internationalization 205
        Dynamic String Internationalization 206
Exploring the Localizable Interface 207
        Understanding Locale-Specific Substitution of Values 207
        Setting and Using the Locale Value in Your Application 208
Tool for Internationalizing Your GWT Applications 209
        Understanding the I18nCreator Tool 209
Creating Your First Internationalized Application 209
        Creating the Project Structure 210
        Working with the Properties Files 211
        Generating the Interface Corresponding to Property Files 212
        Adding Locale Values to a Module's XML File 213
        Setting Up the Host HTML File 213
        Setting the Module's Entry-Point Class 214
        Running the Application 215
Exploring the Constants Interface 218
        Example of Using the Constants Interface 218
        Format of Methods in the Interface Extending the Constants
            Interface 220
        Creating an Entry-Point Class to Access the Interface 221
Exploring the Messages Interface 222
        Format of Methods in the Interface Extending the Messages
            Interface 222
        Creating a Custom Interface 222
        Working with the Properties Files 223
        Creating an Entry-Point Class to Access the Interface 224
        Running the Application 225
        Creating the Messages Interface Using i18nCreator 225
Exploring the ConstantsWithLookup Interface 226
Embedding Data into Your Host HTML Pages 228
        Examining and Using the Dictionary Class 229
Localizing Dates, Times, Numbers, and Currencies 230
        Examining the NumberFormat Class 230
        Examining the DateTimeFormat Class 231
Summary 232

■**CHAPTER 9** **Some Important, Not-to-Be-Missed Techniques** 233

Understanding the History Mechanism 234
    History Class 235
    Steps to Add History Support 235
    Adding History Support to an Application 236
    The Hyperlink Widget and Its Integration with the History
        Mechanism 244
Deploying a GWT-Based Application 245
    Default Directory Structure of a Web Application 245
    Steps for Deploying a GWT Application on a Web Server 246
Maintaining Server Sessions with a GWT Application 249
    Modifying the RemoteService and Its Asynchronous Version 250
    Introducing the Callback Class Corresponding to the New
        Service Method 251
    Adding the Server-Side Implementation for the New Service
        Method 252
    Modifying the Util Class to Support the New Method 253
    Tweaking the Domain Object for Use 254
    Running the Application 254
Creating an ImageBundle of Bundles 256
Understanding and Using the <super-source> Tag 258
Packaging a GWT Module for Reuse 259
    Steps to Package an Application as a Reusable Module 260
    Using the New Module in a Sample Application 261
Summary 262

■**CHAPTER 10** **Peeking Into the Upcoming GWT 1.5 Release** 265

Understanding the Major Changes in Version 1.5 265
Setting Up Your Environment for Using Version 1.5 266
    Testing the New Release 267
Using Version 1.5 of the GWT Framework 269
    Setting Up and Running the BookStore Example on the New
        Version of the Library 269
    Type-Safe Collections by Using Generics 271
    The Type-Safe AsyncCallback Object 272
    Setting Up the LoanServicingSystem Example on the New
        Library 274
    New Package for the Benchmark Classes 274

The New Annotations for Benchmark Tests 274
Setting Up the AdvancedWidgets (ImageGallery) Example on
    the New Library 278
The New Resource Annotation for ImageBundle 278
Exploring the Output Structure of Compilation with the
    New Release 280
Summary 282

INDEX 283

About the Author

VIPUL GUPTA is a software engineer who designs and develops complex web-based applications and distributed software systems. His professional experience includes implementing a virtual file system for a web-based application and developing highly scalable back ends and extremely responsive web-based UIs for high-traffic websites. He has also worked on the prototype of a complex workflow-based solution that is used to handle various business processes. He is an expert in developing enterprise-level applications in the financial domain and has expertise in using a wide range of open source and commercial tools and technologies. Apart from his passion for computer science, he has numerous other interests including Formula 1, table tennis, and water sports.

Acknowledgments

This book would not have been possible without the help of a large number of people, so I would like to sincerely thank everyone involved. Thanks in particular to the team at Apress, especially Tracy Brown Collins and Clay Andres, for helping me keep the book on track and taking care of all the details that go into getting a book printed and on the shelves. I would also like to thank Jason Gilmore for his support during the initial part of the book and Kim Wimpsett for finding and correcting the many mistakes I made during the writing process. I would also like to thank Ellie Fountain and Tina Nielsen for their help in the production and administrative processes during the writing of this book.

Special thanks goes to Chris Mills for getting me excited about the prospect of writing this book and to Eric Briley, my technical reviewer, whose comments helped me polish some of the rough edges of the book.

I would also like to thank my family for their love and support throughout, especially my wonderful wife, Ria, for her patience and enthusiasm during the long hours of writing.

Introduction

Among other things, one of the biggest problems faced by a web application developer is the task of making an application compatible with different browsers. So, how does the idea of writing web applications in Java and testing and debugging them right in your favorite Java IDE sound? Exciting, doesn't it? This is what the Google Web Toolkit (GWT) framework lets you achieve. The GWT framework allows you to write and test your web applications in Java and compile the Java code into JavaScript for deployment purposes. Developing in a mature object-oriented language like Java brings with it all the benefits of object-oriented programming like modular design, type safety, and so on, which are essential for any project of even a moderate size.

I was originally skeptical about the idea of a framework supporting various browsers by converting the Java code into JavaScript and also about the quality of JavaScript code created by it. But once I started using the GWT framework and observed the quality of the generated JavaScript, I became convinced that GWT is going to become the de facto standard to write web-based applications in the future.

During the course of this book, you will learn how to use GWT to build high-quality web-based applications that will run across multiple browsers without the tweaks needed to achieve the same while using JavaScript directly. My aim is to provide you with all the knowledge you need to use GWT effectively in your own applications and to give you insight into what is happening behind the scenes in GWT.

Specifically, you will do the following in this book:

- Learn the fundamentals of using GWT to build UIs for your web applications.

- Learn how the framework works internally so you can solve most common programming problems in web-application development.

- Become aware of remote procedure calls and the asynchronous callback mechanism.

- Effectively write test cases for testing the different parts of your applications, including the asynchronous part of server-side communication.

- Learn how to write benchmark tests for your applications.

- Optimize your web applications by using techniques to bundle multiple images into a single image.

- Learn how to write applications with internationalization in mind.

- Design and implement reusable modules.

- Speed up your web application development by testing your applications right from your favorite Java IDE or from the command line, without the need for deploying them on a web server. You will also learn how to compile and convert the Java code into JavaScript and deploy your applications on a web server.

- Learn how GWT solves the problem of making an application compatible with different browsers without additional coding or development effort.

After reading this book, you will be equipped with all the knowledge you need to build applications using GWT.

Who This Book Is For

This book is for Java-minded web developers seeking to incorporate Ajax capabilities into their web applications without sacrificing sound development principles.

Downloading the Code

The code used in the book's examples will be available in Zip file format in the Downloads section of the Apress website (http://www.apress.com). The instructions for setting up and running the examples will be available in a Readme.txt file, which is bundled along with the source code. The software programs that are used in the book include Eclipse IDE (http://www.eclipse.org), the Tomcat web server (http://tomcat.apache.org) and of course the GWT framework library (http://code.google.com/webtoolkit/download.html).

Contacting the Author

The author can be contacted at vipulgupta.vg@gmail.com.

PART 1

■ ■ ■

Getting Started with GWT

The Google Web Toolkit, better known as GWT, is a Java-based open source framework that helps you develop Ajax-based web applications without having to worry about the quirky cross-browser details. Released in 2006 and with millions of downloads so far, GWT is changing the face of Ajax-based web application development with faster turnaround times in development and testing; it also offers application debugging right in your favorite Java-based IDE.

Chapter 1 will help get you started with GWT. You will learn some basic GWT terminology and understand how to download and set up GWT on your computer. The chapter will also explain details about various libraries in the framework along with the different modes in which the application can be run. This chapter will also guide you through the development and operation of some basic GWT applications with the tools provided in the framework as well as without them.

Chapter 2 will go into details about how the GWT framework works, providing you with a complete picture of GWT's capabilities and its libraries. It will discuss the concept of deferred binding and give you details about autogenerating code for your applications. It will also explain the bootstrap/startup process followed by a GWT application and discuss the various files created by the GWT compiler.

CHAPTER 1

■ ■ ■

GWT Basics and a First Application

GWT is an open source framework that allows you to develop Ajax-based applications in the Java language and provides tools to convert the Java code into JavaScript and HTML. This frees you, the developer, from the burden of rewriting your JavaScript to suit the peculiarities and lack of standards support in all the various browsers in use on people's computers.

Since its June 2006 release, the GWT framework has made a tremendous impact on the developer community engaged in developing Ajax-based web applications. This chapter will help you get started with GWT and help you understand how GWT fits into the next Ajax-based application you develop.

■Note GWT currently supports Internet Explorer 6 and 7; Firefox 1.0, 1.5, and 2.0; Mozilla; Safari 2.0; and Opera 9.0. The GWT compiler converts the Java classes into separate script files in compliance with the JavaScript understood by the various JavaScript engines found in the underlying web browsers. What this means for you as a developer is that Java's original promise of "write once, run anywhere" now applies to the world of Ajax-based applications. This allows you to focus more on the internal domain and application logic, rather than spending precious time making the application work across multiple browsers.

Debugging has long been a major problem for developers tasked with writing JavaScript. Although over the past few years a few very good JavaScript debugging tools have become available, most of them, such as Firebug, are designed to integrate closely with web browsers rather than with the modern IDEs used for Java development, such as Eclipse. GWT solves this problem by providing a mechanism to directly run and test the application from within the IDE as you'd do with typical Java code.

This chapter will start with the details of downloading and setting up GWT on your machine. Then it will go step by step through developing and running a sample application, using the tools and utilities provided by the GWT framework. The chapter will then dissect an entire sample application and explore its various parts to solidify your understanding of the different components of a GWT application. Finally, the chapter will close by showing how to write another application on your own without using the tools provided by GWT so that you have a clear understanding of the process involved in developing an application using GWT.

Setting Up Your GWT Environment

As of this writing, the current version of GWT is 1.4.61. You can download it from `http://code.google.com/webtoolkit/download.html`.

I downloaded the file named `gwt-windows-1.4.61.zip`. Then I extracted the `.zip` file to the root directory (`C:\`) of my system. In my case, I unzipped GWT at the location `C:\gwt-windows-1.4.61`. I renamed the folder to `C:\gwt` and will reference this name across all the code in this book and in the source code for the samples of this book. Figure 1-1 shows the contents of this directory.

Name ▲	Size
doc	
samples	
about.html	3 KB
about.txt	2 KB
applicationCreator.cmd	1 KB
benchmarkViewer.cmd	1 KB
COPYING	13 KB
COPYING.html	16 KB
gwt-benchmark-viewer.jar	3,465 KB
gwt-dev-windows.jar	9,780 KB
gwt-ll.dll	13 KB
gwt-module.dtd	5 KB
gwt-servlet.jar	412 KB
gwt-user.jar	1,889 KB
i18nCreator.cmd	1 KB
index.html	6 KB
junitCreator.cmd	1 KB
lgpl.txt	26 KB
projectCreator.cmd	1 KB
release_notes.html	44 KB
swt-win32-3235.dll	316 KB

Figure 1-1. *List of files after extracting the GWT package*

Hosted Mode vs. Web Mode

Before discussing the files shown in Figure 1-1, it's important to discuss the various modes, web and hosted, in which an application can be run using GWT.

Web Mode

Traditionally, developers of web-based applications had to go through the complete cycle of building, packaging, and deploying the application on a web server to test each new feature that was implemented. This slow and time-consuming process led to overly long development times and project delays.

In *web mode*, the application is run as pure JavaScript and HTML. These files are the result of compiling Java source code of your GWT-based modules by using the Java-to-JavaScript compiler. The JavaScript and HTML files obtained by the compilation step are used for the actual deployment to production environments.

Hosted Mode

In addition to traditional web mode, GWT provides another approach for testing and running applications known as *hosted mode.* In this mode, the actual Java byte code of the classes is run within the Java Virtual Machine (JVM). While web mode requires you to deploy your application to a web server, hosted mode allows a developer to run the application right off their favorite IDE in a web browser embedded in the framework. This greatly reduces the amount of time required to verify, test, and debug changes in an application.

A major advantage of Java byte code being run in hosted mode is the ability to debug the application, in the Java language, by using powerful IDEs available for the Java language. The debugging capabilities of a modern Java IDE are far more mature than the evolving JavaScript-related tools.

Figure 1-2 shows a GWT application being debugged in the Eclipse IDE.

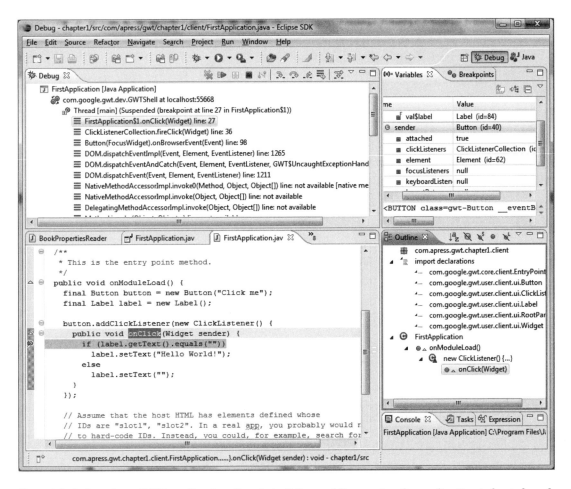

Figure 1-2. *Debugging a GWT application directly in Eclipse while running the application in hosted mode*

What Are All Those GWT Files For?

Here are details about some of the particularly important files shown in Figure 1-1:

gwt-servlet.jar: This provides all the GWT classes (including all the required RPC-related classes) that your application will need. This JAR file should be included in the application when running the application in web mode.

gwt-user.jar: This JAR file is needed when the application is run in hosted mode, that is, inside the web server bundled inside the GWT libraries. (This file should never be included as part of the application when deploying the application to an actual production environment.)

gwt-dev-windows.jar: This JAR file is needed if you want to run your application in hosted mode. Rather than a traditional web application development cycle of building, deploying, and testing the application in a web browser, GWT provides an internal hosted mode that you can use to test and debug the application by running the application in an embedded browser window. When the application is run in hosted mode, the startup class of your application should be com.google.gwt.dev.GWTShell.

gwt-benchmark-viewer.jar: This JAR file contains the benchmarking classes that you can use to create benchmarking tests for your applications (GWT has a Benchmark class that can be subclassed and used for common benchmarking needs). You can use the benchmarkViewer tool (benchmarkViewer.cmd, located in the root of the GWT directory) to derive charts/reports from the XML file that is generated when running the benchmarking tests. You'll learn more about benchmark testing in Chapter 7.

Table 1-1 lists the various JAR files, which should be included in your application when running it in the different modes supported by GWT.

Table 1-1. *JAR Files to Be Included for Web/Hosted Mode*

Application Mode	JARs to Be Included
Web mode	gwt-servlet.jar
Hosted mode	gwt-user.jar and gwt-dev-windows.jar (or gwt-dev-linux.jar)

Creating Your First GWT Application

The following sections will go over the steps needed to create an application using GWT. You will also develop your first application as you go through these steps.

Tools for Creating a Project

The developers of the GWT framework, by providing a number of easy-to-use utilities, have done their part in making starting a project with GWT as easy as possible. The following sections will cover the utilities you'll use to build your first application using GWT in this chapter.

projectCreator

This utility creates the project structure and an empty Eclipse project or Ant build file (or both) for your application. The command takes the following flags/parameters:

```
projectCreator [-ant projectName] [-eclipse projectName] [-out dir]
    [-overwrite] [-ignore]
```

Specifically, the flags/parameters are as follows:

- -ant generates a project build file to compile the source of the application. (The build file is named <projectName>.ant.xml.)

- -eclipse generates an Eclipse project (.project and .classpath files).

- -out is the directory where the output files will be written (default is the current directory).

- -overwrite overwrites any existing files.

- -ignore ignores any existing files (does not overwrite them).

Note You have to specify either the -ant or -eclipse flag to use this command.

For example, if you want to create a new project named chapter1 in a directory named chapter1, then you should run projectCreator -eclipse chapter1 while inside the chapter1 directory.

Listing 1-1 shows the result of executing this command.

Listing 1-1. *Project Structure and Corresponding Files Created by Running* projectCreator

```
C:\gwt\chapter1>projectCreator -eclipse chapter1
Created directory C:\gwt\chapter1\src
Created directory C:\gwt\chapter1\test
Created file C:\gwt\chapter1\.project
Created file C:\gwt\chapter1\.classpath
```

Executing the command shown previously creates the standard project structure in the chapter1 directory (namely, src and test directories for Java source and tests, respectively) and the .project and .classpath files for the Eclipse project for the application.

As another example, say instead that you want to create the project under a subdirectory mysub of your current directory. Then you should use the -out flag as mentioned earlier and pass the name of the subdirectory where the project should be created. Listing 1-2 shows the output of using this flag in the example.

Listing 1-2. *Project Structure and Ant Build File Created in a Specified Folder by Running* projectCreator *with the* -ant *and* -out *Flags*

```
C:\gwt>projectCreator.cmd -ant MySubProject -out mysub
Created directory mysub\src
Created directory mysub\test
Created file mysub\MySubProject.ant.xml
```

■**Note** You should enter the gwt directory to the path of your system so the shell can recognize the utilities when they are called from outside the main gwt directory. In Windows, this would mean adding C:\gwt to your system's path variable.

---

applicationCreator

This utility helps create a basic starter application for a GWT-based Ajax application. By using the -eclipse flag with the utility, you can also create a launch configuration for debugging the application in Eclipse. The command takes the following flags/parameters:

```
applicationCreator [-eclipse projectName] [-out dir] [-overwrite]
    [-ignore] className
```

Specifically, the flags/parameters are as follows:

- -eclipse creates a launch configuration for debugging the application in Eclipse.

- -out is the directory where the output files will be written (default is the current directory).

- -overwrite overwrites any existing files.

- -ignore ignores any existing files (does not overwrite them).

- className is the fully qualified name of the entry-point class in the application.

If you want to create the sample project in the chapter1 directory with the base GWT package location as com.apress.gwt.chapter1, then you should run applicationCreator -eclipse chapter1 com.apress.gwt.chapter1.client.FirstApplication from the shell while in the chapter1 directory. Listing 1-3 demonstrates this scenario.

Listing 1-3. *Sample Project Including Launch Configuration Files Created by Running the* applicationCreator *Command with the* -eclipse *Flag*

```
C:\gwt\chapter1>applicationCreator -eclipse chapter1 ➥
    com.apress.gwt.chapter1.client.FirstApplication
Created directory C:\gwt\chapter1\src\com\apress\gwt\chapter1
Created directory C:\gwt\chapter1\src\com\apress\gwt\chapter1\client
```

```
Created directory C:\gwt\chapter1\src\com\apress\gwt\chapter1\public
Created file C:\gwt\chapter1\src\com\apress\gwt\chapter1\FirstApplication.gwt.xml
Created file ➥
    C:\gwt\chapter1\src\com\apress\gwt\chapter1\public\FirstApplication.html
Created file ➥
    C:\gwt\chapter1\src\com\apress\gwt\chapter1\client\FirstApplication.java
Created file C:\gwt\chapter1\FirstApplication.launch
Created file C:\gwt\chapter1\FirstApplication-shell.cmd
Created file C:\gwt\chapter1\FirstApplication-compile.cmd
```

junitCreator

This utility creates a JUnit test and scripts that you can use for testing the various components of the application in both hosted and web modes. You will learn more about this utility and the details of testing GWT-based applications in Chapter 7.

i18nCreator

This utility creates scripts and a property file for internationalizing your applications. (You'll learn more about internationalization and this utility in Chapter 8.)

Running the Application Using Generated Scripts

You can execute the application in hosted mode by using FirstApplication-shell.cmd. With your current directory being your application's home directory, execute the command <applicationName>-shell.cmd on the command prompt to execute the application. You will see the hosted browser being loaded and the application running. Listing 1-4 shows the snippet with the script being used to run the application.

Listing 1-4. *Command to Run Your First Application in Hosted Mode*

```
C:\gwt\chapter1> FirstApplication-shell.cmd
```

■**Note** You should ensure that all the Java files are compiled before running the application using generated scripts such as FirstApplication-shell.cmd mentioned previously. You can enable autocompile in the Eclipse IDE by select the Project ➤ Build Automatically option if it is not enabled already. This entire book will assume that this option is enabled and the project is fully built before running the application.

Figure 1-3 and Figure 1-4 show the result of running the application in hosted mode by running the script in Listing 1-4.

Specifically, Figure 1-3 shows the web server window. This window displays the application log and stack trace, if any, for the application.

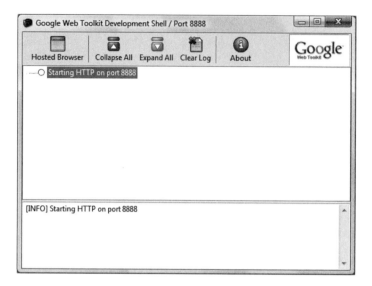

Figure 1-3. *Running your sample application in hosted mode. The embedded web server window shows the application log and stack trace in case of any errors.*

Figure 1-4 shows the actual web browser window with the application running in it.

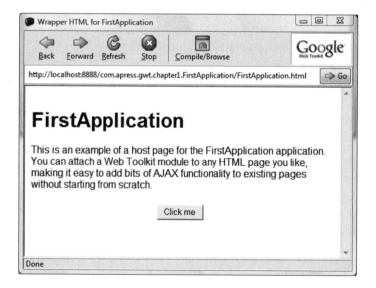

Figure 1-4. *Running your sample application in hosted mode. The embedded web browser window shows the application running in it.*

Understanding the Generated Scripts to Compile and Run the Application

The `applicationCreator` utility creates two script files for helping the development process. These files contain the Java commands to compile the application and to run the application in hosted mode (running the entry-point class). The file contents for the sample application are as follows:

`FirstApplication-shell.cmd`: This file loads the start page of the GWT module in the hosted browser and contains the following Java command:

```
@java -cp "%~dp0\src;%~dp0\bin;C:/gwt/gwt-user.jar;C:/gwt/gwt-dev-windows.jar"
    com.google.gwt.dev.GWTShell -out "%~dp0\www" %*
    com.apress.gwt.chapter1.FirstApplication/FirstApplication.html
```

`FirstApplication-compile.cmd`: This file is responsible for compiling the GWT module and outputs the resultant files in the folder named www. It contains the following Java command:

```
@java -cp "%~dp0\src;%~dp0\bin;C:/gwt/gwt-user.jar;C:/gwt/gwt-dev-windows.jar"
    com.google.gwt.dev.GWTCompiler -out "%~dp0\www" %*
    com.apress.gwt.chapter1.FirstApplication
```

Working with Modules in GWT

GWT applications are basically structured in terms of modules. Each module defines a well-defined functionality or component, and these modules are combined to make a full-fledged application.

Structure of a Module File

The recommended (default) structure of a GWT-based module (with the corresponding structure as an example from your first application) is as follows:

- `moduleName.gwt.xml`: This file includes the configuration of the module. For example:

  ```
  com/apress/gwt/chapter1/ FirstApplication.gwt.xml
  ```

- `client` package: A client subpackage (and corresponding subpackages) with client-side code. For example:

  ```
  com/apress/gwt/chapter1/client
  com/apress/gwt/chapter1/client/data ... and so on
  ```

- `public` package: A public subpackage (and corresponding subpackages) with static web content. For example:

  ```
  com/apress/gwt/chapter1/public
  ```

- `server` package: A server subpackage (and corresponding subpackages) with server-side code. For example:

  ```
  com/apress/gwt/chapter1/server
  com/apress/gwt/chapter1/server/data ... and so on
  ```

■**Note** Even though using the listed module structure is just a recommendation, it's advisable that you stick to the previous structure because the entire community in general is sticking to this, and your modules will therefore be more easily understandable by others.

A *module* in GWT is simply an XML file and combines the entire configuration that your application would need in a single file. GWT modules define the entry point into the application. In the example discussed in this chapter, the module file is located at chapter1/src/com/apress/ gwt/chapter1 and is named FirstApplication.gwt.xml. Listing 1-5 shows the contents of the module file in the sample application.

Listing 1-5. *Contents of the Module File (*FirstApplication.gwt.xml*) for the Sample Application*

```
<module>
    <!-- Inherit the core Web Toolkit stuff. -->
    <inherits name='com.google.gwt.user.User'/>

    <!--Specify the app entry-point class. -->
    <entry-point class='com.apress.gwt.chapter1.client.FirstApplication'/>
</module>
```

Understanding Different Tags in a Module File

You can use the module file to define a number of properties related to the application:

- The entry-point class property

- The inherits property

- The source and public properties

- The servlet property

- The stylesheet property

- The script property

- The extend-property property

These are described in more detail in the following sections.

The entry-point class Property

When a module is loaded, the entry-point classes defined in the module's configuration file are instantiated, and the corresponding onModuleLoad() methods of these entry-point classes are called. This includes the entry-point classes of the inherited modules as well.

In the GWT library, EntryPoint is basically defined as an interface. This interface declares the onModuleLoad() method, which, as defined earlier, is automatically called when the module is loaded. (Adding an entry-point class is optional. However, you can add any number of entry-point classes in your application by including them in the configuration file of your application's module.)

Here's an example:

```
<entry-point class='com.apress.gwt.chapter1.client.FirstApplication'/>
```

As you can see in the application's module file (FirstApplication.gwt.xml), the entry-point class for the application is defined as com.apress.gwt.chapter1.client.FirstApplication. Listing 1-6 shows the code for the entry-point class.

Listing 1-6. *Contents of the Entry-Point Class for the Sample Application*

```java
package com.apress.gwt.chapter1.client;

import com.google.gwt.core.client.EntryPoint;
import com.google.gwt.user.client.ui.Button;
import com.google.gwt.user.client.ui.ClickListener;
import com.google.gwt.user.client.ui.Label;
import com.google.gwt.user.client.ui.RootPanel;
import com.google.gwt.user.client.ui.Widget;

/**
 * Entry-point classes define <code>onModuleLoad()</code>.
 */
public class FirstApplication implements EntryPoint {

  /**
   * This is the entry-point method.
   */
  public void onModuleLoad() {
    final Button button = new Button("Click me");
    final Label label = new Label();

    button.addClickListener(new ClickListener() {
      public void onClick(Widget sender) {
        if (label.getText().equals(""))
          label.setText("Hello World!");
        else
          label.setText("");
      }
    });

    // Assume that the host HTML has elements defined whose
    // IDs are "slot1" and "slot2".  In a real app, you probably would
    // not want to hard-code IDs.  Instead, you could, for example,
    // search for all elements with a particular CSS class and
    // replace them with widgets.
    RootPanel.get("slot1").add(button);
    RootPanel.get("slot2").add(label);
  }
}
```

The inherits Property

Inheriting a module is like including the entire configuration and code of that module in your application. This helps to reuse the existing functionality of other modules in your application. The configuration file has an `inherits` element that is used to inherit other modules in your application's module. You can inherit any number of modules by using this element.

Here's an example:

```
<inherits name='com.google.gwt.user.User'/>
```

The source and public Properties

These two properties help declare the location of the source folder for the client code and for the public path. These two locations are relative to the path where the module XML file containing these attributes is found. If either of these attributes is missing, then default values for these properties are assumed.

For example, `<source path="myModuleClient"/>` defines that the `myModuleClient` directory and all its subpackages contain the client code, and all Java source files found in these locations adhere to the rules of GWT related to client-side code.

If the source element is missing, then `<source path="client">` is assumed as the default definition.

`<public path="myPublic"/>` defines that the `myPublic` directory acts as the root to the public path, and all files found in this folder and all its subfolders are directly accessible by external clients. The files found here are copied to the output directory during the translation steps followed by the GWT compiler.

If the public element is missing, then `<public path="public">` is assumed as the default definition.

If the module containing the previous property is located in the `com/apress/gwt/chapter1` folder and the module defines the public property as `<public path="myPublic"/>`, then the public folder for the application is located in the `com/apress/gwt/chapter1/myPublic` folder.

■**Note** The `public` element allows filtering using patterns. This allows you to decide which resources to copy to the output directory while compiling the GWT module.

The servlet Property

This property allows you to test remote procedure calls (RPCs) by loading the servlets mapped to a specific path. (You are allowed to map all the servlets needed in your application by using this property.)

Here's an example:

```
<servlet path="url-path" class="classname"/>
```

The `url-path` value of the `path` attribute defines the location where the corresponding servlet for the application is mapped. The client should use the same mapping when registering the call using the ServiceDefTarget.setServiceEntryPoint(String) method. (This will be explained in detail in Chapter 4.)

The stylesheet Property

This property allows you to add a CSS file to the module.

Here's an example:

```
<stylesheet src="css/Mycss.css"/>
```

The script Property

This property allows you to add external JavaScript code/libraries to the module.

Here's an example:

```
<script src="js/Mylibrary.js"/>
```

The extend-property Property

This property allows you to add values to a client property. Any number of such values may be introduced by adding them to the comma-separated list of values.

Here's an example:

```
<extend-property name="client-property-name" values="comma-separated-values"/>
```

This feature is most used in specifying locales for your application during internationalization. You will learn more about internationalization and using this property in Chapter 8.

Creating the Host HTML File

Listing 1-7 shows a sample startup HTML file that demonstrates how to add the GWT module to your application so that it is loaded when your application is started. It also shows how to add history support to the application. (Chapter 9 discusses how to handle history support in your applications.)

Listing 1-7. *Sample Host HTML File to Load the Module and Add History Support in the Application*

```
<html>
  <head>
  ...
      <!-- This script loads your compiled module. If you add any GWT meta tags,
          they must  be added before this line -->
      <script language='javascript'
          src='com.apress.gwt.chapter1.FirstApplication.nocache.js'>
      </script>
  </head>
```

```
<body>
  <!-- OPTIONAL: include this if you want history support -->
  <iframe src="javascript:''" id="__gwt_historyFrame"
          style="width:0;height:0;border:0"></iframe>

      <!--Rest of HTML body goes here, for example, we have a table with two
          columns -- >
      <table align=center>
          <tr>
              <td id="slot1"/>
              <td id="slot2"/>
          </tr>
      </table>
  </body>
</html>
```

Here I'll briefly explain some of the important parts of the previous HTML page:

- `<script ... src='com.apress.gwt.chapter1.FirstApplication.nocache.js'>`: After compilation, the application module is stored as a JavaScript file (with a `nocache.js` extension). The path for this file is added to the HTML page so that it can be downloaded and loaded when the page is referenced.

- `<iframe src="javascript:''" id="__gwt_historyFrame" ...>`: This adds history support to the application. This is an interesting functionality provided by the GWT framework that makes adding history management support to your application a simple task. (Chapter 9 discusses how to add history support to your applications.)

Steps to Create a GWT Application

The process of creating a GWT application can be broken down into the following four steps:

1. Create the basic project structure with the corresponding package. Add `client`, `server`, and `public` subpackages.

2. Add the Application module file, named `<appName>.gwt.xml`, to the basic package. Add the corresponding configuration details to the file.

3. Create an entry-point class (by implementing the `EntryPoint` interface) named `<appName>.java` in the `client` subpackage, and override the `onModuleLoad()` method with the required functionality.

4. Create an HTML file named `<appName>.html` in your application's `public` folder, with a script `src` reference to your application's package and with `<appName>.nocache.js` appended.

Creating Another Application Step-by-Step

With all these basic details behind you, let's create another simple application without using the GWT tools in order to solidify your understanding of using and configuring a simple GWT application. There will be numerous situations where you'll want to add GWT support to your existing applications, and this example will serve as good starting point to understanding the integration step required at that point.

In this application, I'll show how to build a simplified version of a news-serving client that will iterate through a set of news stories in the web browser. (In future chapters, you will extend the same application to support displaying real-time news events in a proper news display widget, but for simplicity here, this example will just flash news entries in the browser's window.)

You will follow the steps mentioned earlier to create your application. So, here goes . . .

Creating the Basic Project Structure

As mentioned earlier, the first step is to create the basic project structure with the corresponding base package, as well as the `client`, `server`, and `public` subpackages.

So, let's start by creating a new Java project in Eclipse. I created the project in a folder called `NewsClient` in the gwt directory (`C:\gwt`) of my system. Then I added a source folder named `src` in the project and added necessary packages to it so that the structure looks like the one shown in Figure 1-5. (I also added the JRE system library and `gwt-user.jar` to the build path of the project in Eclipse.) I did not add the server package at this time because the application is not making any RPC calls to server-side logic as of yet. You will learn about RPC (server-side code) starting in Chapter 4 in the book.

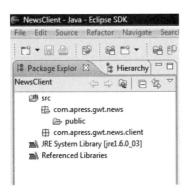

Figure 1-5. *Structure of the NewsClient application*

Adding the Module File

As mentioned earlier, the second step is to add the application's module file, named `NewsClient.gwt.xml`, to the base package, as shown in Figure 1-6.

Figure 1-6. *Adding the module file named* NewsClient.gwt.xml

In addition, let's quickly add the configuration details to the module file (NewsClient. gwt.xml). Listing 1-8 shows the NewsClient application's module configuration file.

Listing 1-8. *Contents of the Module File for the NewsClient Application*

```
<module>
    <!-- Inherit the core Web Toolkit.               -->
    <inherits name='com.google.gwt.user.User'/>

    <!-- Specify the app entry-point class.          -->
    <entry-point class='com.apress.gwt.news.client.NewsClient'/>
</module>
```

As you can see, the module file references the entry-point class as com.google.gwt.news. client.NewsClient, so that takes you to step 3.

■**Caution** The client entry-point class and the module should have the same prefix as part of their names. They're NewsClient.gwt.xml and NewsClient.java in this example.

Creating the Entry-Point Class

As mentioned earlier, the third step is to create an entry-point class, named NewsClient.java, in the client subpackage, as shown in Figure 1-7, and override the onModuleLoad() method of the EntryPoint interface with the required functionality.

```
□·🗗 src
    □·🗃 com.apress.gwt.news
        ·📂 public
        ·📄 NewsClient.gwt.xml
    □·🗃 com.apress.gwt.news.client
        ·🖃·🗊 NewsClient.java
□·📚 JRE System Library [jre1.6.0_01]
□·📚 Referenced Libraries
```

Figure 1-7. *Adding the NewsClient entry-point class to the application*

Listing 1-9 shows the code for the NewsClient entry-point class.

Listing 1-9. *Contents of the Entry-Point Class (Named* NewsClient.java*) for the Application*

```
package com.apress.gwt.news.client;

import com.google.gwt.core.client.EntryPoint;
import com.google.gwt.user.client.Random;
import com.google.gwt.user.client.Timer;
import com.google.gwt.user.client.ui.Label;
import com.google.gwt.user.client.ui.RootPanel;

/**
 * Entry-point class for the news client application displays a news entry
 * every two seconds on the browser window.
 *
 * @author Vipul Gupta (vipulgupta.vg@gmail.com)
 */
public class NewsClient implements EntryPoint{

    private final String[] newsEntries = new String[] {
        "News Entry 1", "Another News Entry", "Yet another news entry",
        "One Final news Entry" };

    public void onModuleLoad() {

        final Label label = new Label();

        // Create a new timer that keeps changing the news text
        Timer t = new Timer() {
          public void run() {
              label.setText(getNewsEntry());
          }
        };

        // Schedule the timer to run every two seconds.
        t.scheduleRepeating (2000);

        RootPanel.get("newsEntryDivId").add(label);
    }

    private String getNewsEntry() {
        return newsEntries[Random.nextInt(newsEntries.length)];
    }
}
```

Let's inspect what's happening in this class in detail:

1. You start by creating a dummy-entry array containing some strings that act as dummy news entries for the class:

```
private final String[] newsEntries = new String[] {  ...
```

Note In an actual production environment, the client will make a call to the server, which will return actual real-time news events for display. We will simulate the same type of application in Chapter 4.

2. You then define the onModuleLoad() method of the EntryPoint interface and give a concrete implementation to it. Eventually this method will be compiled to JavaScript by using the GWT compiler and will be called when the page containing the link to this module is loaded.

In this method definition, I have created a label in which the news-entry text will be shown. I have also created a Timer object and scheduled it to run every two seconds. The overridden run() method of the Timer class is called at every scheduled interval of the Timer object (two seconds in this example):

```
public void run() {
  label.setText(getNewsEntry());
}
```

The Timer object is configured to execute the run() method every two seconds by the following code:

```
t.scheduleRepeating (2000);
```

Note The Timer (com.google.gwt.user.client.Timer) class in the GWT library serves the same purpose as the Timer class in the Java library and has been implemented to be safe across the various browsers. The methods provided by the Timer class are as follows:

- cancel(): Cancels the timer
- run(): Called when the timer is executed
- schedule(int): Schedules the timer to execute once after int milliseconds
- scheduleRepeating(int): Schedules the timer to execute repeatedly after int milliseconds

The run()method in the sample application just updates the text of the label with one of the randomly chosen strings from the newsEntries array that it gets by calling the getNewsEntry() method:

```
private String getNewsEntry() {
  return newsEntries[Random.nextInt(newsEntries.length)];
}
```

The getNewsEntry() method as shown here just uses the Random class to get an index into the newsEntries array, and then the getNewsEntry() method returns the string at that array location.

■**Note** The Random (com.google.gwt.user.client.Random) class in the GWT library serves the same purpose as the Random class in the Java library. The major difference from the Java version is that the class in the GWT library cannot be seeded to start with. As a result, you can never ensure the same sequence of generated values. The methods provided by the Random class in the GWT library are as follows:

- nextBoolean(): Returns true or false with roughly equal probability
- nextDouble(): Returns a random double between 0 (inclusive) and 1 (exclusive)
- nextInt(): Returns a random int between −2147483648 and 2147483647 (inclusive) with roughly equal probability of returning any particular int in this range
- nextInt(int): Returns a random int between 0 (inclusive) and upperBound (exclusive) with roughly equal probability of returning any particular int in this range

---

The onModuleLoad() method in the class shown earlier has the following statement at the end of the method:

```
RootPanel.get("newsEntryDivId").add(label);
```

The RootPanel gets a reference to the panel to which all your application widgets must ultimately be added. (RootPanel returns the reference to the document's body in the browser.) You would generally inject the starting point of your application into an HTML page. You can do this by using the RootPanel class's get() methods. In this example, you added the label to the element with an ID of newsEntryDivId in the HTML page hosting the application. The next step is to create this hosting HTML page.

Creating the Host HTML File

As mentioned earlier, the fourth step is to create an HTML file, named NewsClient.html, in your application's public folder, as shown in Figure 1-8, with a script src reference to the application's package and with NewsClient.nocache.js appended to the package.

Figure 1-8. *Adding the main HTML file named* NewsClient.html

Listing 1-10 shows the code for the host HTML file (NewsClient.html) for the application.

Listing 1-10. *Contents of the Host HTML File (Named* NewsClient.html*) for the Application*

```
<html>
    <head>
        <!-- This script loads your compiled GWT module.    -->
        <script language='javascript'
            src='com.apress.gwt.news.NewsClient.nocache.js'></script>
    </head>

    <body>
        <div id="newsEntryDivId"/>
    </body>
</html>
```

Running the Application in Hosted Mode

With all this behind you, you should now run the NewsClient application in hosted mode to see the application in action. The class named GWTShell is used to run the application in hosted mode and is explained next.

Understanding and Using GWTShell

As mentioned earlier in this chapter, the startup class for running the application in hosted mode is GWTShell (com.google.gwt.dev.GWTShell), and you can use it to run your applications.

The GWTShell class supports the following command-line flags/parameters:

```
GWTShell [-port port-number | "auto"] [-noserver] [-whitelist whitelist-string]
    [-blacklist blacklist-string] [-logLevel level] [-gen dir] [-out dir]
    [-style style] [url]
```

You can find this class in gwt-dev-windows.jar (or gwt-dev-linux.jar). Table 1-2 lists GWTShell's command-line options.

Table 1-2. GWTShell*'s Command-Line Options*

Flag Name	Description
-port	Runs an embedded Tomcat instance on the specified port (defaults to 8888)
-noserver	Prevents the embedded Tomcat server from running, even if a port is specified
-whitelist	Allows the user to browse URLs that match the specified regular expressions (comma separated or space separated)
-blacklist	Prevents the user from browsing URLs that match the specified regexes (comma separated or space separated)
-logLevel	Specifies the level of logging detail: ERROR, WARN, INFO, TRACE, DEBUG, SPAM, or ALL

Flag Name	Description
-gen	Specifies the directory into which generated files will be written for review
-out	Specifies the directory to write output files into (defaults to current)
-style	Specifies the script output style; GWT supports OBF[USCATED], PRETTY, and DETAILED (defaults to OBF)
url	Automatically launches the specified URL

To run your project from the command line, you need to set up the proper classpath for the Java interpreter. The classpath should include gwt-user.jar (needed by the application), gwt-dev-windows.jar (or gwt-dev-linux.jar in case of Linux; the startup class GWTShell is in this JAR), and the src folder of the application (contains the package/classes/module of the application).

So, at your command prompt (from the application's home directory), type the command listed in Listing 1-11 to get the application running.

Listing 1-11. *Command to Run the NewsClient Application*

```
C:\gwt\NewsClient>    java -cp c:\gwt\gwt-dev-windows.jar;c:\gwt\gwt-user.jar;src
                           com.google.gwt.dev.GWTShell
                           com.apress.gwt.news.NewsClient/NewsClient.html
```

■**Note** Listing 1-11 is a single command, but individual elements of it have been broken into multiple lines to fit the width of this page. You can just type the same command on a single line and see the hosted browser load with your application.

I'll now break down the command in Listing 1-11 so you can understand it:

1. You start by setting the classpath for the Java command, as explained earlier:

   ```
   -cp c:\gwt\gwt-dev-windows.jar;c:\gwt\gwt-user.jar;src
   ```

2. Next you pass the main bootstrap class to the Java command to run:

   ```
   com.google.gwt.dev.GWTShell
   ```

3. You then pass the URL to the GWTShell command to launch:

   ```
   com.apress.gwt.news.NewsClient/NewsClient.html
   ```

The URL passed to the GWTShell class shown earlier deserves more explanation. The URL of the application is automatically decided in case of hosted mode and is based on the name of the module (and the corresponding package).

For example, if your module is named NewsClient and it resides in a package named com.apress.gwt.news, then the URL in hosted mode would be com.apress.gwt.news.NewsClient/NewsClient.html, and that's what you used in the earlier example.

So, the format of the URL is <package>.<moduleName>/<moduleName>.html.

Figure 1-9, Figure 1-10, and Figure 1-11 show the NewsClient application in hosted mode at different points of time.

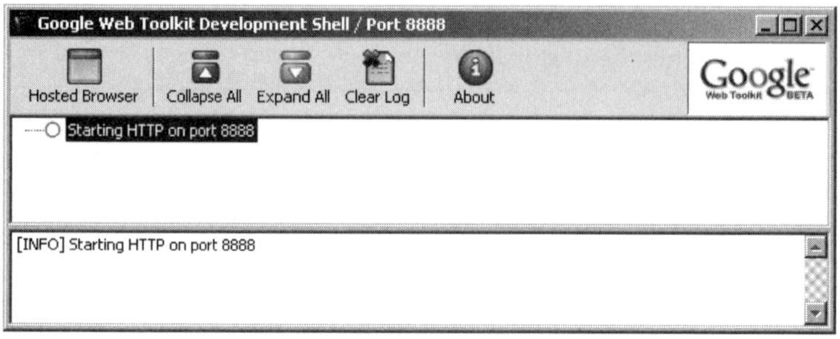

Figure 1-9. *Embedded web server window that shows the application log and error stack trace, if any*

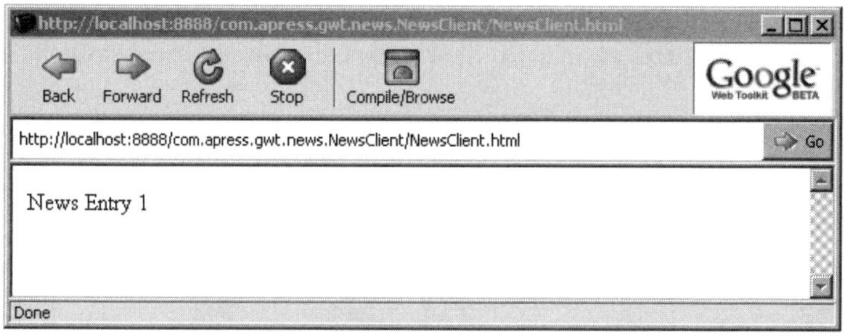

Figure 1-10. *NewsClient application at time T1 showing a news entry*

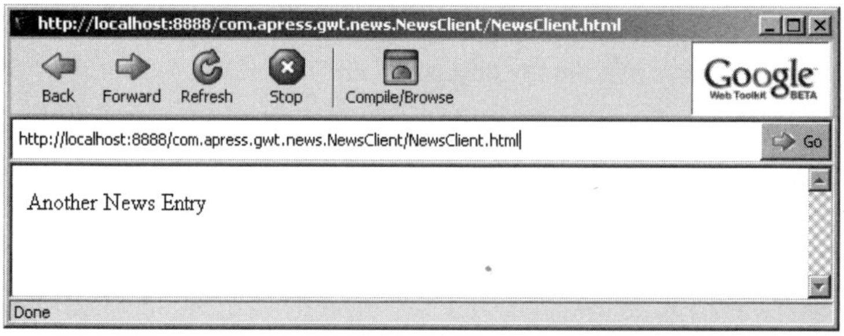

Figure 1-11. *NewsClient application at time T2 showing a different news entry*

Summary

This chapter covered various aspects of the GWT framework, including setting up the GWT environment and basic application development with and without the tools provided by the framework. It also discussed the structure of a GWT application and the configuration required for a GWT module.

In addition, the chapter discussed the various JAR files available in the framework and the various modes in which the application can be run. None of the applications demonstrated in this chapter interfaced with server-side logic and made any RPC calls, even though that would have made much more sense, especially in the NewsClient application. However, this avoided complicating things too much in this first chapter of the book.

Lots of the topics mentioned in this chapter are probably new to you, so it's highly recommended that you try all the examples in this chapter (and the rest of the book too) by hand to solidify your understanding of GWT. The book will delve into a lot more details about all the topics mentioned here and the GWT framework itself in the remaining chapters.

CHAPTER 2

∎∎∎

GWT Architecture and Internal Features

This chapter will focus on the architecture and details of internal features of the GWT framework. You will learn about the various components of the GWT framework and also about the compilation steps in GWT, specifically, the life cycle of the conversion of Java code into its JavaScript equivalent.

You will also learn about the packages/libraries and classes from the Java language that you can use in the GWT application's client code. (The GWT compiler supports a limited set of the most important Java classes, and only these classes are understood by the compiler for the translation process of converting the Java code into its JavaScript equivalent. Therefore, you can use only these classes while developing the client code of your applications.) Finally, you will learn about the important concepts of deferred binding and generators, which will be followed by a discussion about the startup/bootstrap process that a GWT application follows.

So, let's start with the various components that contribute to the GWT architecture.

Understanding the Components That Make Up the GWT Framework

The GWT framework is comprised of four major components. These components are divided into two major groups: the development tools (the compiler and the embedded web browser) and the class libraries (the JRE emulation library and the widget library). The following sections will discuss these components.

Development Tools Explained

GWT provides two core tools to assist in the development of an application. These are the compiler and the embedded web browser (which is used to run the application in hosted mode on a lightweight web server included in the framework). Together these tools form the backbone of the GWT framework.

The Java-to-JavaScript Compiler

One of the most important components of the GWT framework is the compiler. The GWT compiler is responsible for converting the Java code into its JavaScript equivalent so that the application can run in web mode.

The GWT compiler performs various code optimization tasks during the compilation process. The following are the most important ones:

Dead code elimination: Only classes and those methods that are used in the application are translated into JavaScript. For example, say a type X has five methods and only one of these methods is ever called in the application code. The GWT compiler will remove the four methods when converting the code to its JavaScript equivalent.

Method calls inlining: A method call is replaced by the actual code of the method being called.

String interning: Only one single copy of each distinct string object is shared by all strings having the same character sequence.

The Embedded Web Browser

The GWT framework provides an embedded web browser that runs and debugs your applications in hosted mode. The browser runs your Java byte code directly in its own Java Virtual Machine (JVM), without converting it to its JavaScript equivalent. This requires the browser to have direct interaction with the JVM, which is accomplished by the web browser embedding special browser controls (Internet Explorer in Windows and Gecko/Mozilla in Linux), with these controls having hooks to work with the JVM.

Class Libraries Explained

GWT provides two core class libraries to assist in the development of an application. These are the JRE emulation library and the widget library. The following sections will discuss these libraries.

The JRE Emulation Library

The GWT compiler supports only a certain set of the most important JRE libraries and classes. These are accessible to the compiler and the developers as the emulation library in the framework.

The emulation library supports the most important classes from the following packages:

- `java.lang`

- `java.io`

- `java.util`

The following sections will describe all the supported classes/interfaces from these packages.

Classes and Interfaces Available from the java.lang Package

The various interfaces and classes from the java.lang package that form part of the JRE emulation library are listed in this section.

Table 2-1 lists the various interfaces from the java.lang package that form part of the JRE emulation library in GWT.

Table 2-1. *Interfaces in the* java.lang *Package with Support in GWT*

Interfaces	Description
Comparable	Imposes a total ordering on the objects of each class that implements it
Cloneable	Indicates that a class implements clone()
CharSequence	Abstracts a sequence of characters

Table 2-2 lists the various classes from the java.lang package that form part of the JRE emulation library in GWT.

Table 2-2. *Classes in the* java.lang *Package with Support in GWT*

Classes	Description
Object	Base class for all classes. JavaScript is a single-threaded language, so the synchronization methods of wait(), notify(), and notifyAll() from Java's Object class are not available. (GWT does recognize the synchronized keyword, but it has no real effect.)
Boolean, Byte, Character, Double, Float, Integer, Long, Short	Wrapper classes for base types.
Exception, ArrayStoreException, ClassCastException, IllegalArgumentException, IllegalStateException, IndexOutOfBoundsException, NegativeArraySizeException, NullPointerException, NumberFormatException, RuntimeException, UnsupportedOperationException, StringIndexOutOfBoundsException	Classes to signify various exceptional conditions.
Error, AssertionError, Throwable	Error classes.
String, StringBuffer	String handling.
Math, Number	Arithmetic/numeral.
System	Base-level underlying interface.

Interfaces Available from the java.io Package

The various interfaces from the java.io package that form part of the JRE emulation library are listed in this section. Notice that none of the classes from the java.io package is included because JavaScript does not have file access on the client machine except from cookies. So, the various I/O files in this package don't need to be emulated.

Table 2-3 lists the interface from the java.io package that forms part of the JRE emulation library in GWT.

Table 2-3. *Interface in the* java.io *Package with Support in GWT*

Interfaces	Description
Serializable	Marker classes for serializing

■Note Earlier releases of the GWT framework used a marker interface named IsSerializable, and because of the demand by the developer community, the java.io.Serializable interface was also introduced in the 1.4 release of the framework for interoperability. RPC treats this interface synonymously with IsSerializable. The introduction of Serializable interface allowed the developer community to reuse their existing code representing domain objects.

Classes and Interfaces Available from the java.util Package

The various interfaces and classes from the java.util package that form part of the JRE emulation library are listed in this section.

Table 2-4 lists the various interfaces from java.util package that form part of the JRE emulation library in GWT.

Table 2-4. *Interfaces in the* java.util *package with Support in GWT*

Interfaces	Description
Collection, Comparator, Set, List, Map, RandomAccess	Collections
Iterator, ListIterator	Iterators
EventListener	Listeners

Table 2-5 lists the various classes from the java.util package that form part of the JRE emulation library in GWT.

Table 2-5. *Classes in the* java.util *Package with Support in GWT*

Classes	Description
AbstractCollection, AbstractSet, AbstractList, AbstractMap	Base classes for various collections
ArrayList, HashMap, HashSet, Stack, Vector	Implementation of collections
Arrays	Utility methods for native arrays
Collections	Utility methods for collections

Classes	Description
Date	Object representing date and time
EventObject	Superclass of all event objects
ConcurrentModificationException, EmptyStackException, MissingResourceException, NoSuchElementException, TooManyListenersException	Various exceptions

The Widget Library

The GWT framework provides a number of user interface widgets for client-side UI development. The widgets in GWT are divided into container widgets and user-interface widgets. The
collection of all such widgets is what composes the widget library. The various classes in the
library along with details on using them will be explained in Chapter 3.

Before moving on to other details, it's important to understand which version of Java language constructs and syntax the GWT compiler understands for the client code. This will be
explained in the following section.

What Version of the Java Language Does the GWT Support?

As of this writing, the current release of the GWT is version 1.4.61, and this version supports
only Java 1.4 language constructs and syntax for the **client** code. This means that any code
that is written for the client part of your application (as set in the module's configuration file
by using the source tag; the default for which is set as the client folder) should conform to the
language constructs and syntax of Java 1.4.

For all developers used to Java 1.5 language constructs and syntax, there will be a lot of
things missing in terms of language constructs, the most notable being the nonavailability of
generics and annotations.

It's important to understand that the language-level restrictions are applicable only for the
client part of the application, that is, to the code that the compiler will translate to JavaScript.
This also means you are free to use any constructs for the server part of the application.

Let's see what happens if you don't obey the previous restriction of a language construct in
the client code. Let's modify the NewsClient application you developed in Chapter 1. I changed
the entry-point class (NewsClient.java) of the application (see Listing 1-9 in Chapter 1) and
converted the newsEntries String array to an ArrayList that takes String objects (using generics). This modification also required a change in the getNewsEntry() method. The modified
NewsClient class (with changes in bold) is shown here:

```
public class NewsClient implements EntryPoint {

  private static final ArrayList<String> newsEntries = new ArrayList<String>();
  static{
    newsEntries.add("News Entry 1");
```

```
    newsEntries.add("Another News Entry");
    newsEntries.add("Yet another news entry");
    newsEntries.add("One Final news entry");
  }

  public void onModuleLoad() {
    ...
  }

  private String getNewsEntry() {
    return newsEntries.get(Random.nextInt(newsEntries.size()));
  }
}
```

Let's now run the NewsClient application using the command in Listing 1-11 from Chapter 1. GWTShell will attempt to start the application in a hosted browser, and you will get the output shown in Figure 2-1 and Figure 2-2.

Specifically, Figure 2-1 shows the browser window with an alert stating that the application failed to load.

Figure 2-1. *Host browser window demonstrating NewsClient application being run*

Figure 2-2 shows the development shell window. The development shell lists all the errors that are encountered when the application is attempted to be started. The error log clearly states that the GWT framework failed to load the application because it does not support Java 5.0 constructs and the source analyzer found them in the client code.

The next section will focus on the same origin policy, which puts restrictions on the domains that can be contacted by the JavaScript code. The same origin policy has implications on the code written by GWT framework (as it gets converted to JavaScript), so it is important that you understand the implications of same origin policy on the code that you write for your applications.

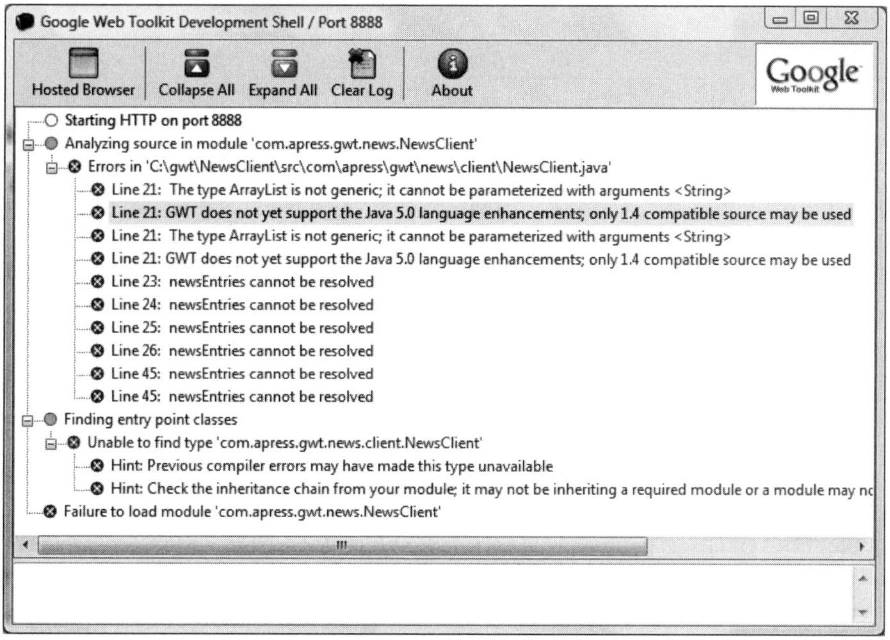

Figure 2-2. *Development shell window showing errors related to Java 5 constructs being used in the client code*

The Same Origin Policy and Its Implications on GWT

In the following sections, I will discuss the same origin policy and how it affects applications developed using the GWT framework.

Same Origin Policy Explained

The *same origin policy* was released a few years ago as part of Netscape Navigator 2.0 and is currently part of all major web browsers in use. The same origin policy is also known as the *single origin* or *same site policy*. The same origin policy prevents JavaScript code loaded from one site (one origin) from interacting with, communicating with, or otherwise accessing any document or JavaScript code loaded from another site (different origin).

The origin includes a combination of the domain name, the port, and the protocol. Table 2-6 lists some examples to show which URLs can and cannot be referenced from a document loaded from `http://apress.com/books/gwt.html`.

Table 2-6. *Set of Valid and Invalid URLs As Per Single Origin Policy*

Referenced URL	Result As Per Same Origin Policy
`http://apress.com/books/Swt.html`	Different documents on the same domain are allowed.
`http://apress.com/books/UI/Awt.html`	Subdirectories on the same domain are allowed.

Continued

Table 2-6. *Continued*

Referenced URL	Result As Per Same Origin Policy
`http://apress.com/cook-books/home.html`	Different directories on the same domain are allowed.
`http://apress.com:8080/books/home.html`	Fails because different port number is not allowed.
`http://someotherpress.com/books/gwt.html`	Fails because different domain is not allowed.
`https://apress.com/books/gwt.html`	Fails because different protocol is not allowed.

Ajax uses the `XMLHttpRequest` object for server-side communication, and this object is restricted under the same origin policy. This means the `XMLHttpRequest` object can make calls only to the location from where the code containing the `XMLHttpRequest` object was loaded.

However, the restrictions imposed by the single origin policy do not apply to all communications between the browser and the web servers like for the data referred to by the tags in an HTML page. For example, many high-traffic web sites have HTML pages being served from one web server and static content such as images, style sheets, and so on, being served from a separate static content server. This is perfectly valid and is a commonly used method of deploying web applications. A page loaded by using a URL such as `http://apress.com/books/gwt.html` could have the snippet mentioned in Listing 2-1 embedded in it. The snippet in Listing 2-1 shows that static content of the site is served from `http://images.press.com`.

Listing 2-1. *Snippet Showing Reference to a Different Server to Serve Static Content for a Page with the URL* `http://apress.com/books/gwt.html`

```
<img src="http://images.press.com/logo/us/logo.gif" />
<link rel="stylesheet" href="http://images.press.com/css/style1.css"
    type="text/css" media="all" />
```

What Are the Implications of the Same Origin Policy on GWT?

As mentioned earlier, the same origin policy is applicable for code written in JavaScript, and since the GWT compiler compiles Java code into JavaScript, the policy is applicable for code written for a GWT application as well. An important implication of this is on the various files generated while compiling a GWT-based application. Since the same origin policy does not allow JavaScript to access resources from a different domain, all the files for the GWT application must reside on the same web server. Another important implication is related to making RPC calls (which are explained in Chapter 4). The same origin policy restricts the `XMLHttpRequest` object to making requests outside the domain from which the page was loaded. Therefore, your GWT application cannot make requests for data to domains different from the one from which the page containing the code was originally loaded.

Deferred Binding

Reflection and dynamic class loading are very powerful concepts used in the Java language, and they open the door to a number of advanced techniques while programming. This section shows how these concepts are used within an example and then relates them back to the GWT.

Suppose you have an object hierarchy with the structure shown in Figure 2-3: a base class called Spacecraft and its two customized subclasses called Orbiter and Lander.

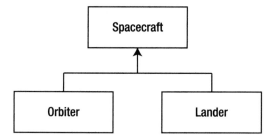

Figure 2-3. *Class hierarchy for a hypothetical example*

In Java, you would use reflection to load a specific type of Spacecraft object, as shown in Listing 2-2.

Listing 2-2. *Dynamically Loading an Object in Java Using Reflection*

```
Spacecraft spacecraft  = (Spacecraft) Class.forName(typeOfSpacecraft).newInstance();
// where typeOfSpacecraft is a String object containing either "Orbiter" or "Lander"
```

The various web browsers in use today have a lot of properties and methods that are proprietary and hence cause differences that need to be handled differently while writing an application supporting all these browsers.

For example, the properties used for getting window dimensions in Firefox and Internet Explorer are different:

Firefox: window.innerWidth and window.innerHeight

Internet Explorer: document.body.clientWidth and document.body.clientHeight

The simplest technique that a programming framework such as the GWT could use to handle such differences is to have a common base class and override such custom behavior in customized subclasses. Then the applications created using such a framework would, at run-time, use reflection and dynamic class loading to create instances of the respective subclasses based on the underlying browser in use.

However, JavaScript is a simple language, and reflection and dynamic class loading are not supported. Although it is possible to create a single .js file containing the translated code of all the various subclasses (representing various browsers), this would be overkill for an application of even a moderately large size because the time taken for downloading a large .js file would lead to a bad user experience associated with the load/startup delay of the application.

To overcome these shortcomings in JavaScript, the GWT framework introduced the concept of *deferred binding*, which works by resolving and inserting the required class during compile time instead of runtime, as is the case in the Java language. You signal the creation of such an instance to the compiler by using the GWT.create(Type.class) method. You must be wondering how the compiler can determine which instance of the class would be needed at runtime and create the compiled version of the application for it. Well, the GWT compiler does this by creating a unique version of the application for each browser supported by it. The version created separately for each browser is tight and compact and contains code relevant only to a specific browser.

The browser version used is just one of the parameters, and you could introduce your own parameters for this scenario. A common use case for this is the language your application will support. Suppose the GWT framework supports eight different browsers and you write your application in two different languages. Then the compilation step would create 16 versions of your application, each file mapping a browser-language combination. This pair and the generated file name are stored in a lookup table of your application's .js file, and the appropriate version is resolved and loaded at runtime.

Unlike Java's refection technique to dynamically load an object at runtime (as shown in Listing 2-2) where you used a string literal, in the GWT framework you must use the name of the type literally (that is, `<TypeName>.class`). As a developer using the GWT framework, it's important for you to understand the difference between the two methods used for creating new objects in GWT: the first method is using the class constructor and calling the constructor explicitly (that is, by using `new <ClassName>()`), and the second method is using the generator and getting the class generated at compile time (by using the `GWT.create(<TypeName>.class)` method).

`new <ClassName>()`: The call to constructor of a class gets converted to JavaScript directly.

`GWT.create(<TypeName>.class)`: The call to `GWT.create(...)` passes through a generator and instantiates a type using deferred binding. (It effectively autogenerates or adds code for you. The next section will discuss generators in more detail. Generators are probably one of the most powerful features at your disposal when using the GWT framework.)

Understanding Generator, Related Classes, and Code Generation Using Generators

The `Generator` class in the `com.google.gwt.core.ext` package acts as the base class for all classes interested in automatic code generation using deferred binding requests. Table 2-7 lists the methods available in the `Generator` class.

Table 2-7. *Methods in the* `Generator` *Class*

Method name	Description
`Generator()`	Constructor.
`escape(String)`	Escapes a string content to be a valid string literal. An escaped literal can be used within double quotes while using the Java language.
`generate(TreeLogger, GeneratorContext, String)`	Generates a default constructable subclass of the type represented by the `String` parameter. This is an abstract method, and all subclasses must override this method and provide a concrete implementation.

The GeneratorContext interface in the com.google.gwt.core.ext package allows the generators to access method metadata, which is used for constructing objects using deferred binding. Table 2-8 lists a few of the most important methods available in the GeneratorContext interface.

Table 2-8. *Important Methods in the* GeneratorContext *Interface*

Method Name	Description
tryCreate(TreeLogger, String, String)	Attempts to get a PrintWriter so that the caller can generate source code for a specific type. If the type already exists, then null is returned. (This takes instances of TreeLogger, packageName, and sourceName of the type to be generated as parameters.)
commit(TreeLogger, PrintWriter)	Commits the source generation begun by a call to the tryCreate(...) method.
getTypeOracle()	Returns the TypeOracle (explained later in this section) for the GeneratorContext.
getPropertyOracle()	Returns the PropertyOracle (explained later in this section) for the GeneratorContext.

■**Note** The source code generation process for a named type, started with a call to the GeneratorContext. tryCreate(...) method, is not committed until the GeneratorContext.commit(...) method is called.

The TreeLogger interface in the com.google.gwt.core.ext package is used to log messages in deferred binding generators. Table 2-9 lists the various methods available in the TreeLogger interface.

Table 2-9. *Methods in the* TreeLogger *Interface*

Method Name	Description
log(TreeLogger.Type, String, Throwable)	Used to log a message and the corresponding exception.
isLoggable(TreeLogger.Type)	Used to determine whether a specific log type can be logged.
branch(TreeLogger.Type, String, Throwable)	Used to branch a new logger under the current logger. The messages that are logged using the branch logger get grouped together under the parent logger.

■**Note** TreeLogger.Type is an enum listing the various logging levels that can be used to differentiate the various logged messages. The various types in the enum are DEBUG, ERROR, INFO, SPAM, TRACE, WARN, and ALL.

The `TypeOracle` class in the `com.google.gwt.core.ext.typeinfo` package is used to get the information (including metadata information such as comments in the documentation of the class/interface/methods) related to a specific type from a set of source files. Table 2-10 lists some of the important methods available in the `TypeOracle` class. The most important methods return an instance of either the `JPackage` or `JClassType` class.

Table 2-10. *Important Methods in the* `TypeOracle` *Class*

Method Name	Description
`getPackage(String packageName)`	Gets a package by name
`getType(String typeName)`	Gets a type (class/interface) by name
`getType(String packageName, String typeName)`	Gets a type (class/interface) by its package relative name

The `PropertyOracle` interface in the `com.google.gwt.core.ext` package is used to retrieve values of the various properties to be used at the time of deferred binding. Table 2-11 lists the methods available in the `PropertyOracle` interface.

Table 2-11. *Methods in the* `PropertyOracle` *Interface*

Method Name	Description
`getPropertyValue(TreeLogger, String)`	This method tries to retrieve the value of a named deferred binding property. The method throws `BadPropertyValueException` if either the property is not defined or it has an unsupported value.

The `JClassType` class in the `com.google.gwt.core.ext.typeinfo` package stores the type information of a Java class or interface. Table 2-12 lists the various methods available in the `JClassType` class. The `JClassType` gives you access to details about a type just as you would be able to do with the Reflection API in the Java language.

Table 2-12. *Important Methods in the* `JClassType` *Class*

Method Name	Description
`getPackage()`	Returns the package of the type
`getSubtypes()`	Returns an array of all subtypes of the type
`getMethods()`	Returns an array of all methods of the type
`getFields()`	Returns an array of all fields of the type
`getField(String fieldName)`	Returns a `JField` object for the specified field
`getMetaData(String tagName)`	Returns an array of array of strings containing the entire metadata for a specified tag name
`getMetaDataTags()`	Returns an array of all the metadata tags

Example of Using Generator to Autogenerate Code for Your Applications

In the following sections, I will go over a concrete example to solidify the understanding of using a generator to autogenerate code for your application. The example I'll discuss is called PropertyFileReader. The Java language provides a `java.util.Properties` class that can be used to read properties from a properties file in the file system. (The properties file contains key-value pairs, and the values corresponding to keys can be retrieved using the `Properties` class.)

For applications configured based on values in property files, this will turn out to be an important missing feature that is required. GWT and JavaScript do not support reading properties files, so you'll want to create a generic feature to reuse this functionality. By using a generator, you will provide the ability to autogenerate code for an interface (which maps different properties to methods in the interface), which can be defined as per an application's needs.

■**Note** You can use generators to autogenerate code for or add code to any existing type (interface or class).

In this example, the developer would only need to define an interface with various methods to access different properties, and the generator will handle the task of generating a class with all the methods implemented to return the values from the corresponding properties file. Once the generator is created and configured properly, a developer would only need to create a properties file and create a corresponding interface. After that, objects for this interface should be created using a call to the `GWT.create(...)` method, which would rebind the variable to instance of the generated class (by deferred binding at compile time).

PropertyFileReader Example Explained

First, you create a properties file named `book.properties` containing the key-value pairs, as shown in Listing 2-3.

Listing 2-3. *Contents of the Sample Properties File*

```
year=2008
name=Accelerated GWT
publisher=Apress
author=Vipul Gupta
```

Next, you create an interface for accessing the properties file, as shown in Listing 2-4.

Listing 2-4. *Contents of the Sample Interface File You Want to Build to Access the Properties File*

```
public interface <InterfaceX_Name > {
  String year();
  String name();
  String publisher();
  String author();
}
```

Once you've created and configured the generator, you need to make a call to the GWT.create(...) method to get an object representing an implementation of the interface. You can use this object to access the property values using the methods in the interface.

The generator will go through the following steps to generate the source code for the class (implementing the logic to return the values corresponding to the keys):

1. Read the key-value pairs in the properties file.

2. Create a new type implementing the accessor interface.

3. Implement all the methods in the interface returning the corresponding values for the keys represented by the method names (or specified by metadata, discussed later).

The class you want to be created and instantiated when you make a call to the GWT.create(InterfaceX_Name.class) method should look like Listing 2-5.

Listing 2-5. *Contents of the File You Want to Be Autogenerated by the Generator*

```
package com.apress.gwt.chapter2.client;

public class InterfaceX_NameGen implements InterfaceX_Name {

    public String author() {
      return "Vipul Gupta" ;
    }

    public String name() {
      return "Accelerated GWT" ;
    }

    public String year() {
      return "2008" ;
    }

    public String publisher() {
      return "Apress" ;
    }
  }
```

Building the Generator-Based Application

The following sections list the steps you should follow to create the PropertyFileReader example discussed previously.

Start by Creating a Sample Project

Start by creating a project in the C:\gwt\Generator directory with the entry-point class for the application set as com.apress.gwt.chapter2.client.PropertyFileReader. (Use the projectCreator and applicationCreator utilities as explained in Chapter 1.)

Generate the Marker Interface Whose Subtypes Should Be Passed the Generator

Next create a new type (a base marker interface) to differentiate all types, whose code should be autogenerated by a specific generator. This interface configures and informs the GWT compiler that any call to GWT.create(...) with this type should pass through the generator registered for this type. I created an interface named PropertiesReader, as shown in Listing 2-6.

Listing 2-6. *New Type to Represent Which Types Should Go to Generator for Reading Properties*

```
package com.apress.gwt.chapter2.client;

/**
 * Marker interface for the PropertyFileReader application
 *
 * @author Vipul Gupta (vipulgupta.vg@gmail.com)
 */
public interface PropertiesReader {
}
```

Set Up the Properties File

Create a properties file named book.properties, and add the contents shown in Listing 2-3 in it. (I put this file in a new folder named res in the C:\gwt\Generator directory and added this folder to the classpath.) You should modify the two script files created by the applicationCreator utility and add the res folder to the classpath in these scripts. Listing 2-7 lists the PropertyFileReader-shell.cmd file, and Listing 2-8 lists the PropertyFileReader-compile.cmd file with the required change to add the res folder to the classpath in bold.

Listing 2-7. PropertyFileReader-shell.cmd *File with Classpath Updated to Include the* res *Folder*

```
@java -cp
    "%~dp0\src;%~dp0\bin;%~dp0\res;C:/gwt/gwt-user.jar;C:/gwt/gwt-dev-windows.jar"
    com.google.gwt.dev.GWTShell -gen "%~dp0\gen" -out "%~dp0\www" %*
    com.apress.gwt.chapter2.PropertyFileReader/PropertyFileReader.html
```

Listing 2-8. PropertyFileReader-compile.cmd *File with Classpath Updated to Include the* res *Folder*

```
@java -cp
    "%~dp0\src;%~dp0\bin;%~dp0\res;C:/gwt/gwt-user.jar;C:/gwt/gwt-dev-windows.jar"
    com.google.gwt.dev.GWTCompiler -gen "%~dp0\gen" -out "%~dp0\www" %*
    com.apress.gwt.chapter2.PropertyFileReader
```

Creating the Interface for PropertyFileReader Application

Create an interface for your application. This interface should have methods with names corresponding to the keys, or the metadata with these methods should specify the name of the key whose value this method should return. The metadata representing the key should be declared by using the gwt.key annotation in the Javadoc of the method. The name of the annotation is as defined by the developer of the generator, and all the implementing types should follow this contract. Also, to simplify things, the return type of all these methods should be String at the moment.

Along with the methods, the interface should also be annotated with metadata specifying the name of the properties file to use. The metadata representing the name of the property file to use should be declared by using the gwt.properties.filename annotation in the Javadoc of the interface. I created an interface named BookPropertiesReader, as shown in Listing 2-9.

Listing 2-9. BookPropertiesReader *Interface with Methods Used to Access the Various Properties*

```
package com.apress.gwt.chapter2.client;

/**
 * Base interface for reading properties from the book.properties file
 *
 * @gwt.properties.filename book.properties
 *
 * @author Vipul Gupta (vipulgupta.vg@gmail.com)
 */
public interface BookPropertiesReader extends PropertiesReader {

   String year();

   /**
    * @gwt.key name
    * @return
    */
   String getBookName();

   String publisher();

   /**
    * @gwt.key author
    * @return
    */
   String getAuthorName();
}
```

I have declared the methods in the interface using the two ways mentioned earlier. The year() method is named after the key year, and hence you don't need an annotation in Javadoc to specify the key. However, this needs to be specified for the method named getBookName() because the name of the method does not match the corresponding key.

■**Note** The `BookPropertiesReader` interface extends the `PropertiesReader` interface so that it represents the same type, and the generator registered (shown in Listing 2-13) to be run on all `WT.create(...)`
calls with the `PropertiesReader` interface runs on a `GWT.create(BookPropertiesReader.class)` call.

Writing the Generator Class

Create the generator class, which will generate the class from the interface you have defined.
Let's define a new class named `PropertyReaderGenerator` in the `com.apress.gwt.chapter2.`
`rebind` package. General convention is to define the generator classes in the `rebind` package
and outside the client package so that you can use all the libraries from the Java language that
are not available for classes in the `client` package.

All generator classes must extend the `com.google.gwt.core.ext.Generator` class and
implement its `generate(...)` method (refer to Table 2-7 for details of this method). Listing 2-10
shows the `PropertyReaderGenerator` class in its initial stage. The listing does not show much
except that the `Generator` class is extended and its `generate(...)` method is overridden.

■**Note** `gwt-dev-windows.jar` needs to be included in the classpath (including that of the IDE) for
accessing, using, and compiling code that uses classes related to `Generator` such as `com.google.gwt.`
`core.ext.Generator`. However, this JAR is already present in the classpath set by the two script files—
namely, `<ModuleName>-compile.cmd` and `<ModuleName>-shell.cmd`—which are generated by the
application by running the `applicationCreator` utility. These script files are used for compiling the code
for web mode and for running the application in hosted mode.

Listing 2-10. *The Generator Class in Its Initial Stage*

```
package com.apress.gwt.chapter2.rebind;

import com.google.gwt.core.ext.Generator;
import com.google.gwt.core.ext.GeneratorContext;
import com.google.gwt.core.ext.TreeLogger;
import com.google.gwt.core.ext.UnableToCompleteException;

/**
 * This class represents the generator for the PropertyFileReader application
 * The generator reads the values of properties from a file and maps them to
 * the implementation of an interface.
 *
 * @author Vipul Gupta (vipulgupta.vg@gmail.com)
 */
```

```
public class PropertyReaderGenerator extends Generator {

  @Override
  public String generate(TreeLogger logger, GeneratorContext context,
      String typeName) throws UnableToCompleteException {

    return null;
  }
}
```

The compiler calls the generate(...) method with the right parameters at compile time. The logger parameter is used to write your own custom log messages; the context gives access to various classes, packages, properties, and metadata; and the typeName is the name of the parameter passed to the GWT.create(...) method.

In Listing 2-10, the generate(...) method returns null, signaling to the compiler that the generator has not constructed any new type and the original type as passed to the GWT.create(...) method should be used for creating the object. As explained in Listing 2-5 earlier, you want to create a new class named BookPropertiesReaderGen for the BookPropertiesReader interface. If any new class is generated, then the generate(...) method should return the fully qualified name of such a class so that the compiler can use it to create an object.

The generate method is modified and shown in Listing 2-11. In Listing 2-11, the responsibility of actually creating the class is delegated to a user-defined method named createClass(...), and the generate(...) method handles returning the name of the newly generated type.

Listing 2-11. generate() *Method of the* PropertyReaderGenerator *Class*

```
  @Override
  public String generate(TreeLogger logger, GeneratorContext context,
      String typeName) throws UnableToCompleteException {

    String generatedClassQualifiedName = createClass(logger, context, typeName);
    if (generatedClassQualifiedName == null) {
      throw new UnableToCompleteException();
    }
    return generatedClassQualifiedName;
  }
```

You should now write the createClass(...) and the other remaining methods that would actually generate the new type with the required functionality. These methods are discussed inline in detail in Listing 2-12, which lists the code for the entire PropertyReaderGenerator class.

Listing 2-12. *Code of the* PropertyReaderGenerator *Class*

```
package com.apress.gwt.chapter2.rebind;

import java.io.IOException;
import java.io.InputStream;
```

```java
import java.io.PrintWriter;
import java.util.Properties;

import com.google.gwt.core.ext.Generator;
import com.google.gwt.core.ext.GeneratorContext;
import com.google.gwt.core.ext.TreeLogger;
import com.google.gwt.core.ext.UnableToCompleteException;
import com.google.gwt.core.ext.typeinfo.JClassType;
import com.google.gwt.core.ext.typeinfo.JMethod;
import com.google.gwt.core.ext.typeinfo.JType;
import com.google.gwt.core.ext.typeinfo.NotFoundException;
import com.google.gwt.core.ext.typeinfo.TypeOracle;
import com.google.gwt.user.rebind.ClassSourceFileComposerFactory;
import com.google.gwt.user.rebind.SourceWriter;

/**
 * This class represents the generator for the PropertyFileReader application
 * The generator reads the values of properties from a file and maps them to
 * the implementation of an interface.
 *
 * @author Vipul Gupta (vipulgupta.vg@gmail.com)
 */
public class PropertyReaderGenerator extends Generator {

  @Override
  public String generate(TreeLogger logger, GeneratorContext context,
      String typeName) throws UnableToCompleteException {

    String generatedClassQualifiedName = createClass(logger, context, typeName);
    if (generatedClassQualifiedName == null) {
      throw new UnableToCompleteException();
    }
    return generatedClassQualifiedName;
  }

  private String createClass(TreeLogger logger, GeneratorContext context,
      String typeName) throws UnableToCompleteException {

    // We start by retrieving the TypeOracle object from the context
    TypeOracle typeOracle = context.getTypeOracle();
    try {

      // We retrieve the JClassType object and the package name for the
      // original type from the typeOracle
      JClassType originalType = typeOracle.getType(typeName);
      String packageName = originalType.getPackage().getName();
```

```
    // We retrieve the name of the properties file to use from the
    // metadata associated with the originalType
    String propertiesFileName = null;
    try {
      propertiesFileName = originalType
          .getMetaData("gwt.properties.filename")[0][0];
    } catch (Exception e) {
      throw new NotFoundException(
          "Properties file name not set using gwt.properties.filename tag");
    }

    // Retrieve the java.util.Properties object associated with the
    // properties file.
    InputStream in = Thread.currentThread().getContextClassLoader()
      .getResourceAsStream(propertiesFileName);
    if (in == null) {
    throw new FileNotFoundException("Property file named "
        + propertiesFileName + " not found in the classpath");
    }
    Properties properties = getProperties(in);


    // Create the name of the generated class from the name of the originalType
    String originalClassName = originalType.getSimpleSourceName();
    String generatedClassName = originalClassName + "Gen";

    // Get a sourceWriter for the generated class
    SourceWriter sourceWriter = getSourceWriter(logger, context,
      originalType, packageName, generatedClassName);

    // Write code for the generated class if the sourceWriter is not null.
    // If it is null then the class has already been created.
    if (sourceWriter != null)
          writeClass(logger, originalType, properties, sourceWriter);

    // Return the fully qualified name of the generated type as this needs
    // to be returned by the overridden generate(...) method
    // of the Generator
    return originalType.getParameterizedQualifiedSourceName() + "Gen";

      // log errors with appropriate messages and return null as the name
      // of the generated class in case of exceptions
  } catch (FileNotFoundException e) {
    logger.log(TreeLogger.ERROR, e.getMessage(), e);
    return null;
  } catch (NotFoundException e) {
```

```
      logger.log(TreeLogger.ERROR, e.getMessage(), e);
      return null;
    } catch (IOException e) {
      logger.log(TreeLogger.ERROR, "Problem in reading properties file", e);
      return null;
    }
  }

  private Properties getProperties(InputStream in) throws IOException {
    if (in == null) {
      throw new IOException("Invalid or null stream for the property file");
    }

    // Create a java.util.Properties object from the InputStream passed to the
    // method and returns this object.
    Properties properties = new Properties();
    properties.load(in);
    return properties;
  }

  /**
   * The getSourceWriter(...) method attempts to create a specific class
   * (represented by generatedClassName) in a specified package (represented by
   * packageName). The generated class is then modified so that it implements
   * the Type whose object was asked to be constructed (represented by
   * originalType). If the class attempted to be generated already exists then
   * the method returns null, otherwise an instance of SourceWriter representing
   * the generated class is returned.
   */
  private SourceWriter getSourceWriter(TreeLogger logger,
      GeneratorContext context, JClassType originalType, String packageName,
      String generatedClassName) {
    ClassSourceFileComposerFactory classFactory =
        new ClassSourceFileComposerFactory(packageName, generatedClassName);

    classFactory.addImplementedInterface(originalType.getName());

    // Initialized as null if the resource already exists
    PrintWriter printWriter = context.tryCreate(logger, packageName,
        generatedClassName);

    // If the resource already exists then return null
    if (printWriter == null) {
      return null;
    }
```

```java
        SourceWriter sourceWriter = classFactory.createSourceWriter(context,
            printWriter);
        return sourceWriter;
    }

    private void writeClass(TreeLogger logger, JClassType originalType,
            Properties properties, SourceWriter sourceWriter) {

        // We start by retrieving the various methods defined in the originalType
        JMethod[] methods = originalType.getMethods();

        // The source file is then indented by a few spaces
        sourceWriter.indent();

        // We create some local variables to use inside the loop
        JMethod method = null;
        JType type = null;
        String[][] keyNameMetadataArray = null;
        String keyName = null;

        // We loop through all the methods in the originalType and then add
        // an implementation for each of those methods in the generated class.
        for (int i = 0; i < methods.length; i++) {
            method = methods[i];
            type = method.getReturnType();

            // Write the method declaration in the generated class. For example for
            // String year() in the interface, this line will add public String year(){
            // in the generated class.
            sourceWriter.println();
            sourceWriter.println("public " + type.getSimpleSourceName() + " "
                + method.getName() + "() {");
            sourceWriter.indent();

             // Retrieve any metadata associated with this method in the original type.
             // We are specifically interested in metadata declared with key as gwt.key
            keyNameMetadataArray = method.getMetaData("gwt.key");

            // If metadata associated with gwt.key exists for this method i.e. if it
            // lists the key that needs to be used for returning the value from this
            // method, then use it. In case the key is missing, then use the
            // name of the method as the key to return the value from the properties file.
            if (keyNameMetadataArray != null && keyNameMetadataArray.length != 0) {
            // Extracting the name of the key into a local variable for brevity
            keyName = keyNameMetadataArray[0][0];
            sourceWriter.println("return \"" + properties.getProperty(keyName)
                + "\" ;");
```

```
    } else {
    sourceWriter.println("return \""
            + properties.getProperty(method.getName()) + "\" ;");

    }
    sourceWriter.outdent();
    sourceWriter.println("}");
  }

  // Commits the source generated for this class
  sourceWriter.commit(logger);
 }
}
```

Registering the Generator in Module's XML File

You should now register the generator, the `PropertyReaderGenerator` class, in the module XML file of the application. Listing 2-13 lists the `PropertyFileReader.gwt.xml` file with the generator registration highlighted in bold.

Listing 2-13. *Module XML File (*`PropertyFileReader.gwt.xml`*) with Generator Registered to Handle the* `PropertiesReader` *Type*

```
<module>

    <!-- Inherit the core Web Toolkit stuff.              -->
    <inherits name='com.google.gwt.user.User'/>

    <!-- Specify the app entry-point class.               -->
    <entry-point class='com.apress.gwt.chapter2.client.PropertyFileReader'/>

    <generate-with class="com.apress.gwt.chapter2.rebind.PropertyReaderGenerator">
        <when-type-assignable
            class="com.apress.gwt.chapter2.client.PropertiesReader"/>
    </generate-with>

</module>
```

The registration in the module XML file states which generator (`PropertyReaderGenerator` in this example) should be run for which types (`PropertiesReader`).

Writing the Entry-Point Class

Next you should make the generator work for your application. This requires modifying the entry-point class. Go ahead and change the `PropertyFileReader.java` file to look like Listing 2-14.

Listing 2-14. *Contents of the* `PropertyFileReader.java` *File*

```java
package com.apress.gwt.chapter2.client;

import com.google.gwt.core.client.EntryPoint;
import com.google.gwt.core.client.GWT;
import com.google.gwt.user.client.ui.Label;
import com.google.gwt.user.client.ui.RootPanel;

/**
 * Entry-point classes define <code>onModuleLoad()</code>.
 */
public class PropertyFileReader implements EntryPoint {

  /**
   * This is the entry-point method.
   */
  public void onModuleLoad() {
    BookPropertiesReader reader = (BookPropertiesReader) GWT
      .create(BookPropertiesReader.class);
    RootPanel.get("slot1").add(new Label(reader.year()));
    RootPanel.get("slot1").add(new Label(reader.getBookName()));
    RootPanel.get("slot1").add(new Label(reader.publisher()));
    RootPanel.get("slot1").add(new Label(reader.getAuthorName()));
  }
}
```

I'll explain the code listed in Listing 2-14 here:

1. You start by creating an object of the `BookPropertiesReader` type, as shown here:

   ```java
   BookPropertiesReader reader = (BookPropertiesReader) GWT
           .create(BookPropertiesReader.class);
   ```

   Since `BookPropertiesReader` is of the `PropertiesReader` type, the call to
   `GWT.create(...)` uses `PropertyReaderGenerator` at compile time to generate the
   `BookPropertiesReaderGen` class at runtime. The compiler then transforms this generated class to its JavaScript equivalent and changes the instantiation call listed earlier
   to new `BookPropertiesReaderGen()`.

2. After the object is generated and instantiated, you make calls to the various methods
   in the object (originally in the interface) and show the values corresponding to the keys
   as labels on the screen:

   ```java
   RootPanel.get("slot1").add(new Label(reader.year()));
   RootPanel.get("slot1").add(new Label(reader.getBookName()));
   RootPanel.get("slot1").add(new Label(reader.publisher()));
   RootPanel.get("slot1").add(new Label(reader.getAuthorName()));
   ```

Creating the Host HTML File

You should also simplify the host HTML file created by the `applicationCreator` utility. Change the `PropertyFileReader.html` file in the `public` folder to the contents shown in Listing 2-15.

Listing 2-15. *Contents of the* `PropertyFileReader.html` *File*

```html
<html>
  <head>
    <title>Wrapper HTML for PropertyFileReader</title>
    <style>
      body,td,a,div,.p{font-family:arial,sans-serif}
      div,td{color:#000000}
    </style>
    <script language='Javascript'
      src='com.apress.gwt.chapter2.PropertyFileReader.nocache.js'></script>
  </head>
  <body>
    <h1>PropertyFileReader</h1>
      <table align=center>
        <tr>
          <td id="slot1"></td >
        </tr>
      </table>
  </body>
</html>
```

Running the Application

You should now execute the application by running the `PropertyFileReader-shell.cmd` script from Eclipse or the command line. Figure 2-4 shows the result of executing the PropertyFileReader application. (You should ensure that the project is built properly before executing the `PropertyFileReader-shell.cmd` script.)

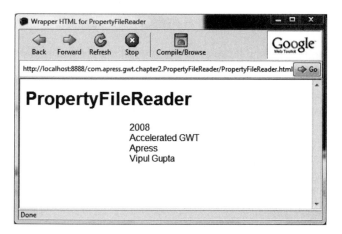

Figure 2-4. *Host browser window demonstrating PropertyFileReader application being run*

The sample PropertyFileReader application demonstrates the power of generators. The application has shown you a very simple but powerful way to autogenerate code for your system. You can use generators to do much more complex things with ease. Generators are used in a lot of internal features in the GWT framework, such as when generating code for RPC and localization. This will be highlighted at relevant places in the book (alongside the features using generators internally).

GWT: Startup/Bootstrap Process

The bootstrap process followed by a GWT application is a point of confusion for many new developers because of an involved process consisting of a lot of files.

The bootstrap process followed by a GWT application goes like this:

1. The client browser makes a request for the host page of the GWT application. The browser then receives the host HTML page from the server and loads it.

2. While processing the host HTML page, the browser encounters the JavaScript tag, which refers to the JavaScript (.js) file of the GWT module. The browser downloads the file and loads it.

3. Apart from other things, the module's JavaScript file contains the code that is responsible for resolving a number of hidden parameters and configurations (also known as *deferred binding* as explained earlier in this chapter). Once these values are resolved, the code then looks up a table generated by the GWT compiler to resolve which .cache.html file (containing all the logic and code of the GWT application) to use. The file is chosen based on the previous parameters. (As explained earlier, the compiler generates different files for different combinations of the various parameters.)

■**Note** Examples of parameters include the browser the client is using, the language, and so on.

---

4. The module's JavaScript code creates and inserts a hidden iframe into the DOM of the page and loads the .cache.html file in this iframe.

To fully understand the compilation output, it is important to understand the various files created by the GWT compiler. The most important ones are listed here:

.cache.html: The files with these extensions contain the JavaScript code and logic of your application. Having the actual JavaScript code in the HTML files allows the web server to compress these files while sending them to the browser. This leads to extremely fast startup times during subsequent runs of the application. The cache part in the extensions of these files represents that the client's web browser can successfully cache these files. The bootstrap process will request a different file from the web server only in the case of changes in your application. These files have an MD5-encoded prefix as their names.

`.cache.xml`: This file lists the various choices made by the compiler while generating the optimized JavaScript code for a specific browser. The names of these files are the same as per the corresponding `.cache.html` file.

Listing 2-16 lists a `.cache.xml` file from the generator example discussed earlier in this chapter. The snippet with `<generated-type-hash...>` reflects the hash generated while using the generator, and the snippet with `<rebind-decision...>` represents the choice made by the compiler while choosing the implementation of history for the Mozilla browser. The compiler decided to use `HistoryImplMozilla` instead of `HistoryImpl` for history support.

Listing 2-16. *The* `3E5E71FAA4A27799CCB015BDCB3B09A0.cache.xml` *File from Generator Example*

```xml
<?xml version="1.0" encoding="UTF-8"?>
    <cache-entry>
        <generated-type-hash
          class="com.apress.gwt.chapter2.client.BookPropertiesReaderGen"
          hash="1A9F325948FC56CD48A02A4368BDC9F8"/>

        <rebind-decision in="com.google.gwt.user.client.ui.impl.TextBoxImpl"
          out="com.google.gwt.user.client.ui.impl.TextBoxImpl"/>

        <rebind-decision in="com.google.gwt.user.client.impl.DOMImpl"
          out="com.google.gwt.user.client.impl.DOMImplMozilla"/>

        <rebind-decision in="com.google.gwt.user.client.impl.HistoryImpl"
          out="com.google.gwt.user.client.impl.HistoryImplMozilla"/>

        <rebind-decision in="com.apress.gwt.chapter2.client.BookPropertiesReader"
          out="com.apress.gwt.chapter2.client.BookPropertiesReaderGen"/>

        <rebind-decision in="com.google.gwt.user.client.ui.ListBox.Impl"
          out="com.google.gwt.user.client.ui.ListBox.Impl"/>

        <rebind-decision in="com.google.gwt.user.client.ui.impl.FormPanelImpl"
          out="com.google.gwt.user.client.ui.impl.FormPanelImpl"/>

        <rebind-decision in="com.apress.gwt.chapter2.client.PropertyFileReader"
          out="com.apress.gwt.chapter2.client.PropertyFileReader"/>

        <rebind-decision in="com.google.gwt.user.client.ui.impl.FocusImpl"
          out="com.google.gwt.user.client.ui.impl.FocusImpl"/>

        <rebind-decision in="com.google.gwt.user.client.ui.impl.PopupImpl"
          out="com.google.gwt.user.client.ui.impl.PopupImplMozilla"/>

    </cache-entry>
```

`.cache.js`: These files represent the stripped-down and optimized version of your application for a specific browser. Just like the `.cache.html` files, these files also contain the entire JavaScript of your application, but these files cannot be compressed by the web server. The cache in the extension of these files represent that these files can be successfully cached by the client's web browser. The bootstrap process will request a different file from the web server only in the case of changes in your application. The names of these files are the same as per the corresponding `.cache.html` and `.cache.xml` files.

■**Note** The compiler generates a set of `.cache.html`, `.cache.xml`, and `.cache.js` files, one set for each supported browser. All the files in the set have the same MD5-coded name as a prefix. The contents of the generated JavaScript are encoded as UTF-8, and the coded name of the files is an MD5 hash of the script contents.

`.nocache.js`: The GWT compiler creates the `<ModuleName>.nocache.js` file (or the cross-site equivalent `<ModuleName>-xs.nocache.js`) for your application. This is the main bootstrap file of the application and should be included in the host HTML file of your application. It is also the first file that is loaded and contains all the properties of the application such as the browser-to-`.cache.js` mapping, locale, and so on.

`history.html`: An HTML file containing code used to maintain the history of a GWT application. The history mechanism is explained in detail in Chapter 9 of the book.

`.gwt.rpc`: This file lists the names of all types that implement the `java.io.Serializable` interface and are allowed to be serialized and used with RPC. In effect, this file acts as a serialization policy file.

■**Note** Earlier releases of the GWT framework provided the `IsSerializable` marker interface for differentiating the classes that can be serialized from the ones that cannot be. The developer community, however, raised the need for `java.io.Serializable`, and the same was added from the GWT release 1.4. The `.gwt.rpc` file must be deployed to your web server as a public resource. If this is not done, then the RPC system built into GWT ignores the serialization of the various types implementing `java.io.Serializable`.

■**Note** There is another file created by the compiler, namely, `gwt.js`. This file is generated to support the bootstrap process followed by the earlier release of the GWT framework (releases prior to 1.4). I won't discuss this file in the book.

Summary

This chapter covered details of the internal architecture and a number of important features of the GWT framework, including details of the basic components and JRE emulation library in the framework. It also discussed the same origin policy and the important concept of deferred binding. While discussing deferred binding, I discussed generators and relevant corresponding classes that can be used to autogenerate code for your needs.

In addition, the chapter showed a comprehensive example listing the various steps that you need to take to write your own generators. Then I discussed the startup/bootstrap process followed by any GWT application. I also listed the various files that are generated by the GWT compiler on compilation. This chapter focused on giving you insights about the internals of the GWT framework.

The next part (Chapters 3–6) will discuss the various UI components and how you can bundle them together to create a GUI for your application. It will also discuss client-server communication including the important concept of RPC and how your application can talk to the server to retrieve/post data in real time.

PART 2

■■■

UI Programming and Client-Server Communication

This part focuses on the UI library and the client-server communication used in GWT. GWT provides a comprehensive UI library and communication mechanism to help you develop rich GUI-based client-server applications. To get you up to speed, the first two chapters in this part will start with the basics of both the UI library and the communication mechanism, and then the remaining chapters will move on to advanced concepts.

Specifically, Chapter 3 will examine the various widgets and layout techniques available in the GWT framework. It will also explain the concept of composites, which help you bundle existing widgets and use composites as widgets.

Chapter 4 will introduce remote procedure calls and how to use RPC in GWT for client-server communication. This chapter will also guide you through the process of developing a basic GWT application using the RPC infrastructure provided by the framework.

Chapter 5 will discuss some of the advanced techniques related to UI development including event handling and other advanced widgets used to create rich GUI applications.

Chapter 6 will discuss some of the advanced techniques and internal details related to communication between client-server components in your GWT application.

CHAPTER 3

■■■

UI Programming:
Basic Widgets

In this chapter, I will discuss the various UI widgets and components available in the GWT framework. A UI *widget* is defined as a graphical component and is used for building graphical user interfaces. Many widgets allow a human to interact with the computer application by performing some action on the widget. For example, a button is a UI widget, and a user can signal an event by clicking it.

Widgets, when grouped together in a meaningful interface, form the contact point of your application to the external world. This chapter will start with some basic widgets offered by the framework, and then it will discuss a few of the basic layouts (container widgets) that are used to group simple widgets. I will wind up the chapter with a simple but comprehensive example, demonstrating how to use widgets to create the GUI of a web-based application.

Widgets in GWT can be divided into user-interface widgets and container widgets. Let's start with some of the basic widgets before jumping into container widgets. Widgets in GWT are rendered using dynamically created HTML. Each widget in the GWT framework has a corresponding HTML representation, and the compiler translates the widget objects in Java into the corresponding HTML equivalent for the widget.

GUI Building with Fundamental Widgets

The most fundamental widget components in any GUI include the following:

Buttons: Button, RadioButton, CheckBox

Text labels: Label, HTML

Input boxes: TextBox, TextArea, PasswordTextBox

Selection lists: ListBox

GWT provides classes for each of these fundamental widgets. Figure 3-1 shows the class hierarchy for the standard UI components in the GWT framework. All the classes above the dotted lines in the figure will be referred to as *base classes* in the rest of the chapter.

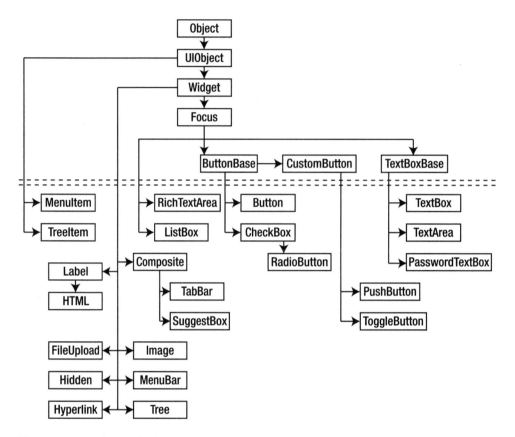

Figure 3-1. *Class hierarchy for the basic UI widgets. (All the classes above the dotted lines are abstract, and all the ones under the dotted lines are concrete widgets available for use by a developer.)*

Hierarchy of Base Classes Explained

All the widgets in the GWT framework are in the com.google.gwt.user.client.ui package. I will discuss the *base classes* in the hierarchy in Figure 3-1 along with their most important methods in the following sections. It's good to know the various APIs in the base classes because the base classes represent the common functionality that all widgets inherit.

The UIObject Class

The UIObject class is an abstract base class for all the UI widgets in the framework. This class provides a large number of methods required for a number of common needs such as checking visibility status, setting/getting height and width, setting/changing CSS styles, and so on. The UIObject class also has a method named setElement() that is used to set the corresponding browser element for the widget.

A Label object has its DOM element set up as an HTML's <div> tag. The following code snippet shows the constructor of a Label widget with the call to setElement() (in bold):

```
public Label() {
    setElement(DOM.createDiv());
    sinkEvents(Event.ONCLICK | Event.MOUSEEVENTS | Event.ONMOUSEWHEEL);
    setStyleName("gwt-Label");
}
```

You can style a UIObject class using CSS classes. Most of the widgets in the GWT framework have their own associated style classes declared for use by the developer. You can use the setStyleName(...) method to specify an object's primary style name. The code for the constructor of the Label shown previously sets the primary style name for the Label object as gwt-Label. You can also add secondary style names using the addStyleName(...) method. Secondary style rules are useful when you want to give a different styling to a widget during different events in its lifetime. In case you want to give specific styling to the Label widgets in your application, you should define a style class named gwt-Label in your application's CSS, as shown in the following example:

```
.gwt-Label {
    background-color: blue;
    font-size: 16pt;
}
```

■**Note** If no primary style is set for a widget, then the style class defaults to gwt-nostyle.

I will discuss more about styling UIObject and the corresponding API in the "How Do You Style UIObject Classes Using CSS?" section later in the chapter.

Being on the base of the class hierarchy for UI widgets, the UIObject class exposes a number of methods for use by all widgets. Table 3-1 lists some of the most important methods in the UIObject class.

Table 3-1. *Some of the Important Methods in the* UIObject *Class*

Method Name	Description
setElement(Element)	Sets the object's browser element. Subclasses must call this method before any other method. If there is an element already associated with this object, this method will copy the events from that element to the parameterized element and then remove the existing element in favor of the new element.
setSize(String, String)	Sets the size of the UIObject class based on the width and height passed as parameters.
isVisible()/setVisible(boolean)	Checks/sets the visibility of a UIObject.

Continued

Table 3-1. *Continued*

Method Name	Description
setStyleName(String)	Clears all the object's style names and sets it to the given style.
addStyleName(String)	Adds a secondary or dependent style name to this object.
removeStyleName(String)	Removes a style name.
setStylePrimaryName(String)	Sets the object's primary style name and updates all dependent style names.
addStyleDependentName(String)	Adds a dependent style name by specifying the style name's suffix.
removeStyleDependentName(String)	Removes a dependent style name by specifying the style name's suffix.

This section discussed briefly how styling is used in the GWT framework. I'll now discuss styling UIObject classes in more detail.

How Do You Style UIObject Classes Using CSS?

GWT allows UIObject classes to be styled using CSS by associating CSS style rule names in your class code. (For each element, the CSS style rule name is the element's CSS class.)

For example, if you use setStyleName("myStyle") in your application code, then the CSS class of the object in which this method is called will be mapped to a myStyle CSS class, as shown in the following code snippet:

```
.myStyle{
  background:#f5f5f5;
  border:1px solid #aaa;
  border-top:1px solid #ddd;
  border-left:1px solid #ddd;
  padding: 2px;
}
```

The UIObject class provides a different set of APIs in setStylePrimaryName(String) and addStyleDependentName(String). These APIs help in setting up the primary style rule and dependent style rules for a widget. You can use the dependent style rules to alter the styling of an object during the state changes in its lifetime.

The following code snippet shows how to use dependent style names for a widget named MyWidget:

```
//Constructor
MyWidget(){
  myWidget.setStylePrimaryName("myWidgetStyle");
  ... // Other logic in Constructor
}

public void select(boolean selected){
  ...
```

```
    if (selected){
    addDependentStyleName("selected");
    }else{
    removeDependentStyleName("selected");
    }
}
```

By using the code listed previously, `MyWidget` will be mapped to the following CSS classes:

```
.myWidgetStyle {
  font-size: 12pt;
}
.myWidgetStyle-selected {
  background-color: #FFDECC;
}
```

When the `myWidget.select(true)` method is called, then *both* the CSS rules declared previously will be applied to the `MyWidget` object.

The dependent style name is mapped in the following format in CSS:

```
<primaryStyleName>-<dependent StyleName>
```

If the primary style name is changed, then all the dependent style names automatically get updated as they are evaluated based on the existing primary style name, as mentioned in the dependent style name form earlier. For example, if the primary style name is changed to `oldWidgetStyle` because of a method call of `setStylePrimaryName("oldWidgetStyle")`, then the object will be mapped to the following CSS classes:

```
.oldWidgetStyle {    }
.oldWidgetStyle-selected {    }
```

The Widget Class

The `Widget` class acts as the base class for most of the UI widgets. Along with the basic functionality inherited from the `UIObject` class, this class adds support for receiving events from the browser as well as the ability for a widget to get added to a panel. Table 3-2 describes the methods in the `Widget` class.

Table 3-2. *Methods in the* `Widget` *Class*

Method Name	Description
getParent()	Returns the object representing the parent panel of this widget.
removeFromParent()	If the widget is attached to a parent widget, then calling this method removes the widget from its parent widget.
isAttached()	Checks whether the widget is currently attached to the browser's document.
onAttach()	Called when the widget is attached to the browser's document.
onDetach()	Called when the widget is detached from the browser's document.

Continued

Table 3-2. *Continued*

Method Name	Description
onLoad()	Called immediately after a widget is attached to the browser's document.
onUnload()	Called immediately before a widget is detached from the browser's document.
onBrowserEvent(Event)	Fired when a browser event is received by the widget.
setElement(Element)	Sets the object's browser element. Subclasses must call this method before any other method. The existing element, if any, is removed, and the events on the existing event are registered on the newly mentioned browser element.

The FocusWidget Class

FocusWidget is the abstract base class for most of the widgets that can receive keyboard focus. This class adds various methods to add and remove different type of event listeners. Table 3-3 describes some of the important methods in the FocusWidget class.

Table 3-3. *Some of the Important Methods in the* FocusWidget *Class*

Method Name	Description
addXXXListener(XXXListener)	Adds a listener to handle corresponding events
removeXXXListener(XXXListener)	Removes the listener previously registered
isEnabled()	Returns whether the widget is enabled or not
setEnabled(boolean)	Enables/disables a widget

■**Note** XXX used in Table 3-3 can be Click/Focus/Keyboard to receive click/mouse/keyboard events, respectively.

The ButtonBase Class

ButtonBase is the abstract base class for all widgets that represent buttons of some sort and adds methods specific to buttons. Table 3-4 describes these methods.

Table 3-4. *Methods in the* ButtonBase *Class*

Method Name	Description
ButtonBase(Element)	Creates a new ButtonBase mapped to the specified browser element
getText()	Returns the text of the object
setText(String)	Sets the object's text
getHTML()	Returns the text of the object as HTML
setHTML(String)	Sets the object's text via HTML

The TextBoxBase Class

TextBoxBase is the abstract base class for all widgets that accept text input. Table 3-5 describes some of the important methods in this class.

Table 3-5. *Some of the Important Methods in the* TextBoxBase *Class*

Method Name	Description
getCursorPos()	Returns the current position of the cursor
setCursorPos(int)	Sets the cursor position
getSelectedText()	Returns the currently selected text
setTextAlignment(TextAlignConstant)	Sets the alignment of the text in the text box
getText()	Gets the object's text
setText(String)	Sets the object's text
selectAll()	Selects all the text in the box

With details about various base classes behind you, let's see few of the widgets available in the UI library offered by GWT. The next sections explain some of the widgets along with the code used to create them.

How Do You Use the Widgets Provided by GWT?

Let's go over some of the widgets offered by the GWT framework and see them in action. You can start by creating a project in the chapter3 directory with the entry-point class set to com.apress.gwt.chapter3.client.SampleWidgets. You can also set the host HTML file as follows:

```
<html>
  <head>
    <style>
      body {font-family:arial,sans-serif; background-color: #C3D9FF;}
    </style>
    <script language='javascript'
        src='com.apress.gwt.chapter3.SampleWidgets.nocache.js'></script>
  </head>
  <body>
    <div id="widgetDiv"/>
  </body>
</html>
```

You have already worked through a few examples of setting up the entry-point class of your application in the earlier chapters. The following sections will go over the relevant code for creating and displaying the widgets. You should add this code in the onModuleLoad() method of the entry-point class. (The code for each widget is accompanied with a figure displaying how the widget looks when used in an application.)

The Label Widget

The Label class represents a Label widget, which is a simple element that just contains arbitrary text for display on the screen. You can add a Label widget to your application as follows:

```
final Label label = new Label("This is a Label");
RootPanel.get("widgetDiv").add(label);
```

When the application containing the earlier code is executed, the Label widget will look like Figure 3-2.

This is a Label

Figure 3-2. *A* Label *widget*

The Button Widget

The Button class represents a standard push button. You can add a Button widget to your application as follows:

```
final Button button = new Button("Button");
RootPanel.get("widgetDiv").add(button);
```

When the application containing the earlier code is executed, the Button will look like Figure 3-3.

Button

Figure 3-3. *A* Button *widget*

The CheckBox Widget

The CheckBox class represents a standard CheckBox widget. You can add a CheckBox to your application as follows:

```
final CheckBox checkBox = new CheckBox("Checkbox");
RootPanel.get("widgetDiv").add(checkBox);
```

Figure 3-4 shows the CheckBox created after the earlier code is executed (and after the CheckBox is clicked).

 ☑ Checkbox

Figure 3-4. *A* CheckBox *widget*

The RadioButton Widget

The RadioButton class represents a standard RadioButton widget. You can add a RadioButton to your application as follows:

```
final RadioButton radioButton = new RadioButton("RadioButton", "RadioButton");
RootPanel.get("widgetDiv").add(radioButton);
```

Figure 3-5 shows the RadioButton created after the earlier code is executed (and the RadioButton is selected).

Figure 3-5. *A* RadioButton *widget*

The PushButton Widget

The PushButton class represents a standard PushButton widget, similar to the Button class described earlier. However, the difference between a PushButton and Button lies in the built-in support for custom styling the PushButton. For example, you can set different text/images that should be shown when the button is in a normal or pressed state. You can add a PushButton that has different text during the default and pressed states to your application as follows:

```
final PushButton pushButton = new PushButton("Push Up", "Push Down");
RootPanel.get("widgetDiv").add(pushButton);
```

When the application containing the earlier code is executed, the PushButton will look like Figure 3-6.

Figure 3-6. *A* PushButton *widget in its initial state*

If the PushButton is clicked, the text on it will change, and the button it will look like Figure 3-7 (until the mouse button is released).

Figure 3-7. PushButton *when it is clicked (it changes to the initial state if the mouse button is released)*

The ToggleButton Widget

The ToggleButton class wraps a button that can be toggled between up and down states. Unlike standard and push buttons where the down state is represented as the time during which the button is kept pressed by the user, in ToggleButton, the state of the button is changed to a down state when it is clicked and persists as down until the user clicks the button again. You can add a ToggleButton that has different text during the default and pressed states to your application as follows:

```
final ToggleButton toggleButton = new ToggleButton("Toggle Up", "Toggle Down");
RootPanel.get("widgetDiv").add(toggleButton);
```

When the application containing the earlier code is executed, the ToggleButton will look like Figure 3-8.

Figure 3-8. *A* ToggleButton *widget in its initial state*

If the ToggleButton is clicked, it will look like Figure 3-9.

Figure 3-9. ToggleButton *widget when it is clicked*

The TextBox Widget

The TextBox class represents a standard TextBox widget that accepts a single line of input. You can add a TextBox to your application as follows:

```
final TextBox textBox = new TextBox();
RootPanel.get("widgetDiv").add(textBox);
```

Figure 3-10 shows the TextBox created by the earlier code in use.

Figure 3-10. *A* TextBox *widget*

The TextArea Widget

The TextArea class is a wrapper around a TextBox that allows multiple line of input. You can add a TextArea to your application as follows:

```
final TextArea textArea = new TextArea();
RootPanel.get("widgetDiv").add(textArea);
```

Figure 3-11 shows the TextArea created by the earlier code in use.

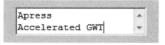

Figure 3-11. *A* TextArea *widget*

The PasswordTextBox Widget

The PasswordTextBox class is a wrapper around a TextBox that masks its input for privacy reasons. You can add a PasswordTextBox to your application as follows:

```
final PasswordTextBox passwordTextBox = new PasswordTextBox();
RootPanel.get("widgetDiv").add(passwordTextBox);
```

Figure 3-12 shows the PasswordTextBox created by the earlier code in use.

Figure 3-12. *A* PasswordTextBox *widget in action*

The ListBox Widget

The ListBox class allows giving a list of choices to the user to choose from. You can add a ListBox with four choices to your application as follows:

```
final ListBox listBox = new ListBox();
listBox.addItem("Item1");
listBox.addItem("Item2");
listBox.addItem("Item3");
listBox.addItem("Item4");
RootPanel.get("widgetDiv").add(listBox);
```

When the application containing the earlier code is executed, the ListBox will look like Figure 3-13.

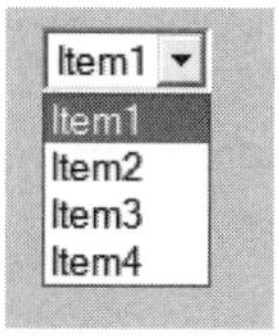

Figure 3-13. *A* ListBox *widget with four choices*

■Note The `ListBox` class provides a method named `setVisibleCount(int itemCount)`, which is used to manipulate the number of items that should be visible to the user from the list box. If this `itemCount` is set to 1, then the list box is displayed as a drop-down list instead.

The RichTextArea Widget

The `RichTextArea` class wraps a rich-text editor that allows the complex styling and formatting of text. You can add a `RichTextArea` to your application as follows:

```
final RichTextArea richTextArea = new RichTextArea();
RootPanel.get("widgetDiv").add(richTextArea);
```

Figure 3-14 shows the `RichTextArea` created by the earlier code (with some of the text formatted in bold and some in italics).

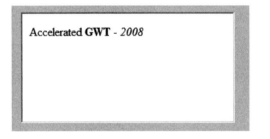

Figure 3-14. *A* `RichTextArea` *widget (displaying text being formatted in bold and italics)*

■Note The GWT framework comes bundled with a few sample applications. One of these is named KitchenSink. You can run this application to play with all the widgets together.

Understanding Layouts Using Panels

Laying out means arranging the UI components on the screen. In GWT, you use *panels* to do this. GWT provides a large number of panels to lay out your widgets. Panels are a special type of widgets that can contain other widgets and that allow you to arrange various widgets in a systematic manner. By organizing or positioning related widgets in a logical manner, the UI becomes much more usable and understandable. Each panel arranges its widgets differently and uses underlying layout logic in browsers for arranging the elements added to it.

■**Note** Panels use the HTML <div> and <table> elements to lay out the GUI.

Figure 3-15 lists the class hierarchy for the various panels included in the UI library of GWT.

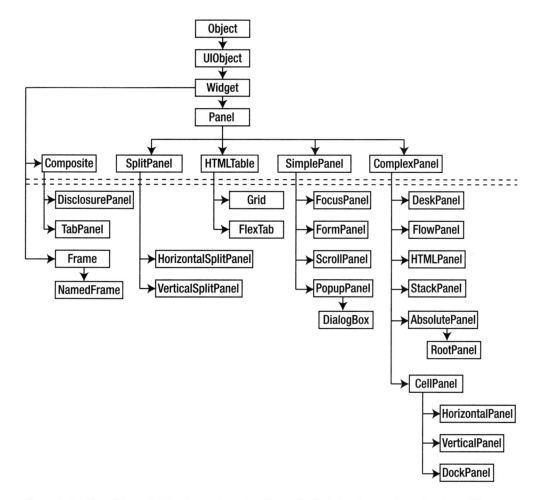

Figure 3-15. *Class hierarchy for the various GWT panels. (All the classes above the dotted lines are abstract panels, and all the ones under the dotted lines are concrete panels available for use by a developer.)*

Let's discuss some of the important panels and their corresponding API methods. I will also discuss the arrangements of child widgets when laid out using specific panels.

Starting with a RootPanel

RootPanel resides on the bottom of all other panels and is used for any UI-based GWT application. It is the base to which any widgets or panels need to be added, before being shown to the user. The RootPanel acts as an abstraction to get access to the document body of the main HTML page, which includes the GWT module (that is, RootPanel represents the <body> element of the containing document). All the widgets in your GWT application should be eventually added to the RootPanel directly or indirectly. RootPanel panels are never created directly and are accessed by using one of the methods from the class, as listed in Table 3-6.

Table 3-6. *Methods in the* RootPanel *Class (All Methods Are Static)*

Method Name	Description
get()	Returns the default RootPanel
get(String elementId)	Returns the RootPanel associated with the browser element having a specific ID
getBodyElement()	Returns an element representing the body of the underlying document

Aligning Widgets Using a CellPanel

In a CellPanel, the child widgets are placed using an HTML <table> tag. Each child widget is contained within the logical cells of a table. This panel allows you to set the size of each cell independently and allows you to align the widget within the cell containing it. Since a table can contain multiple cells, all CellPanel panels can contain multiple child widgets. The CellPanel class adds a number of methods to access and set the border, height, width, spacing, and horizontal/vertical alignment of the cells among others. The different types of cell Panels are HorizontalPanel, VerticalPanel, and DockPanel:

HorizontalPanel: Child widgets are arranged in a horizontal manner from left to right.

VerticalPanel: Child widgets are stacked vertically from top to bottom.

DockPanel: Child widgets are docked at outer edges. This panel allows you to add any number of widgets in the north, south, east, and west corners of the panel. The center widget is special and, if added, takes up the remaining space in the middle (only one widget can be added to the center of this panel).

Let's go through some code to see these panels in action. You already learned how to set up, create, and run a GWT application in earlier chapters, so only the onModuleLoad() method corresponding to the use of the various panels will be listed here. To follow these examples, it is worth setting up a new project using the projectCreator and applicationCreator tools; then modify the onModuleLoad() method of the entry-point class accordingly.

Understanding and Using a HorizontalPanel

If widgets need to be arranged horizontally, then you should use HorizontalPanel. Figure 3-16 shows the template of arrangement done by HorizontalPanel.

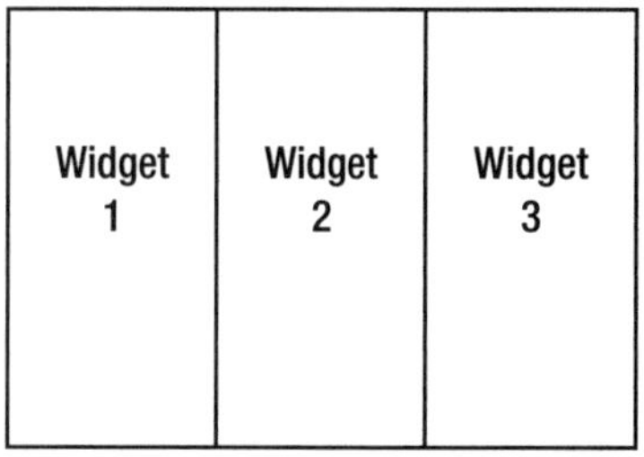

Figure 3-16. HorizontalPanel *template*

Listing 3-1 shows some code to use a HorizontalPanel.

Listing 3-1. *Code Demonstrating the Use of* HorizontalPanel

```
public void onModuleLoad() {
   final Label label = new Label("Sample Label");
   final Button button = new Button("Sample Button");
   final CheckBox checkBox = new CheckBox("Sample CheckBox");
   final RadioButton radioButton = new RadioButton("radio", "Sample RadioButton");

   Panel panel = new HorizontalPanel();
   RootPanel.get().add(panel);

   panel.add(label);
   panel.add(button);
   panel.add(checkBox);
   panel.add(radioButton);
}
```

If you execute the application with the onModuleLoad() method in the entry-point class as listed in Listing 3-1, the application will look like Figure 3-17.

Figure 3-17. *Widgets arranged horizontally by using a* HorizontalPanel

Understanding and Using a VerticalPanel

If widgets need to be arranged vertically, then you should use a VerticalPanel. Figure 3-18 shows the template of arrangement done by VerticalPanel.

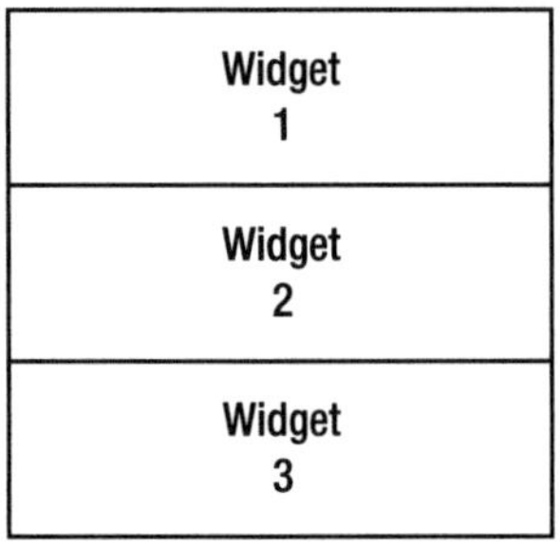

Figure 3-18. VerticalPanel *template*

Listing 3-2 shows some code to use a VerticalPanel.

Listing 3-2. *Code Demonstrating the Use of* VerticalPanel

```
public void onModuleLoad() {
    final Label label = new Label("Sample Label");
    final Button button = new Button("Sample Button");
    final CheckBox checkBox = new CheckBox("Sample CheckBox");
    final RadioButton radioButton = new RadioButton("radio", "Sample RadioButton");

    Panel panel = new VerticalPanel();
    RootPanel.get().add(panel);

    panel.add(label);
    panel.add(button);
    panel.add(checkBox);
    panel.add(radioButton);
}
```

If you execute the application with the onModuleLoad() method in the entry-point class as listed in Listing 3-2, the application will look like Figure 3-19.

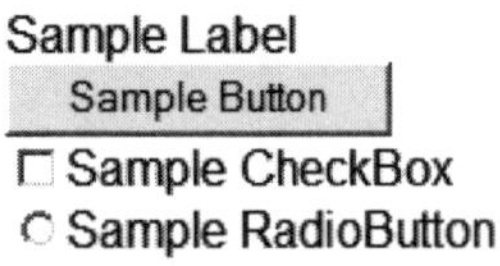

Figure 3-19. *Widgets arranged vertically by using a* VerticalPanel

Understanding and Using a DockPanel

If widgets need to be arranged at edges with the remaining space in the center for a central widget, then you should use a DockPanel. Figure 3-20 shows the template of arrangement done by DockPanel.

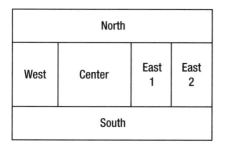

Figure 3-20. DockPanel *template*

Listing 3-3 shows some code to use a DockPanel.

Listing 3-3. *Code Demonstrating the Use of* DockPanel

```
public void onModuleLoad() {
    final Label northLabel = new Label("North");
    final Label southLabel = new Label("South");
    final Label westLabel = new Label("West");
    final Label eastLabel1 = new Label("East 1");
    final Label eastLabel2 = new Label("East 2");
    final Label centerlabel = new Label("Center");

    DockPanel panel = new DockPanel();
    panel.setBorderWidth(2);
    RootPanel.get().add(panel);

    // DockPanel provides constants to specify where the widget should be
    // laid out in the panel. These constants are used to lay out the labels at
    // respective corners of the panel.
    panel.add(northLabel, DockPanel.NORTH);
    panel.add(southLabel, DockPanel.SOUTH);
    panel.add(westLabel, DockPanel.WEST);
    panel.add(eastLabel1, DockPanel.EAST);
    panel.add(eastLabel2, DockPanel.EAST);
    panel.add(centerlabel, DockPanel.CENTER);
}
```

If you execute the application with the onModuleLoad() method in the entry-point class as listed in Listing 3-3, the application will look like Figure 3-21.

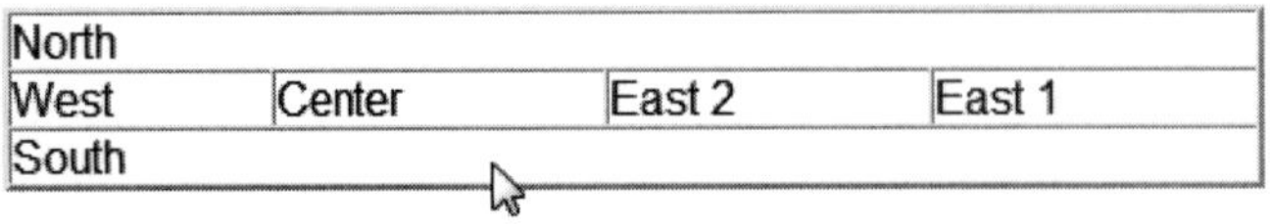

North			
West	Center	East 2	East 1
South			

Figure 3-21. *Application arranged using* DockPanel *by using the code in Listing 3-3*

What Is an HTMLTable Panel?

An HTMLTable panel acts as the base class for few of the table-based panels. The major difference between Cell-based panels and HTMLTable-based panels is that the latter provides an API for handling table-related operations such as getRowCount(), which returns the number of rows in the panel; insertRow(int), which inserts a new row before a specified row in the table; and so on. The different types of HTMLTable-based panels are Grid and FlexTable:

Grid: A rectangular grid that can contain text, HTML, or widget within its cells. It must be resized explicitly to the desired number of rows and columns.

FlexTable: A flexible table that creates cells on demand. Each row can contain a different number of cells, and individual cells can be set to span multiple rows or columns.

Understanding and Using a Grid

If widgets need to be arranged in a table and the application's code explicitly knows and sets the size of the table, then you should use a Grid. Listing 3-4 shows some code to use a Grid.

Listing 3-4. *Code Demonstrating the Use of a* Grid *Panel*

```
public void onModuleLoad() {

    // Grids must be sized explicitly, though they can be resized later.
    Grid grid = new Grid(3, 3);

    int counter = 0;

    // Put some values in the grid cells.
    for (int row = 0; row < 3; ++row) {
      for (int col = 0; col < 3; ++col)
      grid.setText(row, col, String.valueOf(counter++));
    }

    // Set the border for the grid so that you can explicitly see the
    // various cell boundaries.
    grid.setBorderWidth(2);

    RootPanel.get().add(grid);
  }
```

If you execute the application with the onModuleLoad() method in the entry-point class as listed in Listing 3-4, the application will look like Figure 3-22.

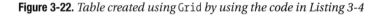

Figure 3-22. *Table created using* Grid *by using the code in Listing 3-4*

Suppose the Grid application created earlier requires the table to have a fourth column value for the first row. In this case, you can resize the grid as follows:

```
grid.resizeColumns(4);
// Other methods to resize are resizeRows(..) and resize(...,...).

grid.setText(0,3,String.valueOf(9));
```

If you execute the application again after the previous change, the application will look like Figure 3-23.

Figure 3-23. *Table after the* Grid *is resized to have an additional column*

Understanding and Using a FlexTable

If widgets need to be arranged in a table and you want the application to take care of managing the size of the table, then you should use a FlexTable. Listing 3-5 shows some code to use a FlexTable.

Listing 3-5. *Code Demonstrating the Use of* FlexTable

```
public void onModuleLoad() {
    // Tables have no explicit size -- they resize automatically on demand.
    FlexTable table = new FlexTable();
    table.setBorderWidth(2);

    table.setText(0, 0, "0-0 Text");

    Button button = new Button("1-1 Button");
    button.setWidth("100%");
    table.setWidget(1, 1, button);
```

```
// Format the cell so that the content, Button in our case, spans
// multiple columns
table.getFlexCellFormatter().setColSpan(1, 1, 2);

table.setWidget(2, 1, new Label("2-1 Label"));
table.setWidget(2, 2, new Label("2-2 Label"));

RootPanel.get().add(table);
}
```

If you execute the application with the onModuleLoad() method in the entry-point class as listed in Listing 3-5, the application will look like Figure 3-24.

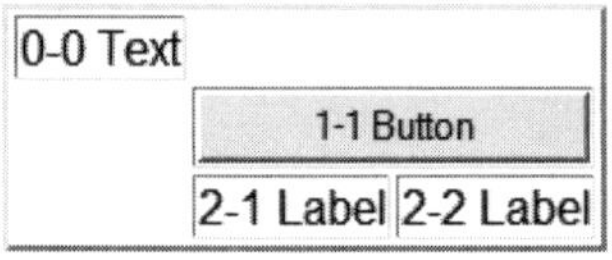

Figure 3-24. *Table created using a* FlexTable *by using the code in Listing 3-5. The* FlexTable *takes care of creating cells based on widgets being added to the table.*

What Is a FlowPanel?

FlowPanel is just an HTML <div> tag that formats its child widgets using the default HTML layout behavior. The widgets added to a FlowPanel get wrapped when the application window containing the widgets is resized. Listing 3-6 shows some code to use a FlowPanel.

Listing 3-6. *Code Demonstrating the Use of* FlowPanel

```
public void onModuleLoad() {
    final Button button = new Button("Sample Button");
    final CheckBox checkBox = new CheckBox("Sample CheckBox");
    final RadioButton radioButton = new RadioButton("radio", "Sample RadioButton");

    Panel panel = new FlowPanel();
    RootPanel.get().add(panel);

    panel.add(button);
    panel.add(checkBox);
    panel.add(radioButton);
}
```

If you execute the application with the onModuleLoad() method in the entry-point class as listed in Listing 3-6, the application will look like Figure 3-25. When the window is resized, the widgets (added in the FlowPanel) get wrapped, as shown in Figure 3-26.

Note I will discuss some of the other panels in Chapter 5.

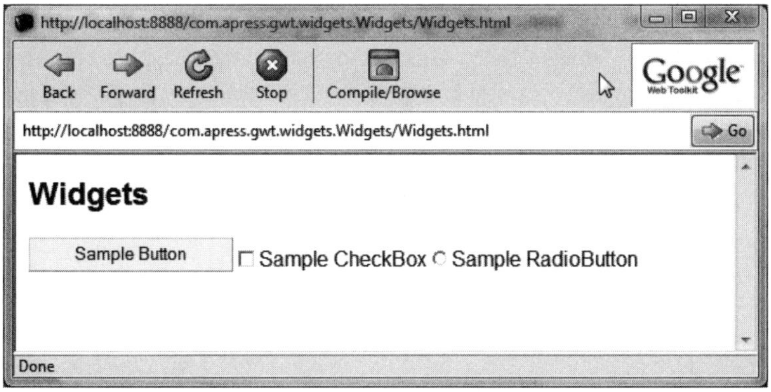

Figure 3-25. *Application using a* FlowPanel *(browser window maximized)*

Figure 3-26. *Application using FlowPanel (browser window resized)*

Creating Complex Widgets Using Composites

Composites are widgets that allow you to create new widgets or panels from the set of existing widgets and panels. Composites allow you to hide the implementation details and API of the internal widgets. You should use composites when you want to control the interface you are exposing for the internal widgets and when you can define your widget in terms of existing widgets. For example, composites are useful for creating a single widget out of an aggregate of multiple widgets contained in a single panel. The initWidget() method provided by the

Composite class sets up the main widget, which is wrapped by your custom composite classes. The initWidget() method must be called on the main user-visible component that has all the other widgets/components added in it directly or indirectly.

Note The call to the initWidget() method should be the *last* call. This is important because the widget passed to this method gets attached to the DOM immediately when this method is called, and some browsers don't work correctly for child elements if the parent element is added to the DOM before they are attached to the parent. This requires that the initWidget() method is never called before the last widget is attached to the main user-visible component.

Developing a Sample Application Using Composites

I'll now present an example to solidify your understanding of creating a GUI-based application. The application you will create is a loan request and servicing system for the loan department at a bank. The module you will develop in this book will handle details about a new loan request. You will create the GUI of the application in this chapter and add other relevant parts of the application such as server-side communication, and so on, in later chapters. The application will allow a customer-care representative of the bank to record the request of a customer along with details about the customer and loan requested.

Start by creating a project named LoanServicingSystem in the C:\gwt\LoanServicingSystem directory with the module's entry-point class as com.apress.gwt.chapter3.client. LoanServicingSystem. Now I'll show how to create the composite object for this application.

Creating the Composite

You should start by creating a composite object representing LoanRequestForm. Every composite type in your application must extend from the Composite class defined in the com.google.gwt.user.client.ui package. The LoanRequestForm composite that you will develop should allow the user to enter some basic information such as contact name, organization name, address, amount, and type of the loan. Listing 3-7 shows the code for the composite representing the loan request form.

Listing 3-7. *First Version of Composite for Loan Request Form*

```
package com.apress.gwt.chapter3.client;

import com.google.gwt.user.client.ui.Button;
import com.google.gwt.user.client.ui.Composite;
import com.google.gwt.user.client.ui.HorizontalPanel;
import com.google.gwt.user.client.ui.Label;
import com.google.gwt.user.client.ui.ListBox;
import com.google.gwt.user.client.ui.TextBox;
import com.google.gwt.user.client.ui.VerticalPanel;
```

```java
/**
 * This class represents the form for taking inputs of a Loan request.
 *
 * @author Vipul Gupta (vipulgupta.vg@gmail.com)
 *
 */
public class LoanRequestForm extends Composite {

  private final Label contactNameLabel;
  private final Label organizationLabel;
  private final Label addressLabel;
  private final Label amountLabel;
  private final Label loanType;
  private final Button submitDetailsButton;
  private final TextBox contactNameTextBox;
  private final TextBox organizationNameTextBox;
  private final TextBox addressTextBox;
  private final TextBox loanAmountTextBox;
  private final Label savedLabel;
 private final ListBox typeOfLoan;

  public LoanRequestForm() {

    // The input widgets will be stacked from top to bottom, so a vertical panel
    // is created and used as the base panel of the composite object.
    final VerticalPanel loanFormMainPanel = new VerticalPanel();

    // Each input element requires a label and input field. These should be
    // displayed together from left to right. So, a horizontal panel needs to be
    // created for each input
    final HorizontalPanel hPanelItem1 = new HorizontalPanel();
    loanFormMainPanel.add(hPanelItem1);
    hPanelItem1.setStyleName("loanForm-Panel");

    contactNameLabel = new Label("Contact Name");
    hPanelItem1.add(contactNameLabel);

    contactNameTextBox = new TextBox();
    hPanelItem1.add(contactNameTextBox);
    contactNameTextBox.setFocus(true);

    // Each Input widget is added with a corresponding Label describing the
    // required input. The widget and corresponding label are added using
    // HorizontalPanel so that they can align horizontally to each other.
    final HorizontalPanel hPanelItem2 = new HorizontalPanel();
    loanFormMainPanel.add(hPanelItem2);
    hPanelItem2.setStyleName("loanForm-Panel");
```

```
organizationLabel = new Label("Organization");
hPanelItem2.add(organizationLabel);

organizationNameTextBox = new TextBox();
hPanelItem2.add(organizationNameTextBox);

final HorizontalPanel hPanelItem3 = new HorizontalPanel();
loanFormMainPanel.add(hPanelItem3);
hPanelItem3.setStyleName("loanForm-Panel");

addressLabel = new Label("Address");
hPanelItem3.add(addressLabel);

addressTextBox = new TextBox();
hPanelItem3.add(addressTextBox);

final HorizontalPanel hPanelItem4 = new HorizontalPanel();
loanFormMainPanel.add(hPanelItem4);
hPanelItem4.setStyleName("loanForm-Panel");

amountLabel = new Label("Amount of Loan");
hPanelItem4.add(amountLabel);

loanAmountTextBox = new TextBox();
hPanelItem4.add(loanAmountTextBox);

final HorizontalPanel hPanelItem5 = new HorizontalPanel();
loanFormMainPanel.add(hPanelItem5);
hPanelItem5.setStyleName("loanForm-Panel");

loanType = new Label("Loan Type");
hPanelItem5.add(loanType);

// Create a new list box with the various types of loans a customer
// can make request for
typeOfLoan = new ListBox();
typeOfLoan.addItem("Home Loan");
typeOfLoan.addItem("Personal Loan");
typeOfLoan.addItem("Auto Loan");
typeOfLoan.addItem("Business installment Loan");
typeOfLoan.addItem("Equipment Loan");

// The visible element count is set as 1, so that the list box behaves
// like a drop-down menu.
typeOfLoan.setVisibleItemCount(1);
hPanelItem5.add(typeOfLoan);
```

```java
    final HorizontalPanel hPanelItem6 = new HorizontalPanel();
    loanFormMainPanel.add(hPanelItem6);
    hPanelItem6.setStyleName("loanForm-Panel");

    submitDetailsButton = new Button();
    hPanelItem6.add(submitDetailsButton);
    submitDetailsButton.setText("Submit Details");

    // Create a hidden label that will be shown the user of the
    // system when the loan is stored on the server.
    // successfully stored on server side.
    savedLabel = new Label("Loan request recorded successfully");
    savedLabel.setVisible(false);
    hPanelItem6.add(savedLabel);

    // The initWidget(...) method is called with the base element of the composite.
    // The base element that contains all other elements is the vertical
    // panel you created in the beginning of this constructor.
    initWidget(loanFormMainPanel);
  }

  public Label getAddressLabel() {
    return addressLabel;
  }

  public Label getContactNameLabel() {
    return contactNameLabel;
  }

  public Label getSavedLabel() {
    return savedLabel;
  }

  public Button getSubmitDetailsButton() {
    return submitDetailsButton;
  }

  ...  // and other getter and setter methods

}
```

Now that you've created the LoanRequestForm class represented by a composite, it's time for you to create the host HTML file for the LoanServicingSystem application.

Creating the Host HTML File

Listing 3-8 shows how to create the host HTML file of the application, which is
LoanServicingSystem.html located in the com.apress.gwt.chapter3.public folder.

Listing 3-8. *The Host HTML File of the LoanServicingSystem Application*

```html
<html>
  <head>
    <title>Wrapper HTML for LoanServicingSystem</title>
    <style>
      body,td,a,div,.p{font-family:arial,sans-serif; background-color: #C3D9FF;}
      div,td{color:#000000}
      a:link,.w,.w a:link{color:#0000cc}
      a:visited{color:#551a8b}
      a:active{color:#ff0000}

      .loanForm-Panel {
        cursor: pointer;
        cursor: hand;
        padding: 1px;
        margin: 5px 5px 5px 5px;
        width: 360px;
      }

      .gwt-Label {
        background-color: #C3D9FF;
        padding: 2px 0px 2px 0px;
        width: 150px;
        text-align: left;
      }

      .gwt-Textbox {
        background-color: #FFDECC;
        padding: 1px;
        width: 190px;
        font-size: smaller;
      }

      .gwt-Button {
          background:#f5f5f5;
          border:1px solid #aaa;
          border-top:1px solid #ddd;
          border-left:1px solid #ddd;
          padding: 2px;
          width: 12em;
      }
```

```
    .gwt-ListBox {
      background-color: #FFDECC;
      width: 190px;
      font-size: smaller;
      text-align: right;
    }


  </style>
  <script language='javascript'
              src='com.apress.gwt.chapter3.LoanServicingSystem.nocache.js'>
  </script>
</head>

<body>
  <h2>New Loan Request</h2>
</body>
</html>
```

Listing 3-8 used CSS to style the widgets in the LoanServicingSystem application. I will discuss the registered CSS classes for various widgets and styling in general in GWT in detail in Chapter 5. The CSS styles in the host HTML file are followed by the application's bootstrap file, which is required to start the application (as explained in Chapter 2).

You should now create the entry-point class for the application. This is explained in the next section.

Creating the Entry-Point Class

You should now modify the default entry-point class named LoanServicingSystem, which is created by using the applicationCreator tool in the com.apress.gwt.chapter3.client package. Since the LoanRequestForm composite contains all the widgets you wanted to add in the application, you can just add this composite to the RootPanel of the application. Listing 3-9 shows the modified entry-point class.

Listing 3-9. *Main Module of Your LoanServicingSystem Application*

```
package com.apress.gwt.chapter3.client;

import com.google.gwt.core.client.EntryPoint;
import com.google.gwt.user.client.ui.RootPanel;

/**
 * Entry point class for the Loan Servicing System.
 *
 * @author Vipul Gupta (vipulgupta.vg@gmail.com)
 *
 */
public class LoanServicingSystem implements EntryPoint {
```

```
/* This is the entry point method. */
public void onModuleLoad() {
    // Get reference to the RootPanel
    final RootPanel rootPanel = RootPanel.get();

    // Create an instance of the LoanRequestForm and add it to the RootPanel
    rootPanel.add(new LoanRequestForm());
  }
}
```

With all the pieces of the application in place, it's now time to execute the application.

Running the Application

You should now run the LoanServicingSystem application. You can do this either by double-clicking the LoanServicingSystem-shell.cmd script in Eclipse or by running this script from the command line. Figure 3-27 shows the output of the application.

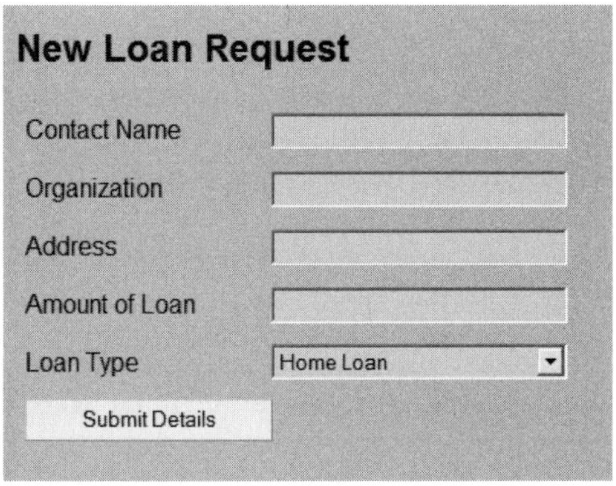

Figure 3-27. *UI of your LoanServicingSystem application, showing the composite representing* LoanRequestForm

Just like with the LoanRequestForm that you developed in this chapter, you can use composites to bundle together widgets and panels to create widgets for your own applications. Using a composite simplifies the reuse of widgets already bundled together and makes the UI code more modular.

Summary

In this chapter, you looked at the UI library in the GWT framework. I discussed the various widgets that are available in the library, and you learned how they can be used. I also discussed the common API that most of the widgets inherit from their base classes.

Then, I discussed layouts and the various panels offered by GWT for arranging the widgets in a GUI. I also discussed how to create composites, which are custom widgets you build from existing widgets, and panels, which you can use to group together a set of widgets to satisfy an application's requirement. Composites allow you to hide the internal implementation and restrict API access to internal components. By using composites, you can expose a restricted API, which you want any component using this composite to be able to access. Finally, you created the initial UI implementation of a sample application that you will build in the remaining chapters of this section.

■■■

Communication: RPC

A *remote procedure call* (RPC) is the standard technique used for server-side communication in the GWT framework. RPC is and has been very commonly used for making distributed client-server applications. In this chapter, we will discuss what RPC is and how it fits into the GWT framework for client-server communication, and then we will go through a sample application to understand how to develop a client-server application using GWT.

Understanding RPC

RPC is used to communicate between the client and server parts of an application in a distributed environment. RPC basically allows an application module (the client) to call or invoke a procedure (the method) in another application's (the server) address space. When an RPC call is made, the server uses the parameters (if any) from the call for processing at its end and then sends the result of the processing to the client application. This turned out to be a very common use case for a large number of distributed applications and led to the development of abstractions for the communication between the client and server components.

The important part of RPC communication is that the programmer is freed from the burden of writing the underlying boilerplate code required for communication between the client and the server (including serializing/deserializing or marshalling/unmarshalling the parameters passed in the call by the client over the wire to the server). Java programmers will be familiar with the concept of remote method invocation (RMI), which is just another name for the RPC calls. RMI calls are, however, synchronous, and the caller waits for the remote method to return before proceeding; however, GWT supports the asynchronous method of making RPC calls. Before going further, it is important that you understand the difference between synchronous and asynchronous calls.

In synchronous mode, a method call blocks the execution until the call can be completed, whereas in asynchronous mode, the call does not block the execution and returns immediately to the caller. The actual results of the asynchronous call are sent back later using an interrupt, which could take many forms such as a function to be called (commonly called a *callback function*) in case of success or failure scenarios.

How to Use RPC in GWT

GWT provides complete support for developing Ajax-based applications where the *A* that is the asynchronous part of the communication is taken care of by using server-side communication (using RPC) provided by the framework.

The asynchronous behavior of Ajax-based applications requires that your application's web pages utilize the JavaScript's XMLHttpRequest object to make asynchronous calls. As mentioned previously, an asynchronous call results in a further call to a registered method (the callback method) with the results of the initial call. (For example, a callback method might manipulate the UI of the application by using the data returned via the RPC call.)

In the asynchronous call model, it's important to understand the idea of the call happening behind the scenes (in a separate thread) and the data being returned from the result of the called method.

JavaScript's XMLHttpRequest object is part of an API that is used to transfer data to and fro from a web server using HTTP by establishing an asynchronous channel of communication. The data returned from XMLHttpRequest calls can come from any source including databases and external systems. You can use XMLHttpRequest to fetch data in multiple formats such as XML, HTML, JavaScript Object Notation (JSON), and plain text.

The biggest problem of developing using the XMLHttpRequest object is that it is implemented differently by different browsers, and this requires the data format and the response to be customized for each specific browser. Most of the Ajax-based packages, including GWT, provide a wrapper to create and use XMLHttpRequest for RPC purposes.

The developer is required to define the remote interface for the client, its implementation for the server, and what to do after the remote call has completed either successfully or unsuccessfully. GWT internally takes care of the problems associated with using the XMLHttpRequest object, and its API, by using the right XMLHttpRequest object, based on the client browser.

Adding RPC support in your GWT application requires creating a few interfaces and setting up your application to make the actual RPC call. Let's go through these requirements one by one.

Creating Service Interface (Also Called the Synchronous Interface)

To use RPC in GWT, you have to start by creating a new Java interface that defines the contract, in other words, the various API calls that will be supported. This interface must extend the com.google.gwt.user.client.rpc.RemoteService interface.

■**Note** The com.google.gwt.user.client.rpc.RemoteService interface is a simple marker/tag interface, and all the RPC interfaces in your application must extend from it.

For example, the following code snippet shows a service interface that has a single remote method:

```
public interface MyServiceInterfaceName extends RemoteService {
  public long remoteMethodName(params.....);
}
```

■**Note** This interface defines the contract of a specific service and is eventually extended by the server-side component of your application. I'll explain more about this later in the chapter.

Creating the Asynchronous Interface

GWT requires that you create an asynchronous interface at the client end corresponding to each service interface you have created. For the service interface defined earlier, the corresponding async service interface is defined here:

```
public interface MyServiceInterfaceNameAsync {
  public void remoteMethodName(params....., AsyncCallback callback);
}
```

You need to take care of two things when creating the asynchronous interface corresponding to the original service interface:

- The async interface requires that an additional parameter of AsyncCallback be passed as a parameter to the method call. This callback object is used to notify the caller with the status and results of the call.

- All asynchronous methods should have no return types; in other words, they must all explicitly return void irrespective of the return type of the original method in the service interface.

In case any of the methods in the service interface throw any specific exceptions, they are not required to be thrown from the asynchronous methods defined in the async interface. If the service interface would have been defined as follows:

```
public interface GameService extends RemoteService {
  public String getPlayer(String playerName) throws PlayerNotFoundException ;
}
```

then the corresponding async interface would be defined as follows:

```
public interface GameServiceAsync extends RemoteService {
  void getPlayer(String playerName, AsyncCallback callback);
}
```

Understanding the AsyncCallback Interface

The AsyncCallback object is used as the last parameter of the async methods defined in the async service interface of your remote services. It represents the type that will handle the response from the server.

Every caller of a service must implement the AsyncCallback interface in order to get a response from the RPC. This interface exposes two methods (listed in Table 4-1) that should be overridden for the desired behavior based on your application. If the RPC goes successfully, then the onSuccess(Object) method of the AsyncCallback object is called. In case of failure or any error conditions, the onFailure(Throwable) method of the AsyncCallback object is called.

Table 4-1. *Methods in AsyncCallback Interface*

Method Name	Description
onFailure(Throwable)	Called when the asynchronous call fails
onSuccess(Object)	Called when the asynchronous call completes successfully

Making an Actual Remote Procedure Call

The steps for using the AsyncCallback object and making an actual remote call are as follows:

1. Create a client-side proxy object for your service. Even though the object of the actual service interface is instantiated, the result of the creation is cast to the asynchronous interface of the service. It is safe to make this cast because the proxy object generated by the GWT.create(...) call actually implements the asynchronous interface.

2. Specify the URL at which the service implementation is running. Note that the target URL must reside on the same domain and port from which the host page was served (adhering to the same origin policy discussed earlier in Chapter 2).

3. Create an asynchronous callback object, and give implementations of the onSuccess() and onFailure() methods to handle the results of executing the call.

4. Finally, actually make the call, passing in the callback object to be used when the call completes at the server end and the response is received.

I'll now go through an example so you can understand the AsyncCallback interface and an actual call to a remote method. You will build this on top of the GameService and GameServiceAsync interfaces defined in the previous section. The code for the sample client-side call is as follows:

```
public void updatePlayerDetails () {
  GameServiceAsync gameService = (GameServiceAsync) GWT.create(GameService.class);

  ServiceDefTarget endpoint = (ServiceDefTarget) gameService;
  String moduleRelativeURL = GWT.getModuleBaseURL() + "game";

  endpoint.setServiceEntryPoint(moduleRelativeURL);

  AsyncCallback callback = new AsyncCallback() {
    public void onSuccess(Object result) {
      // Add code to handle success scenario here
    }
```

```
    public void onFailure(Throwable caught) {
        try {
            // Add code to handle failure scenario here
        } catch(PlayerNotFoundException pnfe) {

        } catch(Throwable te) {

        }
    }
  };
  gameService.getPlayer("playerName", callback);
}
```

■**Note** It is always safe to typecast the parameter of the onSuccess(Object) method to the return type of the original method that has been called. (Primitive return types are converted to their corresponding wrapper objects.)

Your First Complete RPC Example

I'll now present a simple RPC-based example to solidify your understanding of the steps mentioned earlier and to show a working example of using RPC in GWT.

You'll start by creating the project in the chapter4 directory using the projectCreator and applicationCreator utilities as follows:

```
C:\gwt>projectCreator.cmd -eclipse chapter4 -out chapter4
Created directory chapter4\src
Created directory chapter4\test
Created file chapter4\.project
Created file chapter4\.classpath

C:\gwt>applicationCreator -eclipse chapter4 -out chapter4  ➥
                com.apress.gwt.chapter4.client.NewsFeedClient

Created directory chapter4\src\com\apress\gwt\chapter4
Created directory chapter4\src\com\apress\gwt\chapter4\client
Created directory chapter4\src\com\apress\gwt\chapter4\public
Created file chapter4\src\com\apress\gwt\chapter4\NewsFeedClient.gwt.xml
Created file chapter4\src\com\apress\gwt\chapter4\public\NewsFeedClient.html
Created file chapter4\src\com\apress\gwt\chapter4\client\NewsFeedClient.java
Created file chapter4\NewsFeedClient.launch
Created file chapter4\NewsFeedClient-shell.cmd
Created file chapter4\NewsFeedClient-compile.cmd
```

You should now open the project created in Eclipse. Figure 4-1 shows the project structure at this stage.

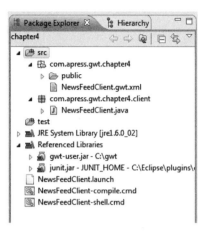

Figure 4-1. *Project structure after running the* `projectCreator` *and* `applicationCreator` *utilities*

You should now define the service interface for the application. As explained earlier, this defines the methods (or contract) between the client and server. You start this by creating a Java interface on the client side, that is, under the `client` package of the application (`NewsFeedService.java`). This interface should extend the `RemoteService` interface provided by GWT. You should also create the corresponding asynchronous interface for the module. Figure 4-2 shows the project structure after adding these interfaces to your project.

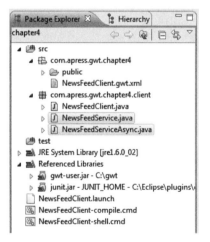

Figure 4-2. *Adding the service interface and corresponding asynchronous interface to your application*

Now you should add a new file representing the server-side implementation called `NewsFeedServer` in the `com.apress.gwt.chapter4.server` package. Figure 4-3 shows the project structure after adding this file.

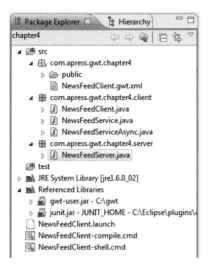

Figure 4-3. NewsFeedServer *being added in the server package of the module*

Now you should modify the service interface (NewsFeedService) and add the method that can be called by the client. In this example, you add a method name getNews(), which takes no parameters and returns a String representing a news feed. Listing 4-1 shows the code for the service interface. (As explained previously, the service interface in the modules has to extend the RemoteService marker interface.)

Listing 4-1. *Code of the Service Interface for Your Application*

```
package com.apress.gwt.chapter4.client;
import com.google.gwt.user.client.rpc.RemoteService;

/**
 * Service interface for the News feed application
 *
 * @author Vipul Gupta (vipulgupta.vg@gmail.com)
 *
 */
public interface NewsFeedService extends RemoteService {
    public String getNews();
}
```

You should also change the async interface (NewsFeedServiceAsync) corresponding to the NewsFeedService interface you just defined. This requires adding the getNews() method to this interface. As explained earlier, the corresponding methods in the async interface should take AsyncCallback as the last parameter and should have no return type (should be void). Listing 4-2 shows the code for the async interface.

Listing 4-2. *Code of the Async Service Interface of Your NewsFeedClient Application*

```
package com.apress.gwt.chapter4.client;

import com.google.gwt.user.client.rpc.AsyncCallback;

/**
 * Async interface corresponding to Service (NewsFeedService) interface
 *
 * @author Vipul Gupta (vipulgupta.vg@gmail.com)
 *
 */
public interface NewsFeedServiceAsync {
    public void getNews(AsyncCallback callback);
}
```

■**Note** The async methods must all have void return types.

Once you have defined the service and async interface at the client end, you need to create an actual implementation for these methods. You must define the NewsFeedServer class that you have created at the server end. This class should extend RemoteServiceServlet and implement the NewsFeedService interface you defined. You also need to give an implementation of the getNews() method in the NewsFeedService interface. Listing 4-3 gives the code for the server-side class.

Listing 4-3. *Server-Side Implementation of the News Service*

```
package com.apress.gwt.chapter4.server;

 import java.util.Random;

import com.apress.gwt.chapter4.client.NewsFeedService;
import com.google.gwt.user.server.rpc.RemoteServiceServlet;

/**
 * Server side implementaion of the NewsFeedService interface.
 *
 * @author Vipul Gupta (vipulgupta.vg@gmail.com)
 *
 */
public class NewsFeedServer extends RemoteServiceServlet implements
    NewsFeedService {

  private static final long serialVersionUID = 1L;
```

```
  private static final Random random = new Random();

  public String[] newsFeeds = { "Feed1", "Feed2", "Feed3" };

  public String getNews() {
    return newsFeeds[random.nextInt(newsFeeds.length)];
  }
}
```

The previous is a simple implementation at the server side for the getNews() method. The implementation in Listing 4-3 just returns one of the text entries from an array of strings when the method is called. In an actual system, you can change this to anything, including making a call to another library or data layer at the server end.

You also need to add the servlet mapping to the module's configuration file. Listing 4-4 shows the module configuration file (NewsFeedClient.gwt.xml).

Listing 4-4. *Code for the Module Configuration File for Your NewsFeedClient Application*

```
<module>

    <!-- Inherit the core Web Toolkit stuff.    -->
    <inherits name='com.google.gwt.user.User'/>

    <!-- Specify the app entry point class.    -->
    <entry-point class='com.apress.gwt.chapter4.client.NewsFeedClient'/>

    <servlet path="/News"
             class="com.apress.gwt.chapter4.server.NewsFeedServer"/>
</module>
```

Now you can go ahead and make the actual RPC call. Listing 4-5 shows the NewsFeedClient class with the onModuleLoad() method making an actual RPC call.

Listing 4-5. *Client-Side Code to Make the Actual Remote Call*

```
package com.apress.gwt.chapter4.client;

import com.google.gwt.core.client.EntryPoint;
import com.google.gwt.core.client.GWT;
import com.google.gwt.user.client.rpc.AsyncCallback;
import com.google.gwt.user.client.rpc.ServiceDefTarget;
import com.google.gwt.user.client.ui.Button;
import com.google.gwt.user.client.ui.ClickListener;
import com.google.gwt.user.client.ui.Label;
import com.google.gwt.user.client.ui.RootPanel;
import com.google.gwt.user.client.ui.Widget;
```

```
/**
  * Entry point class for the News Feed application
  *
  * @author Vipul Gupta (vipulgupta.vg@gmail.com)
  *
  */
public class NewsFeedClient implements EntryPoint {

/**
   * This is the entry point method.
   */
   public void onModuleLoad() {
      final Button button = new Button("Get News Feed");
      final Label label = new Label();

      button.addClickListener(new ClickListener() {
        public void onClick(Widget sender) {
          NewsFeedServiceAsync newsService = (NewsFeedServiceAsync) GWT
              .create(NewsFeedService.class);


        // Specify the URL at which our service implementation is running.
        // Note that the target URL must reside on the same domain and port
        // from which the host page was served.
        ServiceDefTarget endpoint = (ServiceDefTarget) newsService;
        String moduleRelativeURL = GWT.getModuleBaseURL() + "News";
        endpoint.setServiceEntryPoint(moduleRelativeURL);

        // Create an Asynchronous callback to handle the result.
        AsyncCallback callback = new AsyncCallback() {
          public void onSuccess(Object result) {
            // do some UI stuff to show success
            label.setText((String) result);
          }

          public void onFailure(Throwable caught) {
            // do some UI stuff to show failure
            label.setText("Error in getting news feed");
          }
        };
        newsService.getNews(callback);
      }
    });

    // Assume that the host HTML has elements defined whose
    // IDs are "slot1", "slot2". In a real app, you probably would not want
    // to hard-code IDs. Instead, you could, for example, search for all
    // elements with a particular CSS class and replace them with widgets.
```

```
      RootPanel.get("slot1").add(button);
      RootPanel.get("slot2").add(label);
    }
}
```

You should also modify the application's host HTML (NewsFeedClient.html) file to look like Listing 4-6.

Listing 4-6. *Code for the Module's Host HTML File*

```html
<html>
  <head>
    <title>NewsFeedClient</title>

    <style>
      body,td,a{font-family:arial,sans-serif}
      div,td{color:#000000}
    </style>
    <script language='javascript'
      src='com.apress.gwt.chapter4.NewsFeedClient.nocache.js'></script>
  </head>
  <body>
    <h2>NewsFeedClient</h2>
    <table align=center>
      <tr>
        <td id="slot1"></td><td id="slot2"></td>
      </tr>
    </table>
  </body>
</html>
```

After all this code, it's time for us to run the sample application. Double-click the NewsFeedClient-Shell.cmd file in Eclipse to execute the application in hosted mode. Figure 4-4 and Figure 4-5 show two instances of the remote call being made by clicking the Get News Feed button.

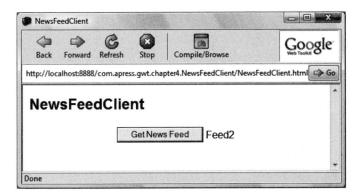

Figure 4-4. *NewsFeedClient application demonstrating the result of an RPC call*

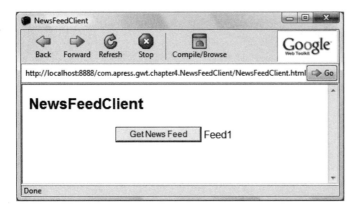

Figure 4-5. *NewsFeedClient application demonstrating the result of an RPC call after a subsequent click*

RPC in GWT: Behind the Scenes

I discussed generators in Chapter 2, and you learned how you can use generators to autogenerate code to match an application's requirements. Using RPC for making server calls is a common requirement for most GWT applications, and all these applications must write boilerplate code for the service. The GWT team realized this requirement and created a generator for autogenerating the boilerplate code required to make the call and get the results back by using the service interface.

The generator class, `ServiceInterfaceProxyGenerator`, generates the proxy object for `RemoteService` objects and is declared in the `com.google.gwt.user.rebind.rpc` package, like so:

```
<generate-with
    class="com.google.gwt.user.rebind.rpc.ServiceInterfaceProxyGenerator">
        <when-type-assignable class="com.google.gwt.user.client.rpc.RemoteService"/>
</generate-with>
```

Creating a client-side proxy object for your service (which implements the `RemoteService` interface) follows these steps:

1. Your application uses deferred binding and makes a call to the `GWT.create(...)` method with the service type as a parameter.

2. The `ServiceInterfaceProxyGenerator` class is called in response to the `GWT.create(...)` call as per the mapping listed previously.

3. The `ServiceInterfaceProxyGenerator` class delegates the responsibility of generating the client-side proxy for the specified `RemoteService` type to the `ProxyCreator` class defined in the `com.google.gwt.user.rebind.rpc` package.

Let's look at the class generated by the `ServiceInterfaceProxyGenerator` class for `NewsFeedService` declared in Listing 4-1. To do this, you have to use the gen flag provided by

GWTCompiler. You use the gen flag to specify the directory into which generated files will be written for review. You should change the compilation script named NewsFeedClient-compile.cmd and add the gen flag to it as shown here in bold:

```
@java -cp "%~dp0\src;%~dp0\bin;C:/gwt/gwt-user.jar;C:/gwt/gwt-dev-windows.jar"
    com.google.gwt.dev.GWTCompiler -gen "%~dp0\gen" -out "%~dp0\www" %*
    com.apress.gwt.chapter4.NewsFeedClient
```

After the change, you should execute the NewsFeedClient-compile.cmd script to compile the application. Along with the compilation step, the compiler will also generate some files, and these files will be written into the gen directory. Among other files, a proxy file named NewsFeedService_Proxy corresponding to the service interface is generated in the C:\gwt\chapter4\gen\com\apress\gwt\chapter4\client folder. Listing 4-7 shows the contents of this file.

Listing 4-7. *Proxy Class Generated by* ServiceInterfaceProxyGenerator *for NewsFeedService Interface Defined in Listing 4-1*

```
package com.apress.gwt.chapter4.client;

import com.google.gwt.core.client.GWT.UncaughtExceptionHandler;
import com.google.gwt.core.client.GWT;

public class NewsFeedService_Proxy implements
    com.google.gwt.user.client.rpc.ServiceDefTarget,
    com.apress.gwt.chapter4.client.NewsFeedServiceAsync {
  private static final com.apress.gwt.chapter4.client.NewsFeedService_TypeSerializer
      SERIALIZER = new
          com.apress.gwt.chapter4.client.NewsFeedService_TypeSerializer();

  private static final String SERIALIZATION_POLICY
      ="A54E696C43E49725CD8446E4171EA2C4";

  String fServiceEntryPoint = null;

  public String getServiceEntryPoint() { return fServiceEntryPoint; }

  public void setServiceEntryPoint(String s) { fServiceEntryPoint = s; }

  private void __getNews(
      com.google.gwt.user.client.rpc.impl. ➡
          ClientSerializationStreamWriter streamWriter)
          throws com.google.gwt.user.client.rpc.SerializationException {
    if (getServiceEntryPoint() == null)
      throw new
          com.google.gwt.user.client.rpc.ServiceDefTarget. ➡
              NoServiceEntryPointSpecifiedException();
```

```
    streamWriter.prepareToWrite();
    streamWriter.writeString("com.apress.gwt.chapter4.client.NewsFeedService");
    streamWriter.writeString("getNews");
    streamWriter.writeInt(0);
  }

  public void getNews(final com.google.gwt.user.client.rpc.AsyncCallback callback) {
    final com.google.gwt.user.client.rpc.impl.ClientSerializationStreamReader ➥
        streamReader = new
            com.google.gwt.user.client.rpc.impl.ClientSerializationStreamReader(➥
                SERIALIZER);
    final com.google.gwt.user.client.rpc.impl.ClientSerializationStreamWriter
      streamWriter = new
          com.google.gwt.user.client.rpc.impl.ClientSerializationStreamWriter(
              SERIALIZER, GWT.getModuleBaseURL(), SERIALIZATION_POLICY);
    try {
      __getNews(streamWriter);
    } catch (com.google.gwt.user.client.rpc.SerializationException e) {
      callback.onFailure(e);
      return;
    }
    com.google.gwt.user.client.ResponseTextHandler handler = new
        com.google.gwt.user.client.ResponseTextHandler() {
      public final void onCompletion(String encodedResponse) {
        UncaughtExceptionHandler handler = GWT.getUncaughtExceptionHandler();
        if (handler != null)
          onCompletionAndCatch(encodedResponse, handler);
        else
          onCompletionImpl(encodedResponse);
      }
      private void onCompletionAndCatch(String encodedResponse,
          UncaughtExceptionHandler handler) {
        try {
          onCompletionImpl(encodedResponse);
        } catch (Throwable e) {
          handler.onUncaughtException(e);
        }
      }
      private void onCompletionImpl(String encodedResponse) {
        Object result = null;
        Throwable caught = null;
        try {
          if (encodedResponse.startsWith("//OK")) {
            streamReader.prepareToRead(encodedResponse.substring(4));
            result = streamReader.readString();
          } else if (encodedResponse.startsWith("//EX")) {
```

```
                streamReader.prepareToRead(encodedResponse.substring(4));
                caught = (Throwable) streamReader.readObject();
              } else {
                caught = new com.google.gwt.user.client.rpc.InvocationException(
                    encodedResponse);
              }
            } catch (com.google.gwt.user.client.rpc.SerializationException e) {
              caught = new
                  com.google.gwt.user.client.rpc.IncompatibleRemoteServiceException();
            } catch (Throwable e) {
              caught = e;
            }
            if (caught == null)
              callback.onSuccess(result);
            else
              callback.onFailure(caught);
          }
        };
        if (!com.google.gwt.user.client.HTTPRequest.asyncPost(getServiceEntryPoint(),
            streamWriter.toString(), handler))
          callback.onFailure(new com.google.gwt.user.client.rpc.InvocationException(
              "Unable to initiate the Asynchronous service invocation -- check the ➡
                  network connection"));
      }
    }
```

A glance at the generated file indicates that this proxy class implements the async interface that you wrote in Listing 4-2 and has all the boilerplate code needed for the serialization and deserialization of the request and response for the RPC.

By studying this example, you can probably see the amount of work that the GWT framework does behind the scenes to make developing applications faster and easier.

Summary

In this chapter, you looked at the basics of making remote procedure calls within the GWT framework. I discussed service interfaces, their async counterparts, the server-side implementation of the service interface, and the APIs or process used to make actual remote calls from the client. I also went through a comprehensive but simple working example of an RPC-based application. I finished the chapter with details about the generator used by RPC to create the proxy code corresponding to the service interface of your application. I have just touched the surface of the details related to server-side communication and making RPC calls using GWT in this chapter. You can find more details of RPC and server-side communication in Chapter 6.

CHAPTER 5

■ ■ ■

UI Programming: Handling Events and Using Advanced Widgets

This chapter will start with a discussion about handling events, that is, performing some action based on the user's action. For example, a `Button` is a UI widget, and a user can signal an event by clicking the button. Clicking the button could trigger a call to a method that can submit the enclosing form or do other useful stuff based on the application's requirements.

After learning about handling events, you'll learn about styling your applications using CSS. You will also learn about the standard CSS classes used for various widgets and about some of the advanced widgets that you can use to create GUIs for your applications.

Later in the chapter, you will learn about `ImageBundles`, which you can use to optimize the performance of your GWT applications by bundling various images into a single image. (An `ImageBundle` helps applications avoid the overhead of making round-trip calls to multiple images on the server.)

In the end, you will learn about the `FormPanel`, which is a GWT wrapper around the classic HTML `<form>` element and provides support for submitting forms of user input and processing the result returned from the server without additional coding effort. This chapter will keep making additions to the LoanServicingSystem application that you started in Chapter 3.

So, let's start this chapter with a discussion about handling events that can be generated by the widgets offered by the GWT framework.

Handling Events Generated by Widgets

All GUI applications are event-driven. User actions on the GUI lead to the generation of events, and based on the event generated, you can program the application to perform some action or ignore it. The following are some sample events:

- A `Button` is a UI widget, and a human can signal an event by clicking the button.

- A mouse pointer entering the boundary of any widget on the GUI generates `MOUSEEVENTS`.

- Pressing a key on the keyboard generates `KEYEVENTS`.

GWT supports various events that a browser can handle/receive. These events are defined in the Event class (in the com.google.gwt.user.client package). The Event class is a wrapper around the native DOM events. Table 5-1 lists the various events defined in the Event class.

Table 5-1. *Various Events with Corresponding Details*

Event Name	Description
BUTTON_LEFT	Left mouse button is clicked
BUTTON_RIGHT	Right mouse button is clicked
BUTTON_MIDDLE	Middle mouse button is clicked
ONFOCUS	When an element receives keyboard focus
ONBLUR	When an element loses keyboard focus
ONLOAD	An element finishes loading
FOCUSEVENTS	Bit mask covering both focus events (focus and blur)
ONCHANGE	When value of an input element changes
ONCLICK	When an element is clicked
ONDBLCLICK	When an element is double-clicked
ONMOUSEMOVE	The mouse moved within an element's area
ONMOUSEOUT	The mouse moved out of an element's area
ONMOUSEOVER	The mouse moved into an element's area
ONMOUSEDOWN	Mouse button pressed over an element
ONMOUSEUP	Mouse button released over an element
ONMOUSEWHEEL	Mouse wheel scrolled over an element
ONLOSECAPTURE	Element having mouse capture loses it
MOUSEEVENTS	Bitmask covering all the mouse events (down, up, move, over, and out)
ONKEYDOWN	When a key is pressed
ONKEYUP	When a key is released
ONKEYPRESS	When a character is generated from a key press (either directly or through autorepeat)
KEYEVENTS	Bitmask covering all the keyboard events (down, up and press)
ONERROR	Error encountered in an image
ONSCROLL	Scroll offset of a scrollable element changes
UNDEFINED	Error code returned by DOM when the actual event value is undefined in the system

GWT follows event-driven architecture for handling events. In an event-driven architecture, there are *source objects*, which are objects/components where the events are generated, and *listener objects*, which are handler objects and are informed by source objects when an event is generated so that appropriate action can be taken by these listener objects. In GWT, events can be generated by the UI components, that is, various widgets/panels in the UI library. You register listener interfaces corresponding to the events to be handled. When the event is generated, it is passed to the appropriate handling method of the listener along with the details of the event. Listeners are discussed in the next sections.

Handling Events Using Listeners

Listeners are interfaces that define methods that can be called to handle specific types of events generated on a widget. The widget just needs to register an actual object corresponding to a listener interface, which will handle the various events.

Let's discuss the various listeners that are available in the GWT framework. Listener interfaces define methods that are invoked on objects that implement them when certain events occur. Table 5-2 lists the various listeners along with the methods that are defined in these listeners. The names of the listeners define what events a particular listener handles. For example, ClickListener is an event listener for click events, and FocusListener is an event listener for focus events (keyboard focus received or lost).

Table 5-2. *Various Event Listeners with Corresponding Methods*

Listener	Methods
EventListener	onBrowserEvent(Event event)
ChangeListener	void onChange(Widget sender)
ClickListener	void onClick(Widget sender)
FocusListener	void onFocus(Widget sender) void onLostFocus(Widget sender)
KeyboardListener	void onKeyDown(Widget sender, char keyCode, int modifiers) void onKeyPress(Widget sender, char keyCode, int modifiers) void onKeyUp(Widget sender, char keyCode, int modifiers)
LoadListener	void onError(Widget sender) void onLoad(Widget sender)
MouseListener	void onMouseDown(Widget sender, int x, int y) void onMouseEnter(Widget sender) void onMouseLeave(Widget sender) void onMouseMove(Widget sender, int x, int y) void onMouseUp(Widget sender, int x, int y)
PopupListener	void onPopupClosed(PopupPanel sender, boolean autoClosed)
ScrollListener	void onScroll(Widget sender, int scrollLeft, int scrollTop)
TableListener	void onCellClicked(SourcedTableEvents sender, int row, int cell)
TabListener	void onBeforeTabSelected(SourcesTabEvents sender, int tabIndex) void onTabSelected(SourcesTabEvents sender, int tabIndex)
TreeListener	void onTreeItemSelected(TreeItem item) void onTreeItemStateChanged(TreeItem item)

Example of Using Listeners

Refer to the LoanRequestForm composite you created in Chapter 3. You'll notice that this composite has a submit button named submitDetailsButton that does nothing so far. Suppose you want to call a method named submitLoanRequest() that submits the request for a loan when this button is clicked. In that case, you will need to register the widget to a `ClickListener` object and provide the implementation of the `onClick()` method defined in the interface.

You can modify the `LoanRequestForm` composite with the code shown in bold in Listing 5-1.

Listing 5-1. *Relevant Portion of* `LoanRequestForm` *with Changes (in Bold) to Handle the Click Event*

```
public LoanRequestForm() {
    ...
  submitDetailsButton = new Button();
  hPanelItem6.add(submitDetailsButton);
  submitDetailsButton.setText("Submit Details");

  submitDetailsButton.addClickListener(new ClickListener() {
    public void onClick(Widget sender) {
    submitLoanRequest();
    }
  });

  savedLabel = new Label("Successfully Saved");
    ...
}

protected void submitLoanRequest() {
    // We will add logic in this method later.
}
}
```

Handling Events Using Adapter Classes

Adapter classes help implement listener interfaces by providing a blank implementation for all the methods defined in the interface. The developers just need to override those methods for which specific behavior is needed in their applications. GWT provides adapter classes corresponding to some of the listeners that have a large number of methods because in many cases the application warrants providing specific behavior corresponding to just one or two events that are mapped to one or two methods in the interface. In such a scenario, adapters come in handy (by providing blank implementations for all the methods) by saving the developer the trouble of writing blank implementations for the remaining methods. Table 5-3 lists the various listeners and the corresponding adapter classes.

Table 5-3. *Event Listeners with Corresponding Adapter Classes*

Name of Listener	Adapter Name
FocusListener	FocusListenerAdapter
KeyboardListener	KeyboardListenerAdapter
MouseListener	MouseListenerAdapter

Example of Using Adapter Classes

Suppose you have a label named highlightingLabel whose text you want to highlight when the mouse moves over the label and unhighlight as soon as the mouse moves away from the label.

Using the MouseListener requires that you provide blank implementations for all the unused methods. Listing 5-2 shows the code for the highlightingLabel example when MouseListener is used.

Listing 5-2. *Using* MouseListener *in the Highlight Label Example*

```
highlightingLabel.addMouseListener ( new MouseListener() {

  void onMouseDown(Widget sender, int x, int y) { }

  void onMouseEnter(Widget sender) {
    highlightLabel(sender);  // Hypothetical method used to highlight the label
  }

  void onMouseLeave(Widget sender) {
    unhighlightLabel(sender); // Hypothetical method used to unhighlight the label
  }

  void onMouseMove(Widget sender, int x, int y) { }

  void onMouseUp(Widget sender, int x, inty) { }
});
```

The MouseListenerAdapter provides blank implementations for all the methods, and hence only the methods that need to be handled by the application (onMouseEnter(...) and onMouseLeave(...)) should be overridden. Listing 5-3 shows the code for the highlightingLabel example when MouseListenerAdapter is used.

Listing 5-3. *Using* MouseListenerAdapter *in the Highlight Label Example*

```
highlightingLabel.addMouseListener ( new MouseListenerAdapter() {

  void onMouseEnter(Widget sender) {
    highlightLabel(sender);  // Hypothetical method used to highlight the label
  }

  void onMouseLeave(Widget sender) {
    unhighlightLabel(sender); // Hypothetical method used to unhighlight the label
  }
});
```

Styling Applications Using CSS

You learned about styling GWT applications using CSS briefly in Chapter 3. This section will go into the details of styling and GWT's support for it. Table 5-4 lists the names of the default CSS style classes for the various widgets in the GWT library. It also describes the corresponding HTML elements that are used to implement the widget. These internal implementation details are useful for styling nested widgets in a GUI by following the styling rules used in CSS and GWT.

Table 5-4. *CSS Style Classes and Underlying HTML Elements Used for Various Widgets*

Widget Name	HTML Element	CSS Style Rules
Button	`<button>`	`.gwt-Button`
CheckBox	`<checkbox>`	`.gwt-CheckBox`
DialogBox	`<div>` (the caption is also a `<div>`)	`.gwt-DialogBox` `.gwt-DialogBox .Caption` (header of the DialogBox)
FlexTable/Grid	`<table>`	
Frame	`<iframe>`	`.gwt-Frame`
HTML	`<div>`	`.gwt-HTML`
HTMLTable	`<table>`	
HyperLink	`<div>` (with an anchor element)	`.gwt-HyperLink`
Image	`<img>`	`.gwt-Image`
Label	`<div>`	`.gwt-Label`
ListBox	`<select>` (with OPTIONS)	`.gwt-ListBox`
MenuBar	`<div>` (with TABLE)	`.gwt-MenuBar` (the menu bar itself) `.gwt-MenuBar .gwt-MenuItem` (menu items) `.gwt-MenuBar .gwt-MenuItem-selected` (selected menu items)
MenuItem	`<td>`	`.gwt-MenuItem` `.gwt-MenuItem .gwt-MenuItem-selected`
PasswordTextBox	`<password>`	`.gwt-PasswordTextBox` `.gwt-PasswordTextBox-readonly` (when text box is read-only)
PushButton		`.gwt-PushButton-up/down/up-hovering/` `down-hovering/up-disabled/down-disabled`
RadioButton	`<input>`	`.gwt-RadioButton`
TabBar	`<table>`	`.gwt-TabBar` (the tab bar itself) `.gwt-TabBar .gwt-TabBarFirst` (left edge of the bar) `.gwt-TabBar .gwt-TabBarRest` (right edge of the bar) `.gwt-TabBar .gwt-TabBarItem` (unselected tabs) `.gwt-TabBar .gwt-TabBarItem-selected` (selected tab)

Widget Name	HTML Element	CSS Style Rules
TextArea	`<textarea>`	`.gwt-TextArea` `.gwt-TextArea-readonly` (when text area is read-only)
TextBox	`<input>` (with type set as text)	`.gwt-TextBox` `.gwt-TextBox-readonly` (When text box is read-only)
Tree	`<div>`	`.gwt-Tree` (the tree itself) `.gwt-Tree .gwt-TreeItem` (a tree item) `.gwt-Tree .gwt-TreeItem-selected` (a selected tree item)
TreeItem	`<div>` (with a TABLE)	`.gwt-TreeItem` `.gwt-TreeItem-selected`

■**Note** The widgets are conventionally named `[project]-[widget name]`, but as mentioned previously, there are some additions to this in terms of dependent style names. `HTMLTable` widgets (`Grid`/`FlexTable`) can be formatted/styled using the `HTMLTable.CellFormatter`, `HTMLTable.ColumnFormatter`, and `HTMLTable.RowFormatter` classes.

Here I'll take the example of the `Button` widget from Table 5-4 and explain the various elements mentioned in it. The first row of this table states that the `Button` widget (represented by the `Button` class) gets translated into the HTML's `<button>` element when the code is compiled using the GWT compiler. It also states that the default CSS class for the generated `Button` element would be set as `gwt-Button`, and this CSS class name would be used by the application to style the buttons. In other words, all the buttons in your application that have not been styled using custom style classes (by using the API explained in Chapter 3) would also be styled using the `gwt-Button` CSS class.

You should be able to interpret the rest of the elements from Table 5-4 in a similar manner as the `Button` widget.

How Do Nested CSS Classes Apply to GWT Widgets?

`DialogBox` is an example of a GWT widget that uses nested CSS classes. The dialog box has a nested element with the style name `Caption`. A `DialogBox` uses `<div>` as the HTML element for its implementation, and after compilation, the `DialogBox` gets converted into the code snippet shown in Listing 5-4; the CSS style classes are highlighted in bold in the snippet.

Listing 5-4. `DialogBox` *After the Java Object Is Converted to Dynamic HTML by the GWT Compiler*

```
<div class="gwt-DialogBox">
  <table  ... >
    <tbody>
      <tr>
        <td >
```

```
      <div class="Caption"> caption </div>
    </td>
  <tr>
  </tr>
    <td >
        ........................
      ... Actual content of the dialog box comes here ...
        ........................
    </td>
  </tr>
  </tbody>
  </table>
</div>
```

The dialog box and its caption can be styled by defining the CSS style classes shown in Listing 5-5 in your style sheets.

Listing 5-5. *CSS Style Classes Defined for Styling* DialogBox *and Its Caption*

```
.gwt-DialogBox {
    border:1px solid #aaa;
    border-top:1px solid #ddd;
    border-left:1px solid #ddd;
}

.gwt-DialogBox  .Caption {
    padding: 2px;
    width: 12em;
}
```

A few panels have CSS style classes set for them. Table 5-5 lists the panels that have CSS style rules set for them along with the corresponding CSS style classes.

Table 5-5. *Panels with CSS Style Classes and Corresponding Class Names*

Panel Name	CSS Class Name
StackPanel	.gwt-StackPanel (the panel itself) .gwt-StackPanel .gwt-StackPanelItem (unselected items) .gwt-StackPanel .gwt-StackPanelItem-selected (selected items)
TabPanel	.gwt-TabPanel (the tab panel itself) .gwt-TabPanelBottom (bottom section of panel, deck containing widget)

Including Style Sheets in Your GWT Application

While creating the LoanServicingSystem application in Chapter 3, you added the CSS styling rules in the application's main HTML file, LoanServicingSystem.html defined in the com/apress/gwt/chapter3/public folder, as shown in Listing 3-8 in Chapter 3. However, the CSS style rules generally become too large, so it is not a good idea to add all of them in the main HTML file. Generally, you'll want to specify the CSS style rules in a separate CSS file (`<name>.css`) and include this file in the host HTML file using HTML's `<link>` tag.

GWT provides a simple way to include the external CSS file in your application by following two simple steps, as described in the following two sections.

Creating a CSS File

The CSS file should be publicly available. This requires that you add the CSS file to the `public` folder of your application. For example, in the LoanServicingSystem application, you can create a CSS file named `LoanServicingSystem.css` in the `com/apress/gwt/chapter3/public` folder. Remove all the CSS styles from the `LoanServicingSystem.html` file, and add them to `LoanServicingSystem.css`.

After moving the CSS styles from the host HTML file to the `.css` file (`LoanServicingSystem.css`), the CSS file should look like Listing 5-6.

Listing 5-6. *Contents of* `LoanServicingSystem.css`

```
body,td,a,div,.p{font-family:arial,sans-serif; background-color: #C3D9FF;}
div,td{color:#000000}
a:link,.w,.w a:link{color:#0000cc}
a:visited{color:#551a8b}
a:active{color:#ff0000}

.loanForm-Panel {
   cursor: pointer;
   cursor: hand;
    padding: 1px;
    margin: 5px 5px 5px 5px;
    width: 360px;
  }

.gwt-Label {
    background-color: #C3D9FF;
    padding: 2px 0px 2px 0px;
    width: 150px;
    text-align: left;
  }

.gwt-Textbox {
    background-color: #FFDECC;
    padding: 1px;
    width: 190px;
    font-size: smaller;
  }

  .gwt-Button {
```

```
        background:#f5f5f5;
        border:1px solid #aaa;
        border-top:1px solid #ddd;
        border-left:1px solid #ddd;
        padding: 2px;
        width: 12em;
    }

    .gwt-ListBox {
        background-color: #FFDECC;
        width: 190px;
        font-size: smaller;
        text-align: right;
    }
```

Including the CSS File in the Module's XML File

The CSS file created previously can be used in your GWT application by including it in the module's XML file. Listing 5-7 shows the module's XML file (LoanServicingSystem.gwt.xml) of the LoanServicingSystem application with the change for adding the style sheet in bold.

Listing 5-7. *Contents of* LoanServicingSystem.gwt.xml

```
<module>

    <!-- Inherit the core Web Toolkit stuff.            -->
    <inherits name='com.google.gwt.user.User'/>

    <!-- Specify the app entry point class.             -->
    <entry-point class='com.apress.gwt.chapter3.client.LoanServicingSystem'/>

    <stylesheet src="LoanServicingSystem.css" />

</module>
```

You can now run the application to verify that all the CSS rules specified in the LoanServicingSystem.css file are properly applied to the corresponding widgets in your application.

In the next section, I will discuss some important widgets, namely, TabBar and TabPanel, and discuss how you can use them in your own applications.

Using the TabBar Widget

A TabBar is just a horizontal bar of tabs and allows one of the tabs to be selected at a time. Creating a TabBar and adding it to your application is an easy task, as shown in Listing 5-8.

Listing 5-8. *Application Startup Method,* onModuleLoad(), *Listing the Code to Add a* TabBar *to Your Application*

```
public void onModuleLoad() {

    // Create a tab bar with few tabs.
    TabBar tabBar = new TabBar();
    tabBar.addTab("Home");
    tabBar.addTab("Products");
    tabBar.addTab("Clients");
    tabBar.addTab("News");
    tabBar.addTab("News");
    tabBar.addTab("Site Map");

    RootPanel.get().add(tabBar);
}
```

With the appropriate style classes set (the sample CSS styles are given in Listing 5-9) in the CSS style sheet of your application, running the application containing the code in Listing 5-8 will create a TabBar, as shown in Figure 5-1. When a tab is selected, the TabBar changes as shown in Figure 5-2.

Listing 5-9. *CSS Rules Used to Style the* TabBar

```
.gwt-TabBar {

    padding-top: 2px;
    border-bottom: 5px solid #336633;
    background-color: #fff;
}

.gwt-TabBar .gwt-TabBarItem {

    padding: 4px;
    cursor: pointer;
    cursor: hand;
    background-color: #ccffcc;
    border-bottom: 2px solid white;
    margin-right: 2px;
}

.gwt-TabBar .gwt-TabBarItem-selected {

    padding: 4px;
    font-weight: bold;
    cursor: default;
    background-color: #00cc00;
    border-bottom: 2px solid #33ff33;
    margin-right: 2px;
}
```

| Home | Products | Clients | News | News | Site Map |

Figure 5-1. TabBar *in its original state (when the application starts)*

| Home | **Products** | Clients | News | News | Site Map |

Figure 5-2. TabBar *after the Products tab is selected*

■Note You can add TabListener to handle various tab-related events.

In most situations, you won't want to use the TabBar directly. You will generally want to associate each tab on the TabBar with a widget that can be shown when a tab is selected. This is what a TabPanel (which I discuss next) lets you do.

Using the TabPanel Widget

TabPanel is a composite that combines a TabBar and a DeckPanel (a panel that displays its child widgets in a "deck," with only one widget visible at a time). This panel associates a widget in a DeckPanel to a tab in the TabPanel. When the user selects a tab in the TabPanel, the widget corresponding to the tab in the DeckPanel is made visible. (Since only one tab can be selected at a time and since only one widget in the DeckPanel can be visible at a time, both of these internal components of the TabPanel go hand in hand.)

This panel is more commonly understood as a set of tabbed pages where each page is associated with a tab and is shown accordingly when a user selects the tab. The tabs themselves can contain any arbitrary HTML that acts as the text of the tab. I'll demonstrate the use of TabPanel by showing how to add it to the LoanServicingSystem application, which needs to have different UIs for handling different tasks.

You already created LoanRequestForm in Chapter 3; the other UIs for the LoanServicingSystem application are an approval system that lists the existing requests along with their status (that is, approved or not) and an accounts information module that lists the details of an account given the ID of a customer in the bank.

■Note The book will concentrate on the UI only for the New Loan Request tab and will add placeholders, represented by HTML text, for the rest of the UIs in the TabPanel. You can fill in replacements for these placeholders as per your application requirements.

You can differentiate these three modules by adding three tabs to the main window of the LoanServicingSystem application, and based on which tab is selected, the widget for the corresponding module can be displayed. So, you'll now modify the onModuleLoad() method of the LoanServicingSystem application to add the TabPanel.

Listing 5-10 and Listing 5-11 show the current and new definition of the module's entry-point class of the LoanServicingSystem application, respectively. The new implementation adds the TabPanel widget, with tabs for exposing different modules of the application.

Listing 5-10. *Current Implementation of the* onModuleLoad() *Method of LoanServicingSystem*

```
public void onModuleLoad() {
  final RootPanel rootPanel = RootPanel.get();
  rootPanel.add(new LoanRequestForm());
}
```

Listing 5-11. *New Implementation of the* onModuleLoad() *Method of LoanServicingSystem*

```
public void onModuleLoad() {
  final RootPanel rootPanel = RootPanel.get();

  TabPanel tabPanel = new TabPanel();
  // Create a new tab titled New Loan Request and associate the
  // LoanRequestForm with it.
  tabPanel.add(new LoanRequestForm(), "New Loan Request");

  // Add two more tabs with HTML text as placeholders for the UI.
  tabPanel.add(new HTML("ApprovalSystem comes here"), "Approve Loan Requests");
  tabPanel.add(new HTML("Under Construction"), "Accounts Information");

  rootPanel.add(tabPanel);
}
```

You should also add the following CSS-style classes to the LoanServicingSystem.css file.

```
.gwt-TabBar {
  padding-top: 2px;
  border-bottom: 5px solid #336633;
  background-color: #ccffcc;
  font-size:0.8em;
}

.gwt-TabBar .gwt-TabBarFirst {
}

.gwt-TabBar .gwt-TabBarRest {
}

.gwt-TabBar .gwt-TabBarItem {
  padding: 4px;
```

```
  cursor: pointer;
  cursor: hand;
  background-color: #ffcccc;
  margin-right: 4px;
}

.gwt-TabBar .gwt-TabBarItem-selected {
  padding: 4px;
  font-weight: bold;
  cursor: default;
  background-color: #ff6666;
  margin-right: 4px;
}

.gwt-TabPanel {
  margin-top: 4px;
}

.gwt-TabPanelBottom {
  background-color: #E8EEF7;
}
```

■**Note** The add(Widget, String) method of TabPanel takes a widget and corresponding text for the tab containing that widget.

Figure 5-3 shows the state of the LoanServicingSystem application after adding TabPanel to it.

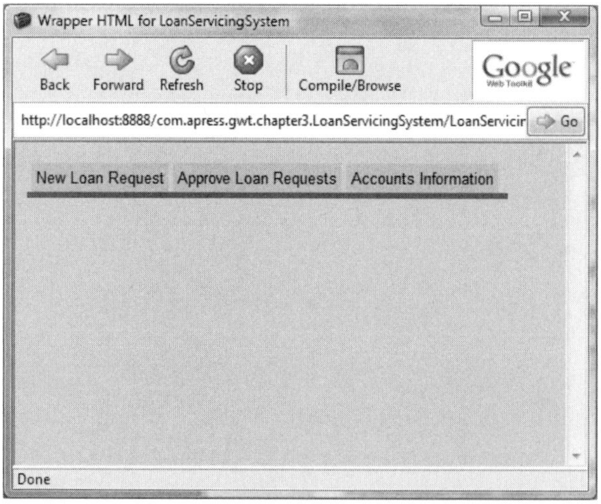

Figure 5-3. *LoanServicingSystem after adding the* TabPanel

Figure 5-4 shows the state of the application after the New Loan Request tab is selected. Since you have mapped the `LoanRequestForm` widget to this tab, it gets displayed when the tab is selected.

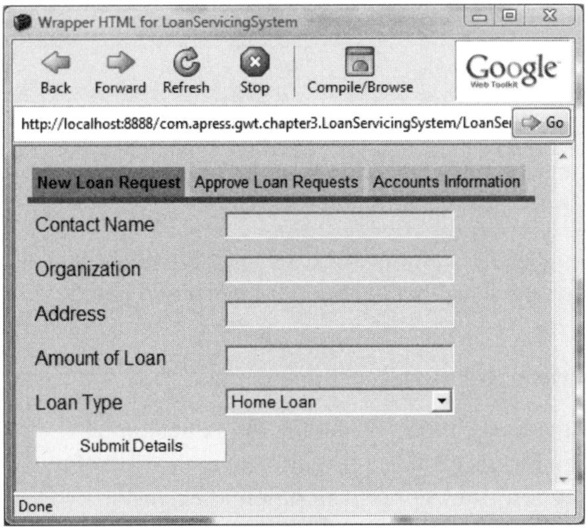

Figure 5-4. *LoanServicingSystem after the first tab for New Loan Request is selected. The LoanRequestForm composite registered with the New Loan Request tab is displayed.*

In the next section, I will discuss the important concept of `ImageBundle` and explain how using a bundle can speed up your applications containing multiple images.

Optimizing Applications Using ImageBundle

Making your Ajax-based applications run fast requires that your application make a minimum number of HTTP requests, be it for script files, images, or anything else. Most web-based applications require multiple images. Lots of HTTP requests are made for small images such as icons, thumbnails for image galleries, and so on. Most of these requests are typically made when the application is starting for the first time, and this leads to bad user experience because the whole application loads and starts slowly. Since this has turned out to be a common use case in a lot of applications, the GWT team came out with the idea of `ImageBundle` to get rid of this pain point in your applications.

`com.google.gwt.user.client.ui.ImageBundle` is a tag interface and is used for generating image bundles in your GWT application. An `ImageBundle` combines all your images into a single large image and contains the logic and code to retrieve (clip out) individual images from this single large image. Being a common use case, the GWT team provided a generator that generates code for the bundle relevant to your application.

■**Note** The generator for creating `ImageBundle`s is named `ImageBundleGenerator` and is located in the `com.google.gwt.user.rebind` package. This generator bundles a set of images specified by the user into a single image, which helps minimize the HTTP requests made to fetch the various images and in effect leads to the faster loading of the application.

To create an `ImageBundle`, a developer has to perform the following simple steps:

1. Create an interface representing your `ImageBundle`, and extend the `ImageBundle` interface.

2. Add method declarations for each image that is supposed to be added to the bundle. The methods declared in this manner must take no parameters and should have a return type of `AbstractImagePrototype`.

3. You can specify the name of the image in two ways:

   • Name the method the same as the image name, excluding the extension. The extension of the image name can be one of `.png`, `.gif`, or `.jpg`. In the case of multiple images having the same name as the method, but different extensions, the extension precedence used to select the image is `.png`, `.gif`, and then `.jpg`. The image specified must also be located in the same package as the `ImageBundle` defined by the user.

   • Use the `gwt.resource` metadata tag, and specify the name of the image as the value to this tag. The valid extensions you can use are `.png`, `.gif`, and `.jpg`. If an absolute image name is given, then the image must be located in the same package as the `ImageBundle` defined by the user. If the name of the image contains a slash (/), then this is evaluated as the name of a resource on the classpath.

Understanding AbstractImagePrototype

`com.google.gwt.user.client.ui.AbstractImagePrototype` is an abstract representation of a particular image and allows accessing the image in two forms, as an image object or as an HTML component. Table 5-6 lists the various methods available in the `AbstractImagePrototype` class.

Table 5-6. *Methods in the* `AbstractImagePrototype` *Class*

Method Name	Description
createImage()	Creates and returns a new image object based on the image that this prototype represents
applyTo(Image)	Transforms an existing image into the image represented by this prototype
getHTML()	Returns a string containing the HTML fragment to display the image represented by this prototype

Sample Application Demonstrating the Use of ImageBundle

In this section, you'll work through an example of using ImageBundle to solidify your understanding of using it. The example I'll present is an image gallery. If you have seen any image gallery applications, you've probably noticed that they start by displaying thumbnails of the various images, and after the user clicks a thumbnail, the full version of the corresponding image appears. A common problem in image gallery applications is that the thumbnails load one by one as the browser makes request for the various images representing the thumbnails to the server. Even if you haven't seen an image gallery application, you can still imagine how much time it would take for the browser to make multiple requests to the web server for the various images representing the thumbnails and to download them individually.

Since the thumbnail images are very small and all of them need to be shown, it makes sense that all of them are bundled into a single image. This will let the browser request a single image that represents all the thumbnails from the web server. This is exactly what you are going to do in this example. The application you will develop will also improve the user experience in the gallery by displaying the full version of the image without having to migrate to a different page. The application will actually respond to mouse movements and will have the functionality to display the full image when the user moves the mouse over a specific thumbnail. The full image will be shown on the same page as the thumbnails and will be hidden when the mouse moves away from the thumbnail. This allows the users to view the full version of the images by just moving the mouse over the thumbnails.

In brief, the example will concentrate on developing an image gallery of flowers where the user can see thumbnails of various flowers and can view the full images of flowers of interest by moving the mouse over specific thumbnails representing the flowers of interest. Let's start by creating the project for the application.

Creating the Project

Start by creating a project named AdvancedWidgets in the C:\gwt\AdvancedWidgets directory with the module's entry-point class as com.apress.gwt.chapter5.client.AdvancedWidgets. Next, create the interface for the ImageBundle in your application.

Creating the ImageBundle Interface

Next you should create a FlowerImages interface in the com.apress.gwt.chapter5.client. images package. This interface represents the ImageBundle interface for the flower gallery project. The interface file should extend the ImageBundle interface, as shown in Listing 5-12.

Listing 5-12. *Flower Images Interface Representing the* ImageBundle *for the Flower Gallery*

```
package com.apress.gwt.chapter5.client.images;

import com.google.gwt.user.client.ui.ImageBundle;

public interface FlowerImages extends ImageBundle {

}
```

Add four thumbnail files—pink.jpg, red.jpg, white.jpg, and yellow.jpg—to the com.apress.gwt.chapter5.client.images package so that the bundle can directly use them. Next, add methods to the FlowerImages interface to access the various thumbnail images. Listing 5-13 shows the FlowerImages interface after adding these methods.

Listing 5-13. FlowerImages *Interface Representing the* ImageBundle *for the Flower Gallery After Adding Methods to Retrieve Thumbnails*

```
package com.apress.gwt.chapter5.client.images;

import com.google.gwt.user.client.ui.AbstractImagePrototype;
import com.google.gwt.user.client.ui.ImageBundle;
/**
 * Interface representing the ImageBundle for the AdvancedWidgets application.
 *
 * @author Vipul Gupta (vipulgupta.vg@gmail.com)
 */
public interface FlowerImages extends ImageBundle {

    /**
     * The metadata tag contains no '/' characters, so pink.jpg
     * must be located in the same package as FlowerImages interface.
     *
     * @gwt.resource pink.jpg
     */
    public AbstractImagePrototype getPinkThumbnail();

    public AbstractImagePrototype red();

    public AbstractImagePrototype yellow();

    public AbstractImagePrototype white();
}
```

The getPinkThumbnail() method is created with the associated metadata tag value of pink.jpg, which in effect maps this method's return value to the image represented by pink.jpg. Other methods are named corresponding to the name of the underlying thumbnail file; namely, red, yellow, and white are directly mapped to images with the corresponding names. Now set up the host HTML page for the application.

Setting Up the Host HTML Page for the Application

Let's modify the host HTML page and create elements where the thumbnails and full image will be displayed. The code in Listing 5-14 creates two tables, one with an element for thumbnail (with the ID thumbnails) and one for the full image (with the ID Content). It also adds a style rule (named gwt-Content) for setting the dimensions of the full image as per the application's requirements. Listing 5-14 shows the modified host HTML file AdvancedWidgets.html.

Listing 5-14. *Host HTML file (*AdvancedWidgets.html*) After Adding Elements for Thumbnails and Full Images for the Flower Gallery*

```html
<html>
  <head>
    <title>Wrapper HTML for AdvancedWidgets</title>
    <style>

      body,td,a,div,.p {font-family:arial,sans-serif}
      div,td{color:#000000}

      a:link,.w,.w a:link{color:#0000cc}
      a:visited{color:#551a8b}
      a:active{color:#ff0000}

      .gwt-Content {
        height: 300px;
        width: 400px;
      }

    </style>

    <script language='javascript'
        src='com.apress.gwt.chapter5.AdvancedWidgets.nocache.js'>
    </script>
  </head>
  <body>

    <h2>AdvancedWidgets</h2>

    <table align=center>
      <tr>
        <td id="thumbnails"></td>
      </tr>
    </table>

    <table align=center>
      <tr>
        <td id="content"></td>
      </tr>
    </table>
  </body>
</html>
```

The full images of the flowers (corresponding to the thumbnails) should be available publicly, and therefore they should be kept in the module's public folder. I added image files named pink_large.jpg, red_large.jpg, white_large.jpg, and yellow_large.jpg to the com/apress/gwt/chapter5/public folder so that they can be directly referenced by the code. It's important to understand that the large images are not added to the bundle because these images would actually slow down the application startup (because of a large bundle getting downloaded). Downloading all the large images as a bundle would also be unnecessary because many of them might never be accessed by the application at all. So, it's also important that the image bundles in your applications are designed with these factors in mind. With all this done, the final step is to create the entry-point class for the application.

Writing the Entry-Point Class

Now let's create the UI of the flower gallery and use the FlowerImages bundle in it. The UI will need a table to add the various thumbnail images, which will be retrieved from the image bundle. The application will need to add mouse listeners and implement mouseEnter(...) and mouseLeave(...) methods to show and hide the full image corresponding to the thumbnail. To show the full image corresponding to a thumbnail, the application needs an image object. The mouse event handlers will modify the URL of this image object to point to the correct image object at runtime.

You need to modify the module entry file for the project (AdvancedWidgets.java) to add the logic described previously. Listing 5-15 shows the code for the module entry class containing the UI and the use of ImageBundle created for the flower image gallery.

Listing 5-15. *Code for the Module's Entry-Point Class (*AdvancedWidgets.java*)*

```
package com.apress.gwt.chapter5.client;

import com.apress.gwt.chapter5.client.images.FlowerImages;
import com.google.gwt.core.client.EntryPoint;
import com.google.gwt.core.client.GWT;
import com.google.gwt.user.client.ui.FlexTable;
import com.google.gwt.user.client.ui.Image;
import com.google.gwt.user.client.ui.MouseListenerAdapter;
import com.google.gwt.user.client.ui.RootPanel;
import com.google.gwt.user.client.ui.SourcesTableEvents;
import com.google.gwt.user.client.ui.TableListener;
import com.google.gwt.user.client.ui.Widget;

/**
 * Entry point class for the AdvancedWidgets application.
 *
 * @author Vipul Gupta (vipulgupta.vg@gmail.com)
 */
public class AdvancedWidgets implements EntryPoint {
```

```
private final Image largeImage = new Image();

public void onModuleLoad() {

  final FlowerImages flowerImages =
      (FlowerImages) GWT.create(FlowerImages.class);  // *(1)

  largeImage.setStylePrimaryName("gwt-Content");

  final FlexTable table = new FlexTable();   //*(2)
  table.setBorderWidth(2);

  Image thumbnailImage = flowerImages.getPinkThumbnail().createImage();   //*(3)
  table.setWidget(0, 1, thumbnailImage);
  addMouseListeners(thumbnailImage, "pink");        //*(4)

  thumbnailImage = flowerImages.red().createImage();
  table.setWidget(0, 2, thumbnailImage);
  addMouseListeners(thumbnailImage, "red");

  thumbnailImage = flowerImages.yellow().createImage();
  table.setWidget(0, 3, thumbnailImage);
  addMouseListeners(thumbnailImage, "yellow");

  thumbnailImage = flowerImages.white().createImage();
  table.setWidget(0, 4, thumbnailImage);
  addMouseListeners(thumbnailImage, "white");

  RootPanel.get("thumbnails").add(table);   //*(5)
}

private void addMouseListeners(final Image thumbnailImage, final String name) {

  thumbnailImage.addMouseListener(new MouseListenerAdapter() {
    public void onMouseEnter(Widget sender) {
      largeImage.setUrl(GWT.getModuleBaseURL() + name + "_large.jpg");
      addContent();
    }

    public void onMouseLeave(Widget sender) {
      removeContent();
    }

  });
}
```

```
  private void removeContent() {
    RootPanel.get("content").remove(largeImage);
  }

  private void addContent() {
    RootPanel.get("content").add(largeImage);
  }
}
```

I'll now discuss the code of this class in detail. The following step numbers correspond to the numbered comments in the code in Listing 5-15:

1. You start by creating an object of type FlowerImages using the GWT.create(...) method so that it can pass through the generator registered for ImageBundle, which is named ImageBundleGenerator.

2. Next you create a FlexTable, which can accommodate as many thumbnails as you want to add. (You could have just used a Grid here, but I used FlexTable to demonstrate that any number of thumbnails can be added in a professional application without having to worry about resizing the table.) You also set the border of the table so that there is little gap between the various thumbnails.

3. Then you use the FlowerImages bundle and extract the images from it by calling the methods defined in the interface. The createImage() method on the returned AbstractImagePrototype object is called to get the Image object representing the underlying image. After the Image object is retrieved, it is added to a cell in the table.

4. You need to handle the mouse events so that the full image corresponding to the thumbnail is shown when the mouse moves over the thumbnail and is hidden when the mouse moves away from the thumbnail. Since mouse events needs to be handled for all images, the logic for this is abstracted into the addMouseListeners(...) method. This method registers MouseListener for the thumbnail image object. Based on the parameters passed to the method, you set the URL for the largeImage and add the largeImage to the "content" element that was added in the host HTML page. You repeat this step for all images retrieved from the FlowerImages bundle.

■**Note** You used GWT.getModuleBaseURL() while setting the URL of the large image. This method returns the URL prefix of the module, which should be prepended to URLs that are intended to be module-relative, such as RPC entry points and files in the module's public path.

---

5. Finally, you add the generated thumbnail table to the "thumbnails" element that was added in the host HTML page.

Running the Sample Application

Now it's time to run the flower image gallery application. You can use AdvancedWidgets-shell.cmd created by the applicationCreator utility to run the application. (As mentioned in previous chapters, the application should be compiled properly before running it using the AdvancedWidgets-shell.cmd script. In Eclipse you can do this by building the project or enabling the automatic build feature as mentioned in Chapter 1.) Figure 5-5 displays the image gallery application when it starts up.

You will notice that all the thumbnails open together without the bouncy effect that occurs when the browser makes multiple requests and resets the screen elements when it gets the resource and evaluates their sizes. With ImageBundle, the size of all images is known in advance, and this lets the browser create proper placeholders for all images, avoiding the bouncy effect.

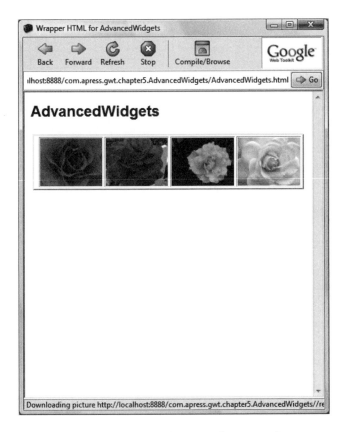

Figure 5-5. *Flower gallery application when started*

You should now drag the mouse over one of the thumbnail images to see the mouse event being handled and the full image being shown. Figure 5-6 shows the state of the flower gallery application when the mouse is moved over the pink flower. (As mentioned previously, the large images are not added to the ImageBundle, so the user has to wait on the large images to be loaded. This was done to avoid slowing down the application during startup because of a large bundle containing the large images getting downloaded. Downloading all the large images as a bundle is also unnecessary because many of them might never be accessed by the user/application at all.)

Figure 5-6. *Flower gallery application when the mouse is moved over one of the thumbnail images*

If you move the mouse away from the thumbnail, the full image will become hidden. Figure 5-7 shows the state of the flower gallery application when the mouse is moved away from the pink flower thumbnail.

Figure 5-7. *Flower gallery application when the mouse is moved away from the thumbnail image*

How Does an ImageBundle Work?

As mentioned earlier, the `ImageBundle` combines all the images into a single image by group-ing them. After you have run the application once, go to the `www\com.apress.gwt.chapter5.` `AdvancedWidgets` directory in your application's directory (`C:\gwt\AdvancedWidgets` in this case). You will find a `<Hash>.cache.png` file (`73D18624F40140FFECC96865020A7401.cache.png` on my machine), which is the bundle created when the application is compiled. If you open this file, you will see that it is just the combination of all images in a single image, as shown in Figure 5-8.

If you compile the application by running the `AdvancedWidgets-compile.cmd` file (with `-style PRETTY` added as the compiler flag), then you can see the generated JavaScript code in the `<hash>.cache.html` or `<hash>.cache.js` file with a function, as listed in Listing 5-16.

Figure 5-8. `ImageBundle` *created by the compiler representing all the images in the flower gallery* (`73D18624F40140FFECC96865020A7401.cache.png`)

Listing 5-16. *An* ImageBundle-*Related JavaScript Method Generated by the GWT Compiler*

```
function $clinit_3(){
  $clinit_3 = nullMethod;

  IMAGE_BUNDLE_URL = getModuleBaseURL() +
      '73D18624F40140FFECC96865020A7401.cache.png';

  getPinkThumbnail_SINGLETON = $ClippedImagePrototype( ➥
      new ClippedImagePrototype(), IMAGE_BUNDLE_URL, 0, 0, 100, 75);

  red_SINGLETON = $ClippedImagePrototype( ➥
      new ClippedImagePrototype(), IMAGE_BUNDLE_URL, 100, 0, 100, 75);

  white_SINGLETON = $ClippedImagePrototype( ➥
      new ClippedImagePrototype(), IMAGE_BUNDLE_URL, 200, 0, 100, 75);

  yellow_SINGLETON = $ClippedImagePrototype( ➥
      new ClippedImagePrototype(), IMAGE_BUNDLE_URL, 300, 0, 100, 75);
}
```

I'll now explain what's happening in this method.

The method first gets a URL reference to the generated image bundle file (73D18624F40140FFECC96865020A7401.cache.png in this example) in the project. Listing 5-17 shows the relevant snippet related to this, from the method in Listing 5-16.

Listing 5-17. *Variable Referring to the Bundled Images File Created by* ImageBundle

```
IMAGE_BUNDLE_URL = getModuleBaseURL() +
    '73D18624F40140FFECC96865020A7401.cache.png';
```

It then creates variables that refer to individual image portions from the bundled image by specifying their coordinates. For example, in this case, the pink image refers to coordinates 0,0 (top-left) to 100,75 (bottom-right) in the bundled image. Listing 5-18 lists the snippet that gets the relevant pink image portion from the combined bundled image.

Listing 5-18. *Pink Image Being Clipped from the Bundled Image*

```
getPinkThumbnail_SINGLETON = $ClippedImagePrototype( ➥
    new ClippedImagePrototype(), IMAGE_BUNDLE_URL, 0, 0, 100, 75);
```

Building Classic HTML Forms Using FormPanel

A FormPanel is a GWT wrapper around HTML's <form> element. A form is generally used to accept a set of inputs from the user and submit them to a server for processing later. Applications developed using JavaScript in general used to do simple client-side validations, and more complex validations were done on the server end. Before Ajax, this required a page refresh, and after Ajax was introduced, the server-side validation could be done by using the `XMLHttpRequest` object and sending across the values to the server for validations.

FormPanel automates this task and provides support for submitting the data given by the user. It also provides hooks for validating the data added by the user before the form is submitted and for getting the result from the server. One area where the use of `FormPanel` becomes necessary is when your application needs to provide support for uploading files. Browsers support file upload using forms only, and in these cases it becomes mandatory to use `FormPanel`.

■**Note** If the `FileUpload` widget needs to be submitted (that is, the file needs to be uploaded to the server), then it should be used only inside a `FormPanel`.

Widgets that implement the `HasName` interface (explained next) will be submitted to the server if they are contained within the `FormPanel`. (`TextBox`, `PasswordTextBox`, `RadioButton`, `CheckBox`, `TextArea`, `ListBox`, `FileUpload`, and `Hidden` all implement `HasName` and are submitted to the server if they are contained within `FormPanel`).

The HasName Interface (in the com.google.gwt.user.client.ui Package)

Any widget implementing the `HasName` interface has a name associated with it and can be used inside a `FormPanel`. The name of the widget along with the value in the widget is sent to the server as a key-value pair when the form is submitted. Table 5-7 lists the methods in this interface.

Table 5-7. *Methods in the HasName Interface*

Method Name	Description
getName()	Returns the string representing the widget's name
setName(String name)	Sets the name of the widget

Sample Application Demonstrating the Use of FormPanel

Listing 5-19 shows the code for an application using `FormPanel`. This code creates a simple résumé upload service. The UI for this application asks the user for e-mail address and the résumé file to be uploaded. The user then clicks the submit button to submit the form.

Listing 5-19. *Code Demonstrating the Use of a* FormPanel

```
package com.apress.gwt.chapter5.client;

import com.google.gwt.core.client.EntryPoint;
import com.google.gwt.user.client.Window;
import com.google.gwt.user.client.ui.Button;
```

```java
import com.google.gwt.user.client.ui.ClickListener;
import com.google.gwt.user.client.ui.FileUpload;
import com.google.gwt.user.client.ui.FormHandler;
import com.google.gwt.user.client.ui.FormPanel;
import com.google.gwt.user.client.ui.FormSubmitCompleteEvent;
import com.google.gwt.user.client.ui.FormSubmitEvent;
import com.google.gwt.user.client.ui.RootPanel;
import com.google.gwt.user.client.ui.TextBox;
import com.google.gwt.user.client.ui.VerticalPanel;
import com.google.gwt.user.client.ui.Widget;

/**
 * Form for a Resume upload service.
 *
 * @author Vipul Gupta (vipulgupta.vg@gmail.com)
 */
public class ResumeUploadForm implements EntryPoint {

  public void onModuleLoad() {

    // We start by creating a FormPanel
    final FormPanel resumeForm = new FormPanel();

    // Map the form panel to a service
    resumeForm.setAction("/resumeUpload");

    // FileUpload widget requires multipart MIME encoding
    resumeForm.setEncoding(FormPanel.ENCODING_MULTIPART);

    // FileUpload widget requires the form to use POST method.
    resumeForm.setMethod(FormPanel.METHOD_POST);

    // Create a vertical panel to put all the widgets in the form vertically.
    Final VerticalPanel verticalPanel = new VerticalPanel();
    resumeForm.setWidget(verticalPanel);

    // Create a text box to take users e-mail as input
    final TextBox emailAddress = new TextBox();
    emailAddress.setText("Enter Your e-mail address");
    emailAddress.selectAll();
    emailAddress.addClickListener(new ClickListener(){
      public void onClick(Widget sender) {
       emailAddress.setText("");
      }
    });
    verticalPanel.add(emailAddress);
```

```java
    // Create a FileUpload widget.
    final FileUpload upload = new FileUpload();
    upload.setName("resume");
    verticalPanel.add(upload);

    // Create a button to submit the form.
    final Button submitButton = new Button("Submit Form");
    submitButton.addClickListener(new ClickListener() {
      public void onClick(Widget sender) {
        resumeForm.submit();
      }
    });
    verticalPanel.add(submitButton);

    /**
     * Create a class to handle the form submission events
     */
    final class ResumeFormHandler implements FormHandler {
      // This method is called just before the form is submitted.
      // It can be used to do validations on the data before submission
      public void onSubmit(FormSubmitEvent event) {
        if (emailAddress.getText().length() == 0) {
          Window.alert("Please enter your e-mail address.");
          event.setCancelled(true);
        }
      }

      // This method is called when the form is successfully submitted
      // and the result is returned from the server.
      public void onSubmitComplete(FormSubmitCompleteEvent event) {
        if (event.getResults().equals("OK")) {
          Window.alert("Resume Successfully uploaded");
        } else {
          Window.alert("Error in uploading your resume");
        }
      }
    };

    // Add an event handler to the form.
    resumeForm.addFormHandler(new ResumeFormHandler());

    RootPanel.get().add(resumeForm);
  }
}
```

The code for the FormPanel in Listing 5-19 maps the panel submission to an endpoint of resumeUpload on the server. You can develop a servlet at your end and map it to this endpoint to handle the form submission event.

■**Note** The Apache Jakarta project provides the Commons FileUpload library for handling file uploads. It provides an API for handling the file and other data submitted as part of the form. This uploaded data can then be processed as per the application requirements. I will not discuss the Commons FileUpload library and its use in this book; you can refer to http://commons.apache.org/fileupload/ for further details on this library.

Summary

In this chapter, you learned about various interesting and powerful widgets including TabBar, TabPanel, and FormPanel. Throughout the chapter, you learned about techniques that can improve the look and feel of your application through modifications in the LoanServicingSystem application (which you started in Chapter 3 of the book).

The chapter started with the important concept of event handling, that is, the steps you should take to handle events generated by the application. Next, the chapter discussed styling applications using CSS and the default CSS classes of the various widgets available in the UI library of GWT. In addition, it discussed the underlying implementation of the various widgets, that is, the mapping of the widgets with the corresponding HTML elements. Later in the discussion on CSS, the chapter covered the steps you take to include an external CSS style sheet in a GWT-based application.

I discussed ImageBundles and the improvement they can bring to your application's speed. I also covered in step-by-step detail the process of writing a customized ImageBundle for your own applications. The discussion emphasized the ease of development and use of ImageBundle with a comprehensive but simplified example of a flower image gallery. The chapter finished with a discussion of building forms using FormPanel, which is a GWT wrapper around HTML's <form> element.

In the next chapter, I'll discuss some of the advanced communication techniques and concepts that are required for interaction between client and server components in a GWT application. You will enhance the LoanServicingSystem application further by adding server communication support and expanding its functionality.

CHAPTER 6

■ ■ ■

Communication: Advanced Techniques

This chapter will discuss some of the advanced concepts and techniques related to client-server communication in a GWT-based application. The chapter will start with details of various objects that can be used for client-server communication in GWT-based applications. It will also discuss the rules that need to be followed to turn a user-defined class into a `Serializable` object (an object that can be used for communication between client-server components).

Next I will discuss serializing collection classes so that you can use them in a client-server environment. You will work on developing a simplified BookStore application to understand how collection classes can be used and transferred across the wire in a GWT-based application.

You will then turn your attention toward understanding custom serializer objects. Custom serializers allow a developer to write serialization and deserialization logic for their application's domain objects.

Finally, the chapter will discuss how to use HTTP requests using `RequestBuilder` objects to communicate with the server in a GWT application. During this chapter, you will build and improve the LoanServicingSystem application and add RPC support to it. You will also develop a custom serializer object and use the `RequestBuilder` object by modifying the LoanServicingSystem application.

What Is Serialization?

An important component of the GWT framework is the support for RPC. By using RPC, it is easy to add support for server-side communication in any GWT application. RPC uses the serialization of objects (data) for communicating between the client and server parts of the application. (The serialization of objects involves converting your application's data into binary form so that it can be transferred over the wire to the client or server component as necessary.)

Examining the Different Type of Objects That Can Be Used in Communication

In Chapter 4, you learned about the basics of client-server communication in a GWT-based application. The objects that are passed around in an RPC environment (be it parameters to the method being called or the return types of these methods) must be Serializable.

A type is considered Serializable if it falls into one of the following categories:

- It is a primitive type such as char, byte, short, int, long, boolean, float, or double.

- It is a wrapper for a primitive type such as Character, Byte, Short, Integer, Boolean, Float, or Double.

- It is an array of Serializable types. Serializable data types from the Java language are present in the JRE emulation library and explained in Chapter 2. These types include ArrayList, HashMap, HashSet, Stack, Vector, String, and Date.

- It is a Serializable user-defined class as explained in the next section.

Making User-Defined Serializable Classes

A user-defined class is Serializable if it follows all of these conditions:

- It is assignable to IsSerializable or Serializable. (In other words, it directly or indirectly implements one of these interfaces.)

- It has a default constructor. (The constructor is declared as public and takes no argument.)

- All the nonfinal and nontransient fields are Serializable by following these same rules.

GWT follows certain rules for transient and final fields as follows:

- Transient values are *not* marshalled and transferred during any remote procedure calls.

- Final fields are also *not* transferred during any remote procedure calls and therefore should normally be marked as transient as well.

Designing an RPC Application

With details of serialization behind you, let's add server communication to the LoanServicing-System application that you started in Chapter 3. One thing to take care of is to isolate various pieces used in communication. This makes the system flexible and allows changes to individual modules in the future. Separating functionality into different pieces also helps you test those pieces individually.

Recall the implementation of the NewsFeedClient entry-point class from Chapter 4. The implementation in Chapter 4 had the logic for creating the service instance and the callback object tightly coupled with the code to create the UI (in the onModuleLoad() method). The

onModuleLoad(...) method of the NewsFeedClient class from Chapter 4 is reproduced in
Listing 6-1 for your reference.

Listing 6-1. *The Entry-Point Method of the* NewsFeedClient *Class*

```
public void onModuleLoad() {
  final Button button = new Button("Get News Feed");
  final Label label = new Label();

  button.addClickListener(new ClickListener() {
      public void onClick(Widget sender) {
        NewsFeedServiceAsync newsService = (NewsFeedServiceAsync) GWT
            .create(NewsFeedService.class);

      // Specify the URL at which our service implementation is running.
      // Note that the target URL must reside on the same domain and port from
      // which the host page was served.
      ServiceDefTarget endpoint = (ServiceDefTarget) newsService;
      String moduleRelativeURL = GWT.getModuleBaseURL() + "News";
      endpoint.setServiceEntryPoint(moduleRelativeURL);

      // Create an asynchronous callback to handle the result.
      AsyncCallback callback = new AsyncCallback() {
        public void onSuccess(Object result) {
          // do some UI stuff to show success
          label.setText((String) result);
        }

        public void onFailure(Throwable caught) {
          // do some UI stuff to show failure
          label.setText("Error in getting news feed");
        }
      };
    newsService.getNews(callback);
}
});
```

The problem with the code in Listing 6-1 is the tight coupling of the various pieces.
The logic for all functionality from the creation of the proxy instance to the callback object
is grouped together. Also, if there is a change in the API in the service interface methods, then
all the clients using it need to be modified. It's good to have a wrapper around the actual RPC
call to handle such situations. Having a wrapper allows you to isolate the code for a specific
functionality to a single class that can be reused multiple times, without having to write the
boilerplate business logic needed to use the API exposed by the service interface multiple
times. The structure of code in Listing 6-1 also makes it hard to change a module or test it in
isolation. Let's take care of all these points and refactor the code to make it more modular. In
the next section, you'll start by creating the objects used for communication.

Creating the Domain Objects Used for Communication

I'll start by introducing the LoanRequest object, which captures details of a new request for a loan in the system. Listing 6-2 shows the LoanRequest class.

Listing 6-2. *The* LoanRequest *Class*

```
package com.apress.gwt.chapter3.client;

import java.io.Serializable;

/**
 * Domain object for capturing details of a loan request in the system.
 *
 * @author Vipul Gupta (vipulgupta.vg@gmail.com)
 */
public class LoanRequest implements Serializable {

  private String contactName;
  private String organizationName;
  private String address;
  private long loanAmount;
  private String typeOfLoan;

  public String getContactName() {
    return contactName;
  }

  public void setContactName(String contactName) {
    this.contactName = contactName;
  }

  public String getOrganizationName() {
    return organizationName;
  }

  public void setOrganizationName(String organizationName) {
    this.organizationName = organizationName;
  }

  public String getAddress() {
    return address;
  }

  public void setAddress(String address) {
    this.address = address;
  }
```

```
public long getLoanAmount() {
    return loanAmount;
}

public void setLoanAmount(long loanAmount) {
    this.loanAmount = loanAmount;
}

public String getTypeOfLoan() {
    return typeOfLoan;
}

public void setTypeOfLoan(String typeOfLoan) {
    this.typeOfLoan = typeOfLoan;
}
}
```

With the domain objects ready, it's time to modify the UI to handle the events that will populate an instance of the LoanRequest object and submit it to the server for processing.

Handling UI Events

Next you need to modify the LoanRequestForm developed in Chapter 3 so that it handles the button click event for the SubmitDetails button. Clicking the SubmitDetails button should collect the details from the UI and send them to the server for storing and processing later.

Let's modify the LoanRequestForm class to handle the event of clicking the SubmitDetails button. Listing 6-3 shows the relevant portion of the LoanRequestForm constructor with the new changes in bold.

Listing 6-3. *Snippet Showing Modification to the* LoanRequestForm *Class to Handle the Button Click Event*

```
public LoanRequestForm() {
    final VerticalPanel loanFormMainPanel = new VerticalPanel();
    ...

    submitDetailsButton = new Button();
    hPanelItem6.add(submitDetailsButton);
    submitDetailsButton.setText("Submit Details");

    // Delegate the handling of the click event for the submitDetails button to the
    // submitLoanRequest() method.
    submitDetailsButton.addClickListener(new ClickListener() {
        public void onClick(Widget sender) {
            submitLoanRequest();
        }
    });
```

```
    savedLabel = new Label("Loan request recorded successfully");
    ...
    initWidget(loanFormMainPanel);
}


protected void submitLoanRequest() {
    //Logic for capturing user data from the form into a
    //LoanRequest object and sending it to server goes here
}
```

The code first added a `ClickListener` to the `submitDetailsButton` and then implemented the `onClick(...)` method of the `ClickListener` interface. The `onClick(...)` method delegated the logic to handle the click event to the `submitLoanRequest()` method by making a call to it.

Defining the Service and Asynchronous Interfaces

Now you should define the service interface (and the corresponding asynchronous interface) for the `LoanServicingSystem` application. As explained in Chapter 4, the service interface defines the methods (or contract) between the client and server. Listing 6-4 shows the code for the service interface, and Listing 6-5 shows the code for the corresponding asynchronous interface. The service interface, `LoanRequestService`, is declared in the `com.apress.gwt.chapter3.client` package and contains only a single method named `storeLoanRequest(...)`, which is used to store `LoanRequest` objects on the server.

Listing 6-4. *Code for the Service Interface for the LoanServicingSystem Application*

```
package com.apress.gwt.chapter3.client;

import com.google.gwt.user.client.rpc.RemoteService;

/**
 * Service interface for the LoanServicingSystem application.
 *
 * @author Vipul Gupta (vipulgupta.vg@gmail.com)
 */
public interface LoanRequestService extends RemoteService {

  public boolean storeLoanRequest(LoanRequest loanRequest);

}
```

Listing 6-5 shows the code for the asynchronous interface, `LoanRequestServiceAsync`, which is also declared in the `com.apress.gwt.chapter3.client` package.

Listing 6-5. *Code for the Asynchronous Service Interface for the LoanServicingSystem Application*

```
package com.apress.gwt.chapter3.client;

import com.google.gwt.user.client.rpc.AsyncCallback;
```

```
/**
 * Async Service interface for the LoanServicingSystem application.
 *
 * @author Vipul Gupta (vipulgupta.vg@gmail.com)
 */
public interface LoanRequestServiceAsync {

  public void storeLoanRequest(LoanRequest loanRequest, AsyncCallback callback);
}
```

To modularize an application, you should separate out the logic for the actual RPC calls, the callback objects, and the UI logic code into different classes.

Creating the Callback Classes

Start by creating the callback class, which handles the server response when an RPC call is made. Since the callback may require manipulating UI elements based on the server's response, you should create an inner class named StoreRequestCallback in the LoanRequestForm class. This allows the callback object to access the enclosing class's member variables and manipulate them as needed. Listing 6-6 shows the code for the callback class (in bold).

Listing 6-6. *Code (in Bold) for the Asynchronous Callback Class for Handling the Server Response for the* storeLoanRequest(...) *RPC Call*

```
public class LoanRequestForm extends Composite {
  ...
  ...

  /**
   * This class represents the Callback object that handles the response to
   * storeLoanRequest() method call.
   *
   * @author Vipul Gupta (vipulgupta.vg@gmail.com)
   */
  public final class StoreRequestCallback implements AsyncCallback {
    public void onFailure(Throwable caught) {
      GWT.log("Error in storing the LoanRequest.", caught);
      Window.alert("Error occurred: " + caught.toString());
    }

    public void onSuccess(Object result) {
      // TODO: Add other logic, if any here
      savedLabel.setVisible(true);
    }
  }
}
```

Listing 6-1 showed the tight coupling of the various pieces including the logic for creating the proxy instance and the actual RPC calls to the methods in the service interface. It's good to have a wrapper around these requirements, as explained in the next section.

Creating the Controller Class

Create a controller class that the LoanRequestForm can use to delegate the responsibility of making an actual instance of the proxy interface for the server and for making the RPC calls. Separating the actual calls by making wrapper methods around the RPC calls helps isolate the different functionalities in the module. Listing 6-7 shows the code for the LoanUtil class (defined in the com.apress.gwt.chapter3.client package).

Listing 6-7. *Code for the* LoanUtil *Controller Class*

```
package com.apress.gwt.chapter3.client;

import com.google.gwt.core.client.GWT;
import com.google.gwt.user.client.rpc.ServiceDefTarget;

/**
 * Wrapper class to encapsulate the creation of service proxy objects.
 * This class also provides wrapper around calls to the service methods.
 *
 * @author Vipul Gupta (vipulgupta.vg@gmail.com)
 */
public class LoanUtil {

  private static LoanRequestServiceAsync serviceInstance;

  /**
   * Utility class for simplifying access to the instance of async service.
   */
  public static class Util {

    // JavaScript is a single-threaded language. This method is synchronized even
    // though the synchronized keyword is ignored by the GWT compiler when
    // converting the code to its JavaScript equivalent.
    public synchronized static void initInstance() {
      if (serviceInstance == null) {
        serviceInstance = (LoanRequestServiceAsync) GWT
            .create(LoanRequestService.class);

        ServiceDefTarget target = (ServiceDefTarget) serviceInstance;
        target.setServiceEntryPoint(GWT.getModuleBaseURL()
            + "LoanRequestService");
      }
    }
  }
}
```

```
static {
  Util.initInstance();
}

public static void storeLoanRequest(LoanRequest loanRequest,
    LoanRequestForm loanRequestForm) {
  serviceInstance.storeLoanRequest(loanRequest,
      loanRequestForm.new StoreRequestCallback());
}

}
```

The LoanUtil class starts with the declaration of an inner class named Util that provides an initInstance() method to create an actual instance of the proxy service interface. The constructor of the LoanUtil class takes the LoanRequestForm as a parameter and uses the initInstance() method to initialize the proxy service interface object.

The LoanUtil class provides a wrapper storeLoanRequest(...) method, which wraps the actual RPC call of storeLoanRequest(...) to the server.

The storeLoanRequest(...) method uses the instance of the proxy server interface, which was created with the call to initInstance() from the constructor of the LoanUtil class. It also uses an instance of StoreRequestCallback for sending back the response to the RPC call.

With all this infrastructure code in place, you should now modify the LoanRequestForm class and use the LoanUtil class to make the actual RPC call to store the request for a loan on the server.

Listing 6-3 shows that the click event for submitDetailsButton delegates the responsibility of handling this event to the submitLoanRequest() method. You should add the code for making the actual RPC call using the LoanUtil class in this method. Listing 6-8 shows the code snippet for the submitLoanRequest() method in the LoanRequestForm class.

Listing 6-8. *Code Snippet for the* submitLoanRequest() *Method in the* LoanRequestForm *Class*

```
protected void submitLoanRequest() {

  LoanRequest loanRequest = new LoanRequest();

  // Any error handling like some values missing from the form should go here.
  loanRequest.setAddress(getAddressTextBox().getText());
  loanRequest.setContactName(getContactNameTextBox().getText());
  loanRequest.setLoanAmount(Integer
      .parseInt(getLoanAmountTextBox().getText()));
  loanRequest.setOrganizationName(getOrganizationNameTextBox().getText());
  loanRequest.setTypeOfLoan(getTypeOfLoan().getValue(
      getTypeOfLoan().getSelectedIndex()));

  LoanUtil.storeLoanRequest(loanRequest, this);

}
```

The method starts by creating a LoanRequest object. It then reads all the values from the UI form and sets them in the LoanRequest object. It then calls the storeLoanRequest(...) method of the LoanUtil class, which makes the actual RPC call.

Writing the Server-Side Implementation

The only thing left for you to do now is to add the server-side implementation of the LoanRequestService interface. Create a class named LoanRequestServiceImpl in the com. apress.gwt.chapter3.server package as the server-side implementation of the service interface defined by you.

Listing 6-9 shows the code for the LoanRequestServiceImpl class.

Listing 6-9. *Code for the* LoanRequestServiceImpl *Class*

```
package com.apress.gwt.chapter3.server;

import com.apress.gwt.chapter3.client.LoanRequest;
import com.apress.gwt.chapter3.client.LoanRequestService;
import com.google.gwt.user.server.rpc.RemoteServiceServlet;

/**
 * @author Vipul Gupta (vipulg@google.com)
 */
public class LoanRequestServiceImpl extends RemoteServiceServlet implements
    LoanRequestService {

  public boolean storeLoanRequest(LoanRequest loanRequest) {
    if (loanRequest == null) {
      return false;
    }
    // You can add the logic for storing the LoanRequest object in any persistence
    // storage like database here
    return true;
  }
}
```

The current implementation of the storeLoanRequest() method as shown in Listing 6-9 checks only whether a null object was passed. The logic for how you want to store the transferred LoanRequest object, say in a database, should go in this method.

Mapping the Server-Side Path in the Module's XML File

You should now add the servlet path entry for the LoanRequestService in the module's XML file of the application. Listing 6-10 shows the module's XML file with the new entry in bold.

Listing 6-10. *Module XML file for the LoanServicingSystem*

```
<module>

    <!-- Inherit the core Web Toolkit stuff.                -->
    <inherits name='com.google.gwt.user.User'/>

    <!-- Specify the app entry point class.                 -->
    <entry-point class='com.apress.gwt.chapter3.client.LoanServicingSystem'/>

    <stylesheet src="LoanServicingSystem.css" />

    <servlet path="/LoanRequestService"
        class="com.apress.gwt.chapter3.server.LoanRequestServiceImpl"/>

</module>
```

Running the Application

Now you should run the LoanServicingSystem application to see all the code you have written until now in action. You can run the application by executing the LoanServicingSystem-shell.cmd script. (You should ensure that the project is built properly before executing the LoanServicingSystem-shell.cmd script.) Figure 6-1 and Figure 6-2 show the application in action at different stages.

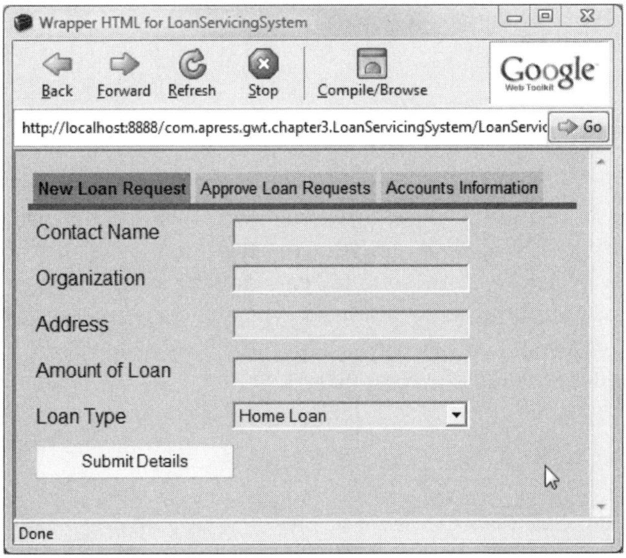

Figure 6-1. *The LoanServicingSystem application showing the* LoanRequestForm

When the form as shown in Figure 6-1 is filled in and the Submit Details button is clicked, it makes a request to the server to store the request for the loan. It then returns a response to the client so it can configure itself accordingly. In your case, based on a positive response from the server (confirming that the object was stored successfully), the application will show a confirmation message to the user, as shown in Figure 6-2.

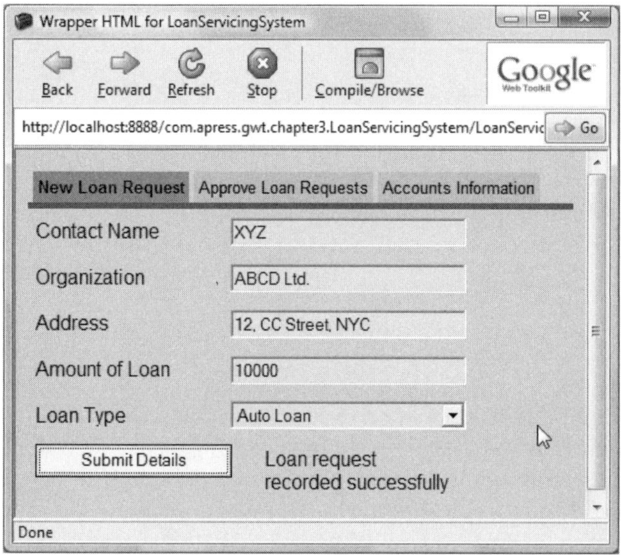

Figure 6-2. *The LoanServicingSystem application showing a confirmation message to the user when the Submit Details button is clicked and the loan request is stored on the server*

Serializing Collection Classes

Collection classes beginning in Java 1.5 operate on objects of a specific type. To make your collections serializable in GWT, you should also specify the type whose objects the collection will contain. GWT provides the gwt.typeArgs annotation for declaring this type. Although defining the type used in the collection is not a necessity, it is important if you want the proxy generator in GWT to generate optimized code for the specific type used in your collections. (As mentioned in Chapter 2, the current version of GWT does not support the Java 1.5 language construct and syntax for the client code. Therefore, you cannot use generics to specify the type associated with the objects in collections.)

■**Note** The Generator class for creating RPC-related code is named ServiceInterfaceProxyGenerator and is located in the com.google.gwt.user.rebind.rpc package. This generator creates all the code for marshalling and unmarshalling the objects and for making the request to the server and getting the response.

Understanding Collection Classes Using a Comprehensive Example

Let's work through an example of annotating parameters and the return type of methods by creating another sample project. In this example, you will create a very simple BookStore application that lists the various categories whose books are available in the store. When the user chooses a category, the system will get the list of books belonging to that category from the server and display them to the user. The user will be allowed to select and order a number of books.

Creating the Project

You should start by creating a project named BookStore in the C:\gwt\bookstore directory with the module's entry-point class as com.apress.gwt.chapter6.client.BookStore.

Creating the Domain Objects

Next you should create a class for representing a book in the system. The Book class is defined in the com.apress.gwt.chapter6.client package and stores the basic information about a book. Listing 6-11 shows the code for the Book class.

Listing 6-11. *Code for the* Book *Class*

```
package com.apress.gwt.chapter6.client;

import java.io.Serializable;

/**
 * Domain object for capturing details of a book in the system.
 *
 * @author Vipul Gupta (vipulgupta.vg@gmail.com)
 */
public class Book implements Serializable {

  String name;
  String author;
  String category;

  public Book() { }

  public Book(String name, String author, String category) {
    super();
    this.name = name;
    this.author = author;
    this.category = category;
  }
```

```java
  public String getName() {
    return name;
  }

  public void setName(String name) {
    this.name = name;
  }

  public String getAuthor() {
    return author;
  }

  public void setAuthor(String author) {
    this.author = author;
  }

  public String getCategory() {
    return category;
  }
  public void setCategory(String category) {
    this.category = category;
  }

}
```

■Note As mentioned previously, the earlier release of the GWT framework provided only the isSerializable interface to mark the types that can be serialized using the RPC mechanism. With the release of version 1.4.60 of the GWT framework, the Serializable interface was introduced for the purpose of marking Serializable classes. With this addition, the RPC mechanism has now also started generating a serialization policy file during compilation. The serialization policy file contains a whitelist of allowed types that may be serialized. Its name is a strong hash name followed by .gwt.rpc.

This file must be deployed to your web server as a public resource, accessible from a RemoteServiceServlet via ServletContext.getResource(). If it is not deployed properly, RPC will run in 1.3.3 compatibility mode and refuse to serialize types implementing Serializable.

Writing the Service and Async Interfaces

Now let's jump into the code for the service interface named BookStoreService declared in the com.apress.gwt.chapter6.client package. Listing 6-12, which shows the code for the service interface, also shows the gwt.typeArgs annotation (highlighted in bold), which is used to specify the type used in the collections in the methods.

Listing 6-12. *Code of the Service Interface for the BookStore Application*

```
package com.apress.gwt.chapter6.client;

import java.util.List;

import com.google.gwt.user.client.rpc.RemoteService;

/**
 * @author Vipul Gupta (vipulgupta.vg@gmail.com)
 */
public interface BookStoreService extends RemoteService {

  /**
   * The annotation indicates that the returned List will only
   * contain objects of type <com.apress.gwt.chapter6.client.Book>
   *
   * @gwt.typeArgs <com.apress.gwt.chapter6.client.Book>
   */
  public List getBooks(String category);

  /**
   * The annotation specifies that the parameter named 'books' is a List
   * that will only contain <com.apress.gwt.chapter6.client.Book> objects.
   *
   * @gwt.typeArgs books <com.apress.gwt.chapter6.client.Book>
   *
   */
  public String storeOrder(List books, String userName);
}
```

■**Note** The getBooks(...) method returns a list of books, and the annotation specifies that the returned list will only contain objects of the Book type.

The storeOrder(...) method takes a list of books selected by the user, and the annotation specifies that the list sent to this method by the client will only contain objects of Book type.

Listing 6-13 shows the corresponding async interface named BookStoreServiceAsync.

Listing 6-13. *Code of the Async* Service *Interface for the BookStore Application*

```
package com.apress.gwt.chapter6.client;

import java.util.List;

import com.google.gwt.user.client.rpc.AsyncCallback;
import com.google.gwt.user.client.rpc.RemoteService;

/**
 * @author Vipul Gupta (vipulgupta.vg@gmail.com)
 */
public interface BookStoreServiceAsync extends RemoteService {

  public void getBooks(String category, AsyncCallback callback);

  public void storeOrder(List books, String userName, AsyncCallback callback);
}
```

Creating the Controller Class

Now, let's create the controller class to which the BookStore class can delegate the responsibility of making an actual instance of the proxy interface for the server and for making the
RPC calls. Listing 6-14 shows the code for the BookUtil class (in the com.apress.gwt.chapter6.
client package).

Listing 6-14. *Code of the* BookUtil *Controller Class*

```
package com.apress.gwt.chapter6.client;

import java.util.List;

import com.google.gwt.core.client.GWT;
import com.google.gwt.user.client.rpc.ServiceDefTarget;

/**
 * @author Vipul Gupta (vipulgupta.vg@gmail.com)
 */
public class BookUtil {

  private static BookStoreServiceAsync serviceInstance;

  /**
   * Utility class for simplifying access to the instance of async service.
   */
  public static class Util {
    public synchronized static void initInstance() {
```

```
      if (serviceInstance == null) {
        serviceInstance = (BookStoreServiceAsync) GWT
            .create(BookStoreService.class);
        ServiceDefTarget target = (ServiceDefTarget) serviceInstance;
        target
            .setServiceEntryPoint(GWT.getModuleBaseURL() + "BookStoreService");
      }
    }
  }


  static {
    Util.initInstance();
  }

  public static void getListOfBooks(String category, BookStore bookStore) {
    serviceInstance.getBooks(category, bookStore.new BookListUpdaterCallback());
  }

  public static void storeOrder(List books, String userName, BookStore bookStore) {
    serviceInstance.storeOrder(books, userName,
        bookStore.new StoreOrderCallback());
  }
}
```

The project will not compile at this stage because you have yet to write the callback objects as used in Listing 6-14. These callback objects are created as part of the entry-point class discussed next.

Creating the Entry-Point Class

Now you should create the UI of the application. The UI of the application will be added in the entry-point class named BookStore. Listing 6-15 lists the entry-point class and explains it inline with the code. (The entry-point class will also define the callback objects used by RPC calls.)

Listing 6-15. *Code of the Entry-Point Class,* BookStore, *Belonging to the BookStore Application*

```
package com.apress.gwt.chapter6.client;

import java.util.ArrayList;

import com.google.gwt.core.client.EntryPoint;
import com.google.gwt.core.client.GWT;
import com.google.gwt.user.client.Window;
import com.google.gwt.user.client.rpc.AsyncCallback;
import com.google.gwt.user.client.ui.Button;
```

```java
import com.google.gwt.user.client.ui.CheckBox;
import com.google.gwt.user.client.ui.ClickListener;
import com.google.gwt.user.client.ui.DeckPanel;
import com.google.gwt.user.client.ui.FlexTable;
import com.google.gwt.user.client.ui.Grid;
import com.google.gwt.user.client.ui.Label;
import com.google.gwt.user.client.ui.Panel;
import com.google.gwt.user.client.ui.RootPanel;
import com.google.gwt.user.client.ui.VerticalPanel;
import com.google.gwt.user.client.ui.Widget;

/**
 * @author Vipul Gupta ( vipulgupta.vg@gmail.com )
 * /
public class BookStore implements EntryPoint, ClickListener {

  private DeckPanel mainPanel;
  private VerticalPanel booksPanel;
  private  ArrayList booksBeingDisplayed;
  private FlexTable table;

  // We have assumed a standard username for our application. In a production
  // environment, this would be assigned based on the logged-in user.
  private String userName = "VG";

  private int CATEGORY_PANEL_INDEX = 0;
  private int BOOKS_PANEL_INDEX = 1;

  /**
   * Create a DeckPanel with CategoryPanel and Books display panel. Then show
   * the category panel when the application is started.
   */
  public void onModuleLoad() {

    mainPanel = new DeckPanel();
    booksPanel = new VerticalPanel();
    booksBeingDisplayed = new ArrayList();
    table = new FlexTable();

    mainPanel.add(createCategoryPanel());
    mainPanel.add(booksPanel);

    mainPanel.showWidget(CATEGORY_PANEL_INDEX);
    RootPanel.get("slot1").add(mainPanel);
  }
```

```java
/**
 * Create the category panel and add the various categories to it.
 */
private Panel createCategoryPanel() {
  VerticalPanel categoryPanel = new VerticalPanel();
  Label categoryHeading = new Label("Books Categories");
  categoryHeading.addStyleName("heading");

  Grid grid = new Grid(5, 1);
  grid.setWidget(0, 0, categoryHeading);
  grid.setWidget(1, 0, addCategories("Computer"));
  grid.setWidget(2, 0, addCategories("Fiction"));
  grid.setWidget(3, 0, addCategories("Horror"));
  grid.setWidget(4, 0, addCategories("Romance"));

  categoryPanel.add(grid);
  return categoryPanel;
}

/**
 * Utility method to add a category label having a click listener registered
 * to it.
 */
private Widget addCategories(final String categoryName) {

  Label categoryLabel = new Label(categoryName);
  categoryLabel.addClickListener(new ClickListener() {

    public void onClick(Widget sender) {
    createBooksPanel(categoryName);
    }
  });
  return categoryLabel;
}

/**
 * Utility method to create the books panel. The method first removes the existing
 * books panel from the deck and then creates a new panel and adds and shows
 * the same. The method calls the helper getBooks(...) method to retrieve the
 * books belonging to a specified category.
 */
private void createBooksPanel(String categoryName) {
  mainPanel.remove(booksPanel);
  booksPanel = new VerticalPanel();
  table = new FlexTable();
```

```
    mainPanel.add(booksPanel);
    mainPanel.showWidget(BOOKS_PANEL_INDEX);

    Label bookCategoryHeading = new Label(categoryName + " Books");
    bookCategoryHeading.addStyleName("book-category-heading");
    booksPanel.add(bookCategoryHeading);

    getBooks(categoryName);
  }

  /**
   * The getBooks() method just makes a call to the wrapper getListOfBooks(...)
   * method in the BookUtil class. The getListOfBooks(...) method internally
   * makes the actual RPC call to the server.
   */
  private void getBooks(String categoryName) {
    BookUtil.getListOfBooks(categoryName, this);
  }

  /**
   * Asynchronous callback object class to handle the servers
   * response to getBooks(...) method call.
   */
  public class BookListUpdaterCallback implements AsyncCallback {

    public void onFailure(Throwable caught) {
      GWT.log("Error in retrieving books list.", caught);
      Window.alert("Error in retrieving books list. Try again later.");
    }

    public void onSuccess(Object result) {
      booksBeingDisplayed = (ArrayList) result;
      displayBooks((ArrayList) result);
    }
  }

  /**
   * Asynchronous callback object class to handle the servers
   * response to storeOrder (...) method call.
   */
  public class StoreOrderCallback implements AsyncCallback {
    public void onFailure(Throwable caught) {
      GWT.log("Error in storing order.", caught);
      Window.alert("Error in storing order. Try again later.");
    }
```

```java
  public void onSuccess(Object result) {
    showSuccessMessage((String) result);
  }
}


/*
 * Implementation of ClickListeners onClick(...) method to handle the button
 * click event. We just accumulate the list of all books selected by the user
 * and send the same to the server to store it accordingly.
 */
public void onClick(Widget sender) {
  ArrayList selectedList = new ArrayList();
  for (int i = 0; i < booksBeingDisplayed.size(); i++) {
    if (((CheckBox) table.getWidget(i + 1, 0)).isChecked()) {
    selectedList.add(booksBeingDisplayed.get(i));
    }
  }

  BookUtil.storeOrder(selectedList, userName, this);  }

/**
 * Utility method to display the list of books returned by the server and
 * belonging to a specific category to the user.
 */
private void displayBooks(ArrayList booksList) {
  Label nameHeading = new Label("Name");
  Label authorHeading = new Label("Author");

  nameHeading.addStyleName("heading");
  authorHeading.addStyleName("heading");

  int rowNum = 0;

  table.setWidget(rowNum, 1, nameHeading);
  table.setWidget(rowNum, 2, authorHeading);

  Book book = null;
  Label name = null;
  Label author = null;
  CheckBox selectBook = null;

  for (int i = 0; i < booksList.size(); i++) {
    rowNum++;
    book = (Book) booksList.get(i);
    name = new Label(book.getName());
    author = new Label(book.getAuthor());
```

```
      selectBook = new CheckBox();
      table.setWidget(rowNum, 0, selectBook);
      table.setWidget(rowNum, 1, name);
      table.setWidget(rowNum, 2, author);
    }

    Button button = new Button("Order books");
    button.addClickListener(this);

    table.getFlexCellFormatter().setColSpan(++rowNum, 0, 2);
    table.setWidget(rowNum, 0, button);
    booksPanel.add(table);
  }

  /**
   * Simple utility method to display a message as an alert to the user. In the
   * BookStore application we use this method to show the message returned
   * by the server and affirming the confirmation of books ordered by the user.
   */
  private void showSuccessMessage(String message) {
    Window.alert("[Server] : " + message);
  }
}
```

The `BookUtil` class provides a wrapper method around the actual RPC calls using the proxy service interface. It also contains the logic to create an instance of the proxy server interface.

Creating the Server-Side Implementation of the Service Interface

Next you should add the server-side implementation of the `BookStoreService` interface. Create a class named `BookStoreServiceImpl` in the `com.apress.gwt.chapter6.server` package to represent the server-side implementation of the service interface defined by you. Listing 6-16 shows the code for the `BookStoreServiceImpl` class; the code is explained inline.

Listing 6-16. *Code of the Class Representing the Server-Side Implementation of the* `BookStoreService` *Interface*

```
package com.apress.gwt.chapter6.server;

import java.util.ArrayList;
import java.util.List;

import com.apress.gwt.chapter6.client.Book;
import com.apress.gwt.chapter6.client.BookStoreService;
import com.google.gwt.user.server.rpc.RemoteServiceServlet;
```

```java
/**
 * @author Vipul Gupta (vipulgupta.vg@gmail.com)
 */
public class BookStoreServiceImpl extends RemoteServiceServlet implements
    BookStoreService {

  // We start by creating a list of different books in the bookstore. We just added
  // books in Computer category for our application for demonstration purpose.
  private static ArrayList<Book> booksInStore = new ArrayList<Book>();
  static {
    booksInStore.add(new Book("Java 1", "XYZ", "Computer"));
    booksInStore.add(new Book("Java 2", "ABC", "Computer"));
    booksInStore.add(new Book("GWT 1", "DEF", "Computer"));
    booksInStore.add(new Book("GWT 2", "LMN", "Computer"));
  }

  /**
   * This method just filters out the books of a specified category and
   * returns it back to the client for displaying to the user
   */
  public List<Book> getBooks(String category) {
    ArrayList<Book> books = new ArrayList<Book>();

    for (Book book : booksInStore) {
      if (book.getCategory().equals(category)) {
      books.add(book);
      }
    }
    return books;
  }

  /**
   * This method receives a list of books which were selected by the user.
   * This is the place where an application in production should store the
   * books selected by the user. In our sample application we just compile
   * the list of books selected by the user into a message which can be
   * displayed back to the user.
   */
  @SuppressWarnings("unchecked")
  public String storeOrder(List books, String userName) {
    StringBuilder builder = new StringBuilder();
    builder.append("Order by ");
    builder.append(userName);
    builder.append(" for ");
    for (int i = 0; i < books.size(); i++) {
      Book book = (Book) books.get(i);
```

```
        builder.append(book.getName());
        if (i < (books.size() - 1)) {
        builder.append(", ");
        }
    }

    builder.append(" has been successfully recorded.");
    return builder.toString();
  }
}
```

Configuring the Module's XML File

Add the servlet path entry for the BookStoreService in the module's XML file of the application. Listing 6-17 shows the module's XML with the new entry in bold. The module's XML file
also shows the entry for the style sheet for the BookStore application.

Listing 6-17. *Contents of the Configuration Module File (*BookStore.gwt.xml*) of the BookStore*
Application

```
<module>

    <!-- Inherit the core Web Toolkit stuff.              -->
    <inherits name='com.google.gwt.user.User'/>

    <!-- Specify the app entry point class.               -->
    <entry-point class='com.apress.gwt.chapter6.client.BookStore'/>

    <stylesheet src="BookStore.css" />

    <servlet path="/BookStoreService"
        class="com.apress.gwt.chapter6.server.BookStoreServiceImpl"/>
</module>
```

Creating the CSS Style Sheet for the Application

Create the style sheet file named BookStore.css in the com/apress/gwt/chapter6/public
folder. Listing 6-18 shows the contents of the style sheet.

Listing 6-18. *Contents of the Style Sheet File*

```
body,td,a,div,.p{font-family:arial,sans-serif; background-color: #ccffcc;}
div,td{color:#000000}
a:link,.w,.w a:link{color:#0000cc}
a:visited{color:#551a8b}
a:active{color:#ff0000}
```

```
.gwt-Label {
  background-color: #cccc66;
  padding: 2px 0px 2px 0px;
  width: 150px;
  text-align: center;
  cursor: hand;
}

.heading {
  background-color: #cccc66;
  padding: 2px 0px 2px 0px;
  width: 150px;
  text-align: center;
  font-weight: bold;
  cursor: default;
}

.book-category-heading{
  background-color: #ccffcc;
  padding: 2px 0px 2px 0px;
  width: 300px;
  text-align: center;
  font-weight: bold;
}

.gwt-Button {
  background:#f5f5f5;
  border:1px solid #aaa;
  border-top:1px solid #ddd;
  border-left:1px solid #ddd;
  padding: 2px;
  width: 12em;
}
```

Writing the Host HTML File

Modify the host HTML file of the application, BookStore.html in the com/apress/gwt/chapter6/ public folder, to look like Listing 6-19.

Listing 6-19. *Contents of the Host HTML of the BookStore Application*

```
<html>
  <head>
    <script language='javascript'
        src='com.apress.gwt.chapter6.BookStore.nocache.js'></script>
  </head>
```

```
<body>
  <center>
    <h2>BookStore</h2>
  </center>
  <table align=center>
    <tr>
      <td id="slot1"></td>
    </tr>
  </table>
</body>
</html>
```

Running the Application

It's now time for you to run the BookStore application and observe the RPC mechanism passing collections to and fro between the client and server. I ran the application by executing the
BookStore-shell.cmd script. (You should ensure that the project is built properly before executing the BookStore-shell.cmd script.) Figure 6-3 to Figure 6-6 show the BookStore application in
various stages.

Specifically, Figure 6-3 displays the initial screen of the BookStore application, listing the
various categories of books in the store.

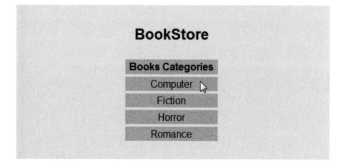

Figure 6-3. *Initial screen of the BookStore application listing the various categories whose books
are available in the store*

Figure 6-4 displays the lists of books in the BookStore application when the Computer
link in Figure 6-3 is clicked. Behind the scenes, a call is made to the server to retrieve the list of
books in the Computer category in the store.

The user can select books of interest by selecting the corresponding check boxes. Figure 6-5
displays the BookStore application showing multiple books selected by the user.

By clicking the Order Books button, the user can order the books. The application we have
developed just sends the list of books selected by the user to the server, and the server just
compiles the names of the books selected by the user from this list and returns an informative
message to the user. (In an actual application, the server would store the details of the user as
well as the books requested by the user in a database so that the books could be shipped to the
user.) Figure 6-6 shows the message returned by the server being displayed to the user.

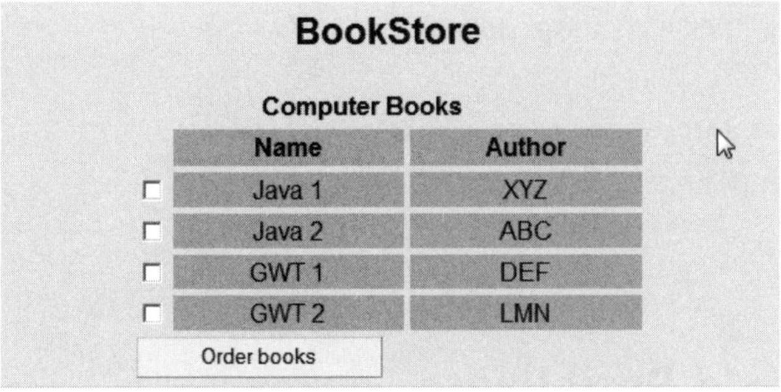

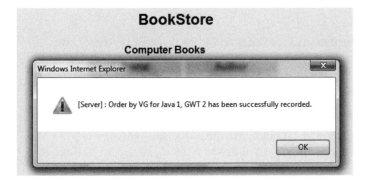

Figure 6-4. *BookStore application displaying various books belonging to the Computer category*

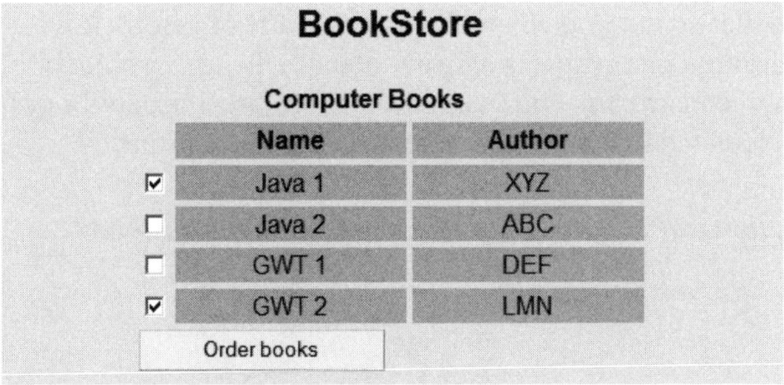

Figure 6-5. *BookStore application displaying books being selected by the user*

Figure 6-6. *BookStore application displaying the message from the server stating that books being selected by the user were properly recorded*

Example of Using HashMap

Suppose an object in your application needs to transport a HashMap of pending requests as part of the object (mapping Integer to String). Then your domain object should contain the map definition as listed in Listing 6-20.

Listing 6-20. *Demonstrating the Use of the* gwt.typeArgs *Annotation for a* HashMap

```
/**
    * HashMap that will contain Integer for keys and String for values
    * @gwt.typeArgs <java.lang.Integer, java.lang.String >
    */
   private HashMap pendingRequests;
```

Creating Custom Field Serializers

GWT handles the serialization and deserialization complexity of most objects (implementing Serializable or IsSerializable) needed in your applications. However, sometimes the default handling is not suitable for your application's needs. This could be because of various reasons, including legacy objects being used that do not implement the Serializable or IsSerializable interface, the serialization/deserialization performance of heavy objects, the legacy objects not having the default zero-argument constructor, and so on. Listing 6-21 lists the bare-bones structure of the LoanRequest object (created in the beginning of this chapter in Listing 6-2).

Listing 6-21. *Bare-Bones Structure of the* LoanRequest *Object Used for Custom Serialization*

```
public class LoanRequest implements Serializable {

  private String contactName;
  private String organizationName;
  private String address;
  private long loanAmount;
  private String typeOfLoan;
}
```

Before starting the implementation of the serializer for the LoanRequest object, you should look at two different interfaces, which are used for writing and reading data to and from a stream.

Understanding the SerializationStreamWriter Interface

The SerializationStreamWriter interface is defined in the com.google.gwt.user.client.rpc package and provides methods for writing data of different types to the stream, as listed in Table 6-1.

Table 6-1. *Methods in the* SerializationStreamWriter *Interface*

Method Name	Description
writeBoolean(boolean value)	Write a boolean.
writeByte(byte value)	Write a byte.
writeChar(char value)	Write a char.

Method Name	Description
writeDouble(double value)	Write a double.
writeFloat(float value)	Write a float.
writeInt(int value)	Write an int.
writeLong(long value)	Write a long.
writeObject(java.lang.Object value)	Write an Object.
writeShort(short value)	Write a short.
writeString(java.lang.String value)	Write a String.

Understanding the SerializationStreamReader Interface

The SerializationStreamReader interface is defined in the com.google.gwt.user.client.rpc package and provides methods for reading data of different types from a stream, as listed in Table 6-2.

Table 6-2. *Methods in the* SerializationStreamReader *Interface*

Method Name	Description
readBoolean(boolean value)	Read a boolean.
readByte(byte value)	Read a byte.
readChar(char value)	Read a char.
readDouble(double value)	Read a double.
readFloat(float value)	Read a float.
readInt(int value)	Read an int.
readLong(long value)	Read a long.
readObject(java.lang.Object value)	Read an Object.
readShort(short value)	Read a short.
readString(java.lang.String value)	Read a String.

With the details of the serialization reader and writer behind you, let's create a custom serializer for the LoanRequest object, as listed in Listing 6-21. The development of a custom serializer follows certain rules. These rules, along with the description for developing the serializer, are as follows:

1. A custom serializer must reside in the same package as the object being serialized and must have the same name as the object being serialized, but the name of the serializer must have a suffix of _CustomFieldSerializer added to it.

   Add the serializer for the LoanRequest object in the com.apress.gwt.chapter3.client package, and name it LoanRequest_CustomFieldSerializer, as shown in Listing 6-22.

Listing 6-22. *Custom Field Serializer for the* LoanRequest *Object Being Declared*

```
package com.apress.gwt.chapter3.client;

public class LoanRequest_CustomFieldSerializer {

}
```

2. The serializer should optionally declare a static instantiate(...) method that takes an instance of a SerializationStreamReader and returns an instance of the type for which this custom serializer is being written. The method must also throw a SerializationException. Listing 6-23 shows the definition of the instantiate(...) method in the current example.

Listing 6-23. *The* instantiate(...)*Method Being Implemented for the Custom Field Serializer of the* LoanRequest *Object*

```
public static LoanRequest instantiate(SerializationStreamReader reader)
    throws SerializationException {

  return new LoanRequest();
}
```

■**Note** The instantiate(...)method is definitely required when the type to be serialized and deserialized does not have a default or zero-argument constructor.

The instantiate(...) method in this example just creates an instance of the LoanRequest object, which is also the default implementation of the instantiate(...) method when the object has a default or zero-argument constructor.

---

3. To serialize the object, you should declare a static serialize(...) method, which takes two parameters: a SerializationStreamWriter and an instance of the object that is serialized (LoanRequest in this example). The method must also throw a SerializationException. Listing 6-24 shows the definition of the serialize(...) method in this example.

Listing 6-24. *The* serialize(...)*Method Being Implemented for the Custom Field Serializer of the* LoanRequest *Object*

```
public static void serialize(SerializationStreamWriter writer,
    LoanRequest instance) throws SerializationException {

  if (instance == null)
    throw new NullPointerException ("LoanRequest object is null");
```

```
    writer.writeString(instance.getContactName());
    writer.writeString(instance.getOrganizationName());
    writer.writeString(instance.getAddress());
    writer.writeLong(instance.getLoanAmount());
    writer.writeString(instance.getTypeOfLoan());
}
```

The only thing being done in the implementation of the serialize(...) method in Listing 6-24 is writing the relevant fields to the stream by using the various methods provided by the SerializationStreamWriter interface. You can use more custom serialization logic in your own applications, and the fields can then be written in the same way. The only thing to remember is that the fields have to be deserialized in the same order in which they are serialized; that is, while writing your serializer, you are allowed to write the fields in your object to the stream in any desired order, but this same order has to be followed while deserializing these fields as well.

4. Like the serialize(...) method earlier, you declare a static deserialize(...) method to deserialize your object. This method takes two parameters: a SerializationStreamReader and an instance of the object that is being deserialized (LoanRequest in this example). The method must also throw a SerializationException. Listing 6-25 shows the definition of the deserialize(...) method in this example.

Listing 6-25. *The* deserialize(...) *Method Being Implemented for the Custom Field Serializer of the* LoanRequest *Object*

```
public static void deserialize(SerializationStreamReader reader,
    LoanRequest instance) throws SerializationException {

    if (instance == null)
        throw new NullPointerException ("LoanRequest object is null");

    instance.setContactName(reader.readString());
    instance.setOrganizationName(reader.readString());
    instance.setAddress(reader.readString());
    instance.setLoanAmount(reader.readLong());
    instance.setTypeOfLoan(reader.readString());
}
```

The only thing being done in the implementation of the deserialize(...) method is reading the relevant fields from the stream using the various methods provided by the SerializationStreamReader interface. You can use more custom deserialization logic as per the needs of your applications, and the fields can then be read and processed before being set in the object's instance. As mentioned earlier, the fields have been deserialized in the same order in which they were serialized in the serialize(...) method.

■**Note** The instance passed to the deserialize(...) method is the same that is constructed when the instantiate(...) method explained in step 2 is run.

Communicating with Server Using HTTP Requests

Apart from RPCs, GWT provides an alternative mechanism for making your application communicate with the server. This mechanism allows building HTTP requests (GET and POST) that can be sent to the server for further processing. By using this mechanism, the developers are free to choose a server-side framework of their choice for incoming requests. The key class available for this purpose is the RequestBuilder class available in the com.google.gwt.http.client package. Table 6-3 lists the various methods in this class.

Table 6-3. *Methods in the* RequestBuilder *Class*

Method Name	Description
RequestBuilder(RequestBuilder.Method, String)	Constructor that takes the HTTP request type and URL.
RequestBuilder(String, String)	Constructor that takes the HTTP request type and URL.
sendRequest(String, RequestCallback)	Sends an HTTP request based on the builder's configuration. If no request headers have been set, the header "Content-Type" will be used with a value of "text/plain; charset=utf-8".
setHeader(String, String)	Sets a request header with the given name and value. If a header with the specified name has already been set, then the new value overwrites the current value.
setPassword(String)	Sets the password to use in the request URL. This is ignored if there is no user specified.
setTimeoutMillis(int)	Sets the number of milliseconds to wait for a request to complete. If the request times out, the onError(...) method will be called on the callback instance given to the sendRequest(...) method.
setUser(String)	Sets the username that will be used in the request URL.

■**Note** Modules that use the RequestBuilder class should inherit com.google.gwt.http.HTTP by including it in the module's XML file, as shown here:

```
<module>
    ...
    <inherits name="com.google.gwt.http.HTTP"/>
    ...
</module>
```

GWT also provides a utility class named URL (in the com.google.gwt.http.client package) for encoding and decoding URLs in their entirety or by their individual components/fields. Table 6-4 lists the various methods in the URL class.

Table 6-4. *Methods in the* URL *Class*

Method Name	Description
decode(String)	Returns a string where all URL escape sequences have been converted to their original character representations
decodeComponent(String)	Returns a string where all URL component escape sequences have been converted to their original character representations
encode(String)	Returns a string where all characters that are not valid for a complete URL have been escaped
encodeComponent(String)	Returns a string where all characters that are not valid for a URL component have been escaped

With the details of the various methods in these classes behind you, let's work through an example of creating a RequestBuilder for the LoanServicingSystem application. Let's assume you want to implement the back-end service as a regular CGI/PHP script, and based on the LoanRequest being approved, the script makes entries into a database to record the loan approval, which eventually starts the disbursement of the loan amount by different departments. The request takes in two parameters: the ID of the LoanRequest and the status of the request (that is whether the loan is approved or denied).

Assuming that the URI of the script in the web server hosting your application is mapped as approveLoan, the steps to create the RequestBuilder object and to connect to the script are listed in Listing 6-26 and are explained inline with comments. You can add this method to any class in your application and call it in response to, say, the click of a button.

Listing 6-26. *Method Demonstrating the Use of* RequestBuilder *Object to Make a Call to the* approveLoan *Service Registered As a CGI/PHP Script on the Web Server Hosting the Application*

```
private void approveLoan(int requestId, String status) {

  // Create the parameters that you want to add to the request. The parameters
  // should be encoded so that any special characters like blanks and
  // special symbols can be part of the URL string.
  StringBuffer params = new StringBuffer();
  params.append("id=");
  params.append(URL.encodeComponent(String.valueOf(requestId)));
  params.append("&");
  params.append("status=");
  params.append(URL.encodeComponent(status));

  //  Create the RequestBuilder object appending the parameters created
  // earlier to the URL string as well.
  RequestBuilder builder = new RequestBuilder(RequestBuilder.GET, GWT
      .getModuleBaseURL() + "approveLoan?" + params.toString());

  try {

    // A request is then created and a callback is passed to handle the
    // response from server
```

```
      Request request = builder.sendRequest(null, new RequestCallback() {

        public void onError(Request request, Throwable exception) {
        }

        public void onResponseReceived(Request request, Response response) {
          if (response.getStatusCode() == 200) {
            Window.alert(response.getText());
          } else if (response.getStatusCode() == 404) {
            Window.alert("Loan Approval service not available. Try again later.");
          } else {
            GWT.log("The request returned an error", null);
          }
        }
      });
    } catch (RequestException requestException) {
      GWT.log("Error ", requestException);
    }
  }
```

Summary

We discussed a number of things related to client-server communication in this chapter. I started the chapter with a discussion of serialization concepts, namely, objects that can be serialized in GWT. Next I showed how to enhance the LoanServicingSystem application by adding RPC support to it.

The chapter then moved onto a discussion of serializing collection classes and got into developing a simplified BookStore application that demonstrated how collection classes can be used over RPC. While working on both the LoanServicingSystem and BookStore applications, you learned techniques to make your applications more modular.

Next you turned your attention toward understanding custom serializer objects, which are used to write custom serialization and deserialization logic for objects in your applications. In the end, I discussed RequestBuilder objects that can be used to create HTTP requests to communicate to the server.

PART 3

■■■

Making Applications Ready for the Real World

This part focuses on some important tools and techniques that you should fully understand and use in your development routine to make your GWT applications ready for use in the real world. GWT provides support for testing and internationalizing your applications, and the first two chapters in this part will deal with these topics in detail. This will be followed by the deployment process and the various optimization techniques that you can use to improve your applications in the next chapter.

Specifically, Chapter 7 will introduce testing, and it will explain how you can test your GWT-based applications. It will also explain the different tools and techniques you should use to test various components of a GWT application including asynchronous calls and benchmark testing.

Chapter 8 will introduce internationalization and explain why it is important to think about internationalization requirements for your applications during the design stage. It will also explain the various internationalization techniques that are available in the GWT framework. This chapter will also guide you through the process of developing a complete internationalized application.

Chapter 9 will discuss a number of important topics, including a few that are necessary for any production-level application, such as the steps you should follow for deploying a GWT application on a web server. It will also explain the support provided by the GWT framework to add the history feature to your applications as well as a few techniques to optimize and enhance your applications.

Chapter 10 will introduce you to the most important changes in the upcoming 1.5 release of the framework, such as the support for Java 5 language constructs and the syntax for the client code of your GWT applications. This chapter will explain the minor changes that you should make to your applications to make them fully compatible with this upcoming release.

CHAPTER 7

■■■

Testing GWT Applications

Testing is a fundamental part of the entire software development process, and you should aim to write a test for all situations handled by the code. Testing is not something that should be left to a specific stage in the development cycle of the software project; rather, testing is an integral part of the entire development process. Writing good unit tests by covering all possible scenarios is an art that is acquired with practice and time. Tests basically assert that given a specific set of inputs, the method produces a desired output.

A good test suite gives you confidence about the underlying software system, while revealing any bugs or missed use cases. A set of good unit test cases also helps catch bugs early in the development process and lets you understand and refactor the code with ease. Unit tests also act as good documentation for the underlying classes being tested. They basically represent a set of use cases that the underlying code adheres to fulfill. Test cases also ensure that any existing functionality is not broken as new features and modules are added to the system.

Unit tests are generally written from the point of view of the programmer and ensure that the various methods of the classes perform the specific tasks they are assigned to do successfully. A number of open source testing frameworks are available for automated testing today. The most popular among these is JUnit. The GWT framework actively supports JUnit by providing integration with it. The GWT framework provides tools and classes to speed up the testing process using the JUnit testing framework for your application. These integrated tools allow you to test the code in both hosted and web modes.

In general, a developer should aim for a unit test for every public method of the class being written unless they are very straightforward like simple methods without any significant computation and getter and setter methods. Unit tests also act as supplementary documentation for the methods in your class.

The integration between GWT and JUnit allows developers who are creating and running test cases for their Ajax-based applications to do so with ease. In this chapter, we will look at the various ways a developer can test GWT-based applications using the built-in utilities and testing support provided by the GWT framework.

It's important to remember that you should write your GWT tests in a manner that they verify the logic behind user interactions, rather than validating user actions such as click events. For example, clicking the submit button on a new loan request form (in LoanServicingSystem, explained in Chapter 3) submits the loan details to the server asynchronously. The tests for your application should validate that the asynchronous behavior of validating a loan request is working as desired, rather than testing the event of clicking a button. This requires advanced planning and designing your application code to facilitate testing later. It further requires a clear application design so that the application's processing logic is separate from the UI logic and events.

JUnit has become the standard testing framework while testing applications written in Java. If you have never worked with JUnit before, then you should check the online documentation and samples of JUnit at `http://www.junit.org`.

Testing applications in GWT can be broken down into four broad categories. These categories are dealt with in different sections as follows:

- Understanding the `junitCreator` utility

- Writing GWT-based unit tests

- Testing asynchronous calls

- Using the `Benchmark` utility and writing tests for gathering benchmark results

Let's start with the `junitCreator` utility and create sample test cases using it.

Understanding the junitCreator Utility

This utility creates a JUnit test class and scripts that can be used for testing the different components of the application in both hosted and web modes. The template for using `junitCreator` tool is as follows:

```
junitCreator -junit pathToJUnitJar [-eclipse projectName] [-out dir] [-overwrite]
    [-ignore] className
```

Specifically, the flags/parameters are as follows:

- `-junit` is the path to the JUnit JAR file.

- `-module` is the name of the application module to use (and is mandatory).

- `-eclipse` creates a debug launch configuration for the named Eclipse project.

- `-ignore` ignores any existing files (does not overwrite them).

- `-overwrite` overwrites any existing files.

- `-out` is the directory to write output files into (the default is `current`).

- `className` is the fully qualified name of the test class that should be created.

Creating Sample Tests Using the junitCreator Utility

In this section, I'll show an example of using the `junitCreator` utility. For the LoanServicingSystem application (created in Chapter 3), you can use the `junitCreator` utility to create the test class and scripts and run these tests either from the command line or from within Eclipse. The `junitCreator` command to use for the LoanServicingSystem application is as follows:

```
junitCreator -junit C:/gwt/junit.jar -module ➥
  com.apress.gwt.chapter3.LoanServicingSystem -eclipse LoanServicingSystem ➥
  com.apress.gwt.chapter3.client.TestLoanServicingSystem
```

The output of running the previous command is as follows:

```
Created file ➥
  C:\gwt\chapter3\test\com\apress\gwt\chapter3\client\TestLoanServicingSystem.java
Created file C:\gwt\chapter3\TestLoanServicingSystem-hosted.launch
Created file C:\gwt\chapter3\TestLoanServicingSystem-web.launch
Created file C:\gwt\chapter3\TestLoanServicingSystem-hosted.cmd
Created file C:\gwt\chapter3\TestLoanServicingSystem-web.cmd
```

The script files created previously are used to execute the test cases. Table 7-1 explains these script files in detail.

Table 7-1. *Details of Different Files Generated by the* junitCreator *Utility*

Generated File Name	Description
TestLoanServicingSystem-hosted.cmd	Used to run the tests as Java byte code in a JVM
TestLoanServicingSystem-hosted.launch	Used to run the tests as Java byte code in a JVM from Eclipse
TestLoanServicingSystem-web.cmd	Used to run tests after compiling the code into JavaScript
TestLoanServicingSystem-web.launch	Used to run tests from Eclipse after compiling the code into JavaScript

The contents of the script files that display the commands to execute the TestLoanServicingSystem test file in hosted mode are as follows (TestLoanServicingSystem-hosted.cmd):

```
@java -Dgwt.args="-out www-test" -cp
  "%~dp0\src;%~dp0\test;%~dp0\bin;C:/gwt/junit.jar;C:/gwt/gwt-user.jar;➥
  C:/gwt/gwt-dev-windows.jar" junit.textui.TestRunner ➥
  com.apress.gwt.chapter3.client.TestLoanServicingSystem %*
```

The contents of the script files that display the commands to execute the TestLoanServicingSystem test file in web mode are as follows (TestLoanServicingSystem-web.cmd):

```
@java -Dgwt.args="-web -out www-test" -cp
  "%~dp0\src;%~dp0\test;%~dp0\bin;C:/gwt/junit.jar;C:/gwt/gwt-user.jar;➥
  C:/gwt/gwt-dev-windows.jar" junit.textui.TestRunner
  com.apress.gwt.chapter3.client.TestLoanServicingSystem %*
```

I'll now break down the hosted mode test script so you can understand what's happening.

The Java interpreter is called with a command-line parameter gwt.args. The value of this parameter is "-out www-test", which specifies that the result of compilation should be written to the www-test directory:

```
@java -Dgwt.args="-out www-test"
```

The classpath is set to the src, test, and bin directories of the project. The path for the JAR files for JUnit, gwt-user, and gwt-dev-windows is also set as part of the classpath. All these entries are required in the classpath for the test to run:

```
-cp "%~dp0\src;%~dp0\test;%~dp0\bin;C:/gwt/junit.jar;C:/gwt/gwt-user.jar;➥
C:/gwt/gwt-dev-windows.jar"
```

Use the class junit.testui.TestRunner as your main class, and pass the full name of the test class, com.apress.gwt.chapter3.client.TestLoanServicingSystem, as a command-line argument to the main class:

```
junit.textui.TestRunner com.apress.gwt.chapter3.client.TestLoanServicingSystem
```

The main difference in the hosted and web mode scripts is the value of the gwt.args parameter. For hosted mode, the value of the gwt.args parameter is "-out www-test", while for web mode it is "-web -out www-test". In summary, by passing an additional flag of -web to the gwt.args parameter, the test runs in web mode rather than hosted mode.

Writing GWT-Based Unit Tests

In this section, you'll continue working with the test file named TestLoanServicingSystem, which was created by running the junitCreator command previously, to write the tests. Later in this section I'll also list the steps required for creating tests without using the junitCreator tool.

Listing 7-1 shows the contents of the test file named TestLoanServicingSystem after running the junitCreator tool.

Listing 7-1. *Contents of* TestLoanServicingSystem.java *Created by Running the* junitCreator *Utility*

```
package com.apress.gwt.chapter3.client;

import com.google.gwt.junit.client.GWTTestCase;

/**
 * GWT JUnit tests must extend GWTTestCase.
 */
public class TestLoanServicingSystem extends GWTTestCase {

  /**
   * Must refer to a valid module that sources this class.
   */
  public String getModuleName() {
    return "com.apress.gwt.chapter3.LoanServicingSystem";
  }
```

```
  /**
   * Add as many tests as you like.
   */
  public void testSimple() {
  }
}
```

I'll now break down this generated test class so you can understand its various parts:

- The generated class (TestLoanServicingSystem) extends the GWTTestCase class. All GWT test classes must extend from the GWTTestCase class. This class provides integration between JUnit and the GWT framework. It is important to understand that the GWTTestCase class was not created to test UI-related code. It allows you to test asynchronous code, which is generally triggered by external events.

- The GWTTestCase class has an abstract method named getModuleName() that must be implemented by all test subclasses and should return a string representing the fully qualified name of the GWT module associated with the test. This module is used internally when the test is run. In this case, the module is LoanServicingSystem, and the getModuleName() method returns its fully qualified name, as shown in Listing 7-2.

Listing 7-2. getModuleName() *Method of* GWTTestCase *Being Implemented by the Test Class*

```
  /**
   * Must refer to a valid module that sources this class.
   */
  public String getModuleName() {
    return "com.apress.gwt.chapter3.LoanServicingSystem";
  }
```

Examining the GWTTestCase Class

The GWTTestCase class acts as the base class for all JUnit tests for GWT-based applications and provides integration with the JUnit framework. An invisible browser is started in the background when any test cases derived from the GWTTestCase class are launched. This browser acts as the sandbox inside which the tests run. This class sets up the testing and related environments (including loading the module, the hidden browser, and so on) inside which the user's written tests are eventually run.

An important thing to remember is that GWTTestCase is not meant to help you test the UI code and UI events. Rather, it allows you to test the asynchronous code and logic, which gets triggered because of UI events.

Table 7-2 lists the various methods available in the GWTTestCase class.

Table 7-2. *Methods in the* GWTTestCase *Class*

Method Name	Description
addCheckPoint(String)	Adds a checkpoint message to the current test. This is useful in web mode to determine how far the test progressed before a failure occurred.
catchExceptions()	Determines whether exceptions will be caught by the test fixture. By default this method returns true to facilitate the normal JUnit error-reporting mechanism. By overriding the method and returning false, you can ensure that exceptions go to the browser.
clearCheckpoints()	Clears the accumulated list of checkpoint messages.
delayTestFinish(int)	Puts the current test in asynchronous mode. The test waits for int milliseconds passed as a parameter to this method. (You'll learn about this in more detail in the note after the table.)
finishTest()	Causes this test to succeed during asynchronous mode. Calling this method during the delay period introduced by GWTTestCase.delayTestFinish(int) causes the test to succeed.
getCheckpoints()	Returns the current set of checkpoint messages.
getModuleName()	Specifies a module to use when running this test case. All the subclasses of this class must override this method and return the fully qualified name of the module for which the test is being written.
getTestResults()	Returns the overall test results for this unit test.
run(TestResult)	Stashes the result so that it can be accessed during the runTest() method.
runTest()	Runs the test via the JUnitShell environment.

■Note As mentioned in Table 7-2, calling the delayTestFinish(int timeoutInMilliSeconds) method causes a delay in the test as the test is put into asynchronous mode. One of the following two things can happen during the delay period:

- If GWTTestCase.finishTest() is called before the expiry of the timeout (in milliseconds) passed to the delayTestFinish(int) method, then the test succeeds.

- If any exception is thrown during the delay period in any of the event handlers, then the test will fail and throw the same exception.

If neither of these two events occurs during the timeout period and the timeout period lapses, then the test fails with a TimeoutException.

Let's now add a sample unit test to the previous test class and test the LoanRequestForm that was created in Chapter 3 (as part of the LoanServicingSystem application). Follow these steps to add the test:

1. Open the TestLoanServicingSystem class under the com.apress.gwt.chapter3.client package (inside the test directory) in the Eclipse IDE.

2. You should now add a new test method named testLoanRequestForm() to test the LoanRequestForm of the TestLoanServicingSystem class, as shown here:

    ```
    public void testLoanRequestForm() {
    }
    ```

3. Create some assertions to the newly added test, testLoanRequestForm(). You can start with some basic assertions such as testing the name of a label and button and testing the style being used for the label. Listing 7-3 shows the code for the test case.

Listing 7-3. *Test Case to Test the* LoanRequestForm *After Adding Some Assertions*

```
/**
 * Test case to validate the Loan Request Form.
 */
public void testLoanRequestForm() {

    // Create an instance of the loan request form.
    final LoanRequestForm loanRequestForm = new LoanRequestForm();

    // Assert the name of the contact label
    assertEquals("Contact Name", loanRequestForm.getContactNameLabel()
        .getText());

    // Assert the style of the contact label
    assertEquals("gwt-Label", loanRequestForm.getContactNameLabel()
        .getStyleName());

    // Assert the name of the submit details button
    assertEquals("Submit Details", loanRequestForm.getSubmitDetailsButton()
        .getText());
}
```

At this stage, you should run the test class to validate whether the tests you've written are passing.

Until now you have been working with a sample test class created by the junitCreator tool. However, sometimes you don't want to use the junitCreator tool (such as when adding some GWT code to a legacy application) but you still want to test the newly written code. The next section will discuss the steps to take to create tests without using the junitCreator tool.

Creating Tests Without Using the junitCreator Utility

If for any reason you don't want to use the junitCreator tool for generating the test class and associated scripts, then the steps in this section will come in handy to help you to manually set up test classes to test your GWT code. This section will also explain how you could run these tests. Let's start with the steps to create tests for your GWT-based applications:

1. Create a new Java file for your test cases. For example, let's create a Java file named TestLoanService in the test folder under the com.apress.gwt.chapter3.client package.

2. Ensure that your test class extends the GWTTestCase class defined under the com.google.gwt.junit.client package.

    For example, the TestLoanService class at this stage is as follows:

    ```
    package com.apress.gwt.chapter3.client;

    import com.google.gwt.junit.client.GWTTestCase;

    /**
     * @author Vipul Gupta (vipulgupta.vg@gmail.com)
     */
    public class TestLoanService extends GWTTestCase {
    }
    ```

3. The GWTTestCase class defines an abstract method named getModuleName() that must be implemented and must return a string representing the fully qualified name of the module (in other words, the name of the module for which the test is being written) that has the code to be tested.

    For example, Listing 7-4 shows the TestLoanService class with the code implementing the getModuleName() method.

    Listing 7-4. *Test Case Class After Implementing the* getModuleName() *Method of the* GWTTestCase *Class*

    ```
    package com.apress.gwt.chapter3.client;

    import com.google.gwt.junit.client.GWTTestCase;

    /**
     * @author Vipul Gupta (vipulgupta.vg@gmail.com)
     */
    public class TestLoanService extends GWTTestCase {
    ```

```
      public String getModuleName() {
         return "com.apress.gwt.chapter3.LoanServicingSystem";
      }
   }
```

4. Next you should add tests for the various scenarios you want to test. Let's start by adding a simple test to the TestLoanService class.

For example, you can add a test to validate the style used by the addressLabel in the LoanRequestForm created as part of the LoanServicingSystem application. After implementing the testAddressLabelStyle() method, the TestLoanService class is as shown in Listing 7-5.

Listing 7-5. *Test Case Class After Implementing the* testAddressLabelStyle() *Method to Test the Style Used on* addressLabel

```
package com.apress.gwt.chapter3.client;

import com.google.gwt.junit.client.GWTTestCase;

/**
 * @author Vipul Gupta (vipulgupta.vg@gmail.com)
 */
public class TestLoanService extends GWTTestCase {

  public String getModuleName() {
    return "com.apress.gwt.chapter3.LoanServicingSystem";
  }

  public void testAddressLabelStyle() {

    // Create an instance of the loan request form.
    final LoanRequestForm loanRequestForm = new LoanRequestForm();

    // Assert the style of the address label
    assertEquals("gwt-Label", loanRequestForm.getAddressLabel().getStyleName());
  }
}
```

With the test class and test cases behind you, the next step is to run the tests. The next sections will detail the steps to run the tests written for your GWT-based applications.

Running the Tests

You can run the tests in two ways: from within Eclipse or via the command line. The following sections will use the TestLoanService example discussed previously to explain these two ways of running the tests.

Steps to Run the Tests from Eclipse

The steps required to run the tests in Eclipse involve configuring the IDE with different settings. The following steps explain the process required to run the tests in Eclipse:

1. You should start by creating a new launch configuration. To do this, click the Run menu item in the main Eclipse window, and click the Open Run Dialog option. In the newly opened window, click JUnit, and then click the New Launch Configuration button, as shown in Figure 7-1.

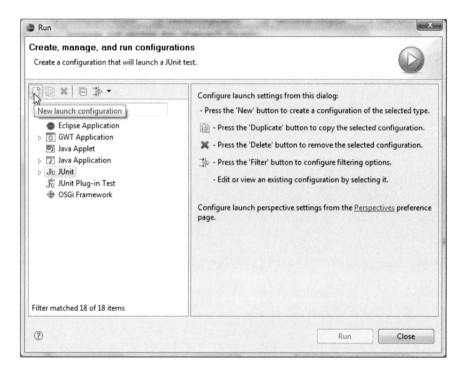

Figure 7-1. *New launch configuration button in Eclipse*

2. In the dialog box that opens, enter the launch details to create the new launch configuration. Name the new launch configuration **TestLoanService** after the test file, and name the project **LoanServicingSystem** after the Eclipse project. Name the test class **com.apress.gwt.chapter3.client.TestLoanService**, and set the test runner to Junit3. (If you selected the TestLoanService.java file in the Package Explorer in Eclipse before doing step 1, then all these values should be already filled in.) Refer to Figure 7-2 for details.

3. Next you should click the Arguments tab and type the string **-Dgwt.args="-out www-test"** in the VM Arguments field. (If you want to run the tests in web mode, then the VM argument string should be -Dgwt.args="-web -out www-test".) Figure 7-3 displays the hosted mode string being set up.

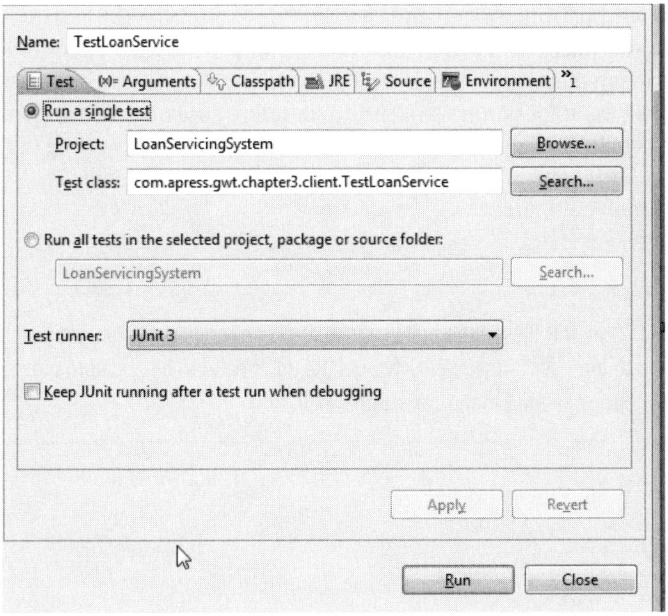

Figure 7-2. *TestLoanService configuration with values filled in*

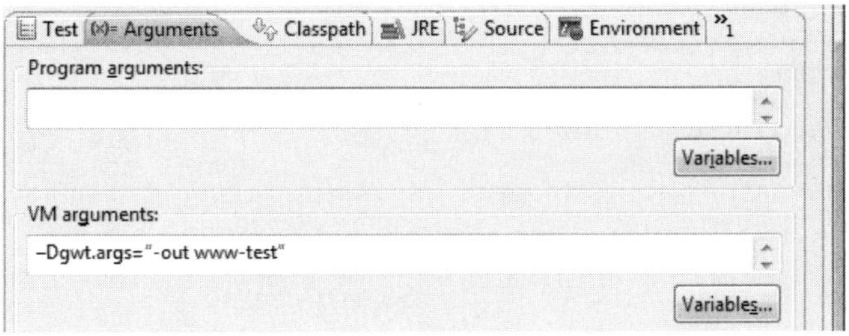

Figure 7-3. *VM arguments being filled in on the Arguments tab*

4. Now click the Classpath tab, and ensure that the following directories and libraries are present in the classpath:

- Your project's src, test, and bin directories

- The gwt-user.jar and junit.jar libraries

- Either one of gwt-dev-windows.jar, gwt-dev-linux.jar, or gwt-dev-mac.jar depending on which platform you are running the tests

You should add anything from the previous list if it is missing from the classpath. You do this by clicking the User Entries item and then clicking the Advanced button. In the dialog box that opens, select Add Folders, and then click OK. After this, a new dialog box will open; select the folders you want to add (definitely the ones missing from the previous list), and click OK. Figure 7-4 shows the Classpath tab after adding the missing entries. You should then click the Apply button on the main window to save these settings for the launch configuration.

■**Note** I added the GWT and JUnit JAR files in the build path of the LoanServicingSystem project, and since the project is added by default to the User Entries item, these JARs don't need to be added to the classpath separately because they are indirectly added to the classpath.

Figure 7-4. *State of the Classpath tab after adding the directories and libraries from the earlier list*

5. Now you should run the tests by clicking the Run button in the window, as shown in Figure 7-5.

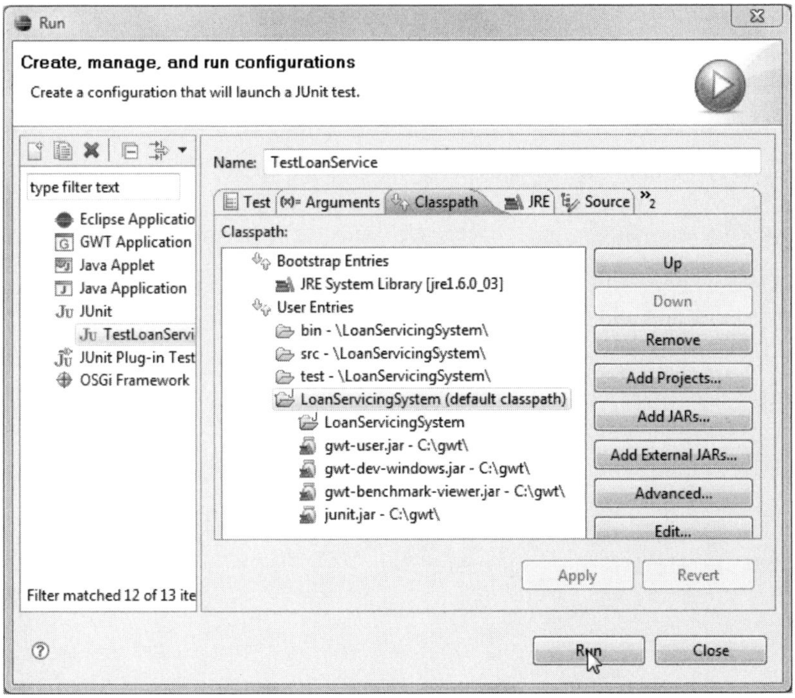

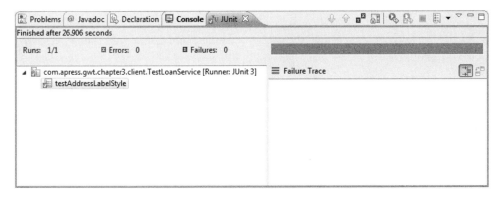

Figure 7-5. *Running the test from Eclipse*

After you click the Run button, the test will be started in Eclipse, and the JUnit window will open. Figure 7-6 shows the successful execution of the test in Eclipse IDE.

Figure 7-6. *Status of the test execution in Eclipse*

With the steps to run tests from Eclipse under your belt, the only thing left for you is to be able to run the tests from the command line.

Steps to Run the Tests from the Command Line

You can take the reference from the test script created by the `junitCreator` tool for the `TestLoanServicingSystem` example discussed earlier in the chapter. The contents of this script file are as follows:

```
@java -Dgwt.args="-out www-test" -cp "%~dp0\src;%~dp0\test;%~dp0\bin;➥
  C:/gwt/junit.jar;C:/gwt/gwt-user.jar;C:/gwt/gwt-dev-windows.jar"
  junit.textui.TestRunner com.apress.gwt.chapter3.client.TestLoanServicingSystem %*
```

You can follow the same code and use it for `TestLoanService`. You can create a file named `TestLoanService-hosted.cmd` and add the following code in it. (In this example, the only change is the name of the test file and is highlighted in bold.)

```
@java -Dgwt.args="-out www-test" -cp "%~dp0\src;%~dp0\test;%~dp0\bin;➥
  C:/gwt/junit.jar;C:/gwt/gwt-user.jar;C:/gwt/gwt-dev-windows.jar"
  junit.textui.TestRunner  com.apress.gwt.chapter3.client.TestLoanService %*
```

Now you can run the test from the command line by using this script file:

```
C:\gwt\LoanServicingSystem>TestLoanService-hosted.cmd
.
Time: 23.209

OK (1 test)
```

Now let's go over the important points that you should keep in mind while creating JUnit-based test cases for an application.

Points to Remember While Creating a JUnit-Based GWT Test Case

Here are some points to remember while creating JUnit-based test cases for a GWT application:

- A valid test in GWT must extend the `GWTTestCase` class and reside in the same package as the module being tested.

- The test class must implement the `getModuleName()` method. This method returns a string object representing the fully qualified XML file representing your module.

  For example, for the `LoanServicingSystem` module created in Chapter 3, the module's XML file is `com.apress.gwt.chapter3.LoanServicingSystem.gwt.xml`. The test class named `TestLoanServicingSystem` must implement the `getModuleName()` method as follows:

  ```
  public String getModuleName() {
    return "com.apress.gwt.chapter3.LoanServicingSystem";
  }
  ```

- The `Timer` object provided by GWT should be used for testing asynchronous code on the server side. If you don't use the `Timer` object, then the test written using JUnit will just fly away, not stopping for the asynchronous code to run, and the test will fail. Using the `Timer` object allows testing the asynchronous code in a separate thread of execution. This is the topic of the next section and will be dealt in detail as part of writing asynchronous tests.

Testing Asynchronous Calls

Sooner or later you will probably look into testing your asynchronous code, which generally forms the most important part of any Ajax-based application. The GWTTestCase class provides support for doing this by providing special methods that can be used to test the delayed response received in case of asynchronous calls. JUnit does not support threads, and all tests run in a sequence; hence, each individual test stops execution when the end of the test method is reached.

Since any GWT application of even a moderate size uses AsyncCallback objects, a mechanism is needed to delay the running of the tests to completion. If this is not done, the test will fail because no reply will be received from the server. By using GWT's support for asynchronous testing, the tests are run in a separate thread that in effect blocks the test (for a specified period of time) before the result is received from the asynchronous calls.

The two important methods defined in the GWTTestCase class (which extends the junit.framework.TestCase class) that help in achieving this are delayTestFinish(int) and finishTest(). With the help of these two methods, you can test asynchronous methods in JUnit.

An asynchronous method can be tested by setting up an event in the test method and calling GWTTestCase.delayTestFinish() with a timeout long enough to receive a response from the asynchronous service implementation. The event handler is also set up to validate (by asserting) the event's return values and then calling GWTTestCase.finishTest(), which successfully finishes the test.

You can schedule the testing of your asynchronous code in two ways, either by using the Timer object or by using mock callback objects. The template code of these two methods, along with examples for both, is discussed in following sections.

Testing by Using a Timer Object

You can test the asynchronous code of your GWT application with the help of a Timer object. The return values of the actual Ajax-based functionality (that is, the asynchronous code) are asserted/validated in the Timer object's run() method. Listing 7-6 displays the template code for using the Timer object while testing your asynchronous code.

Listing 7-6. *Testing an Asynchronous Call Using the* Timer *Object*

```
public void testUsingTimer() {

  // (1) Set up an asynchronous event handler and call an asynchronous
  //       method directly or indirectly.
  ...

  // (2)
  Timer timer = new Timer() {
    public void run() {

      // (3) Validations and assertions-related code comes here
      ...
```

```
    // (4) Brings the test out of asynchronous mode and the test succeeds.
    finishTest();
  }
};


// (5) Set a long enough delay period for the asynchronous event handling
// on the server side to complete
delayTestFinish(2000);

// (6) Schedule the event and return control to JUnit runtime.
timer.schedule(100);
}
```

I'll now dissect this template code so you can understand it. The numbers given with the comments in the template code earlier are used for reference during this explanation:

1. The test code starts by setting up the asynchronous event handler, which involves making a call to an asynchronous method directly or indirectly.

2. A Timer object is created, and its run() method is overridden.

3. All the functionality and data values are verified/asserted inside the run() method of the Timer object created in step 2.

4. The last step in the overridden run() method is to call the GWTTestCase.finishTest() method. This method internally signals to the runtime that everything went as expected and JUnit should unblock and start running normally again.

5. After the Timer object is created and its run() method is overridden properly, the GWTTestCase.delayTestFinish(int) method is called in the test with a delay period long enough to allow the asynchronous call made to the server to finish and return the results. You would have to carefully set up this timeout delay when calling the delayTestFinish(int) method to ensure that the asynchronous call completes.

6. Finally, the Timer object created earlier is scheduled to run after a certain amount of time by a call to the Timer.schedule(int) method. The timer fires after the given delay, and the run() method of the timer is called, where we validate the expected results.

Example of Using a Timer Object

Listing 7-7 lists the code for an actual example of using the Timer object. This code tests the LoanServicingSystem application developed earlier in the book. You should add this test to the TestLoanService.java class and run it.

Listing 7-7. *Example of Using the* Timer *Object to Test LoanServicingSystem*

```
public void testUsingTimer() {

  // (1) Set up an asynchronous event handler and call an asynchronous
  // method directly or indirectly.
```

```
  final LoanRequestForm loanRequestForm = new LoanRequestForm();
  LoanUtil.storeLoanRequest(new LoanRequest(), loanRequestForm);

  // (2)
  Timer timer = new Timer() {
    public void run() {

        // (3) Validations and assertions-related code comes here
        assertEquals(Boolean.TRUE.booleanValue(), loanRequestForm
            .getSavedLabel().isVisible());

        // (4) Brings the test out of asynchronous mode and the test succeeds.
        finishTest();
    }
  };

  delayTestFinish(2000); // (5) Set a long enough delay period for the
  // asynchronous event handling on the server side to complete

  timer.schedule(100);
  // (6) Schedule the event and return control to JUnit runtime.
}
```

Testing by Using a Mock Callback Object

You can also test the asynchronous code of your GWT application by using mock callback objects. The return values of the actual Ajax-based functionality (that is, the asynchronous code) are asserted/validated in the callback object's onSuccess(Object) method. Listing 7-8 lists the template code for using a mock callback object for testing asynchronous code.

Listing 7-8. *Testing an Asynchronous Call Using a Mock Callback Object*

```
public void testUsingMockCallbacks () throws Exception {

  // (1)
  final XYZServiceAsync xyzService = (XYZServiceAsync) GWT.create(XYZService.class);

  // (2)
  ServiceDefTarget endPoint = (ServiceDefTarget) xyzService;
  endPoint.setServiceEntryPoint(GWT.getModuleBaseURL() + "serviceEndPointMapping");
  // (3)
  AsyncCallback callback = new AsyncCallback() {
      public void onSuccess(Object result) {
          // (4) Assert the returned values here
          finishTest();
      }
```

```
      public void onFailure(Throwable caught) {
         // (5)
         fail();
      }
   };

   // (6)
   delayTestFinish(2000);

   // (7)
   xyzService.asyncMethodName(parameter1, ... , callback) ;
}
```

I'll now dissect this template code so you can understand it. The numbers given with the comments in the template code earlier are used for reference during this explanation:

1. The code starts by creating an object of the asynchronous service.

2. A ServiceDefTarget object is created, and its entry point is mapped to the correct URL where the async service is mapped to run (in the module's configuration XML file). ServiceDefTarget is the interface implemented by client-side RPC proxy objects. (Objects returned by the GWT.create(class) method call are cast to this interface to initialize the target URL for the remote service.)

3. An AsyncCallback object (explained in Chapter 3) is created, and its onSuccess() and onFailure() methods are overridden to handle the actual occurrence of events.

4. All valid assertions should be added in the onSuccess() method and verified. This helps in testing that the results generated are as expected.

5. Any failure scenarios should be added and asserted in the onFailure(...) method. The fail() method is called to signal the failure of the test.

6. After the AsyncCallback object is created and its onSuccess() and onFailure() methods are overridden properly, the GWTTestCase.delayTestFinish(int) method is called in the test with a delay period long enough to allow the asynchronous call made to the server to finish and return the results. You have to carefully set up this timeout delay when calling the delayTestFinish(int) method to ensure that the asynchronous call completes.

7. Finally, the service object is used, and an asynchronous call is made, passing all the required parameters as well as the callback object created in step 3.

Example of Using a Mock Callback Object

Listing 7-9 shows the code for an actual example of using a mock Callback object. This code tests the LoanServicingSystem application developed earlier in the book. You should add this test to the TestLoanService.java class and run it.

Listing 7-9. *Example of Using a Mock Callback Object to Test LoanServicingSystem*

```
public void testStoreLoanRequest() throws Exception {
  final LoanRequestServiceAsync loanRequestService =
      (LoanRequestServiceAsync) GWT.create(LoanRequestService.class);

  ServiceDefTarget endPoint = (ServiceDefTarget) loanRequestService;
  endPoint.setServiceEntryPoint(GWT.getModuleBaseURL() + "LoanRequestService");

  AsyncCallback callback = new AsyncCallback() {
    public void onSuccess(Object result) {
      assertEquals(Boolean.TRUE, result);
      finishTest();
    }

    public void onFailure(Throwable caught) {
      fail();
    }
  };

  delayTestFinish(2000);
  loanRequestService.storeLoanRequest(new LoanRequest(), callback);
}
```

The next section will help you understand the benchmarking support provided by GWT. It will go into the details of using benchmarking classes as well as viewing reports generated by the test runs visually.

Using the Benchmark Utility and Writing Tests for Gathering Benchmark Results

As part of its support for testing, GWT also provides support for creating benchmarking tests. Benchmark tests are different from the regular JUnit tests because these tests are called repeatedly with different values and because the results generated by these runs are stored for further analysis post-runs. GWT provides a tool to read the results generated by running the benchmarking tests and to create graphs from these results. The steps needed to create benchmark tests and read reports generated by them can be summarized in five simple steps:

1. Use the junitCreator tool to create basic JUnit test classes and launch configuration scripts.

2. Change the autogenerated test class to extend from the Benchmark class (com.google. gwt.junit.client.Benchmark) instead of GWTTestCase. Benchmark is actually a type of GWTTestCase because it extends GWTTestCase and adds the functionality to store the results of running the tests.

3. Create as many parameters as you want with ranges, over which the tests should iterate. For every parameter declared, you will need to provide a constant containing the various values on which the test should iterate. The framework does provide built-in classes such as `IntRange` to help in defining such parameters. You can create any range of values (with any objects), as long as an instance of class `java.lang.Iterable` is specified in the annotation (`gwt.benchmark.param`) for the parameter of the test methods.

4. Write your benchmark tests and then run them like you would run your regular JUnit tests. The tests results are written to an XML file in the working directory.

5. Run the `benchmarkViewer` tool provided with the GWT framework to view benchmark reports containing graphs and charts of the test results generated by the test runs.

Examining the Benchmark Class

The `Benchmark` class in the `com.google.gwt.junit.client` package is a type of `GWTTestCase` because it extends the `GWTTestCase` class. This class adds the functionality of storing the results of running the tests in a benchmark report. `Benchmark` also adds support for multiple things over the standard JUnit's `TestCase` class, and these additional functionalities are as follows:

- Support for test methods with parameters is added. Each method in the `Benchmark` test class is executed multiple times with different values covering the entire range of the specified parameters. The methods should be annotated with the `@gwt.benchmark.param` annotation for each such parameter. The syntax for this annotation requires adding the parameter as `<parameter name> = <Iterable>`. You can also add `-limit` to flag that the tests should stop executing when the execution time becomes too long.

  In the following example, `size` is a parameter to the test function, and the range of values is defined by the `Iterable` instance named `sizeRange`:

  ```
  /**
   * @gwt.benchmark.param size = sizeRange
   */
  ```

- Support for separating the setup and teardown costs from the actual work being benchmarked is provided. The `setup()` and `tearDown()` methods of the `TestCase` class don't take parameters, but sometimes you'll want to add some setup and teardown logic for different tests using certain parameters.

  GWT provides beginning and ending methods to separate the setup and teardown costs. You can customize these methods by passing parameters for different runs of the tests. To do this, simply name your methods `"begin[TestMethodName]"` and `"end[TestMethodName]"`, and these methods will be executed before and after each test method in your test class. The time taken by these methods will not be included in the generated test reports.

- Extreme cases are removed from the test runs so that the results are not affected by such scenarios. It is ensured that the benchmark methods are run for a minimum period of time (150ms). You can optionally also limit the maximum time for which the execution of a method run can continue (1000ms) by providing an additional flag (-limit) while declaring the annotation for the parameters.

Table 7-3 lists the method and fields available in the Benchmark class.

Table 7-3. *Methods/Fields in the* Benchmark *Class*

Method/Field Name	Description
Benchmark()	Constructor for creating a Benchmark object.
REPORT_PATH	String field representing the name of the system property that specifies the location where the benchmark reports are written to and read from. The system property's value is com.google.gwt.junit.reportPath, and if this property is not set, then the value is defaulted to the user's current working directory.

Examining the IntRange Class

The com.google.gwt.junit.client.IntRange class is used to specify a range of integer parameters to be used in your benchmark tests. IntRange basically creates a new range with start and end values and a stepping function that is described by a com.google.gwt.junit.client. Operator and step value. The Operator class provides mathematical operations of addition and multiplication specified by Operator.ADD and Operator.MULTIPLY, respectively, and these can be used when specifying the stepping function. Table 7-4 lists the methods available in the IntRange class.

Table 7-4. *Methods in the* IntRange *Class*

Method/Constructor	Description
IntRange (int start, int end, Operator operator, int step)	Constructor used to create a new range that produces iterators that begin at start, end at end, and increment by the stepping function described by operator and step.
iterator()	Used to get an iterator over the range of values represented by the IntRange object.

Benchmarks do not support asynchronous testing. Calling the delayTestFinish(int) or finishTest() method of the GWTTestCase class will result in an UnsupportedOperationException being thrown.

Benchmarking helps in deciding among multiple algorithms or data structures for doing a single task. By looking at the performance of the different algorithms or data structures over the varied set of actual inputs, the developer can choose the best among the options available.

Benchmarks also help in optimizing a module and in effect the entire application. By benchmarking a piece of code over a set of expected inputs, you can visualize the runtime of that piece of code over the input set, and this helps reflect which modules should be optimized before being deployed for actual use.

Sample Application for Benchmarking

Let's take a hypothetical example to understand benchmarking and the various tools in the GWT framework related to it. Assume you have a system that has two requirements:

- You need to store a large number of values in a data structure.

- You should be able to ask (a large number of times) whether a number is present in the data structure. This should be done very efficiently.

The entire system can be mimicked in the test case itself. You can use the ideas from this example when writing a benchmark test for your actual production systems.

Assume that the system needs to choose between HashSet and ArrayList as the data structure. The Test class should have the following code for declaring these data structures:

```
public HashSet hashSet = new HashSet();
public ArrayList arrayList = new ArrayList();
```

To mimic this system, you should create a simple IntRange variable named sizeRange, as shown next. This variable will be used as a parameter in the test methods so that the actual functions could be called multiple times with these values and the runtime corresponding to this parameter value will be stored.

```
final IntRange sizeRange = new IntRange(500000, 550000, Operator.ADD, 200);
```

Next you should add methods to populate the data structures with data up to a certain range. Listing 7-10 details two simple methods that populate the data structures with all values from 0 to the limit specified by the parameter passed to the method. This parameter declares the upper range of values.

Listing 7-10. *Methods for Populating the Two Data Structures*

```
/**
 * Populates the ArrayList with integers 0 <= x <= size
 * @param size Upper limit of the integers to add in the structure
 */
public void populateArrayList(Integer size) {
  for (int i = 0; i <= size.intValue(); i++)
    arrayList.add(new Integer(i));
}

/**
 * Populates the HashSet with integers 0 <= x <= size
 * @param size Upper limit of the integers to add in the structure
 */
public void populateHashSet(Integer size) {
  for (int i = 0; i <= size.intValue(); i++)
    hashSet.add(new Integer(i));
}
```

Now you should add a method to test the `ArrayList` structure. Each run of the method should first clear the existing array list and then populate the array list using the `populateArrayList(...)` method listed in Listing 7-10. After populating the structure, the test method loops through all the values in the data structure, checking whether they exist (doing this efficiently is the fundamental requirement of the system, as mentioned earlier).

Listing 7-11 details the test method used for testing the array list structure. Notice that JUnit requires that along with the test method with parameters, a method with the same name that takes no parameters should also be mentioned in the test file created for benchmarking purposes.

Listing 7-11. *Method for Testing the Efficiency of Array List*

```
/**
 * JUnit requires a method that takes no arguments. This method is not
 * used for benchmarking.
 */
public void testArrayList() {
}

/**
 * @gwt.benchmark.param size = sizeRange
 */
public void testArrayList(Integer size) {
  arrayList.clear();
  populateArrayList(size);
  for (int i = 1; i < size.intValue(); i++) {
    arrayList.contains(new Integer(i));
  }
}
```

Similar to the test for the array list, you should create a test case for the hash set as well, as shown in Listing 7-12.

Listing 7-12. *Method for Testing the Efficiency of the Hash Set*

```
/**
 * JUnit requires a method that takes no arguments. This method is not
 * used for benchmarking.
 */
public void testHashSet() {
}

/**
 * @gwt.benchmark.param size = sizeRange
 */
public void testHashSet(Integer size) {
  hashSet.clear();
```

```
    populateHashSet(size);
    for (int i = 1; i < size.intValue(); i++) {
      hashSet.contains(new Integer(i));
    }
  }
}
```

You should write the benchmark test in a class named StructureBenchmark.java under the test folder in the com.apress.gwt.chapter3.client package. Listing 7-13 shows the test class for your reference.

Listing 7-13. *Code of* StructureBenchmark.java

```
package com.apress.gwt.chapter3.client;

import java.util.ArrayList;
import java.util.HashSet;

import com.google.gwt.junit.client.Benchmark;
import com.google.gwt.junit.client.IntRange;
import com.google.gwt.junit.client.Operator;

/**
 * @author Vipul Gupta (vipulgupta.vg@gmail.com)
 */
public class StructureBenchmark extends Benchmark {

  public HashSet hashSet = new HashSet();
  public ArrayList arrayList = new ArrayList();

  final IntRange sizeRange = new IntRange(500000, 550000, Operator.ADD, 200);

  /**
   * Must refer to a valid module that sources this class.
   */
  public String getModuleName() {
    return "com.apress.gwt.chapter3.LoanServicingSystem";
  }

  /**
   * Populates the ArrayList with integers 0 <= x <= size
   * @param size Upper limit of the integers to add in the structure
   */
  public void populateArrayList(Integer size) {
    for (int i = 0; i <= size.intValue(); i++)
      arrayList.add(new Integer(i));
  }
```

```java
/**
 * Populates the HashSet with integers 0 <= x <= size
 * @param size Upper limit of the integers to add in the structure
 */
public void populateHashSet(Integer size) {
  for (int i = 0; i <= size.intValue(); i++)
    hashSet.add(new Integer(i));
}

/**
 * JUnit requires a method that takes no arguments. It is not used for
 * Benchmarking.
 */
public void testArrayList() {
}

/**
 * @gwt.benchmark.param size = sizeRange
 */
public void testArrayList(Integer size) {
  arrayList.clear();
  populateArrayList(size);
  for (int i = 1; i < size.intValue(); i++) {
    arrayList.contains(new Integer(i));
  }
}

public void testHashSet() {
}


/**
 * @gwt.benchmark.param size = sizeRange
 */
public void testHashSet(Integer size) {
  hashSet.clear();
  populateHashSet(size);
  for (int i = 1; i < size.intValue(); i++) {
    hashSet.contains(new Integer(i));
  }
}
}
```

Now it's time to run this class and generate the report file with results. Referring to the scripts created by junitCreator earlier, you can write the hosted mode script for this test case as follows:

```
@java -Dgwt.args="-out www-test"
  -cp "%~dp0\src;%~dp0\test;%~dp0\bin;c:/gwt/junit.jar;C:/gwt/gwt-user.jar;➥
  C:/gwt/gwt-dev-windows.jar" junit.textui.TestRunner
  com.apress.gwt.chapter3.client.StructureBenchmark %*
```

You should create a file named StructureBenchmark-hosted.cmd in the project's root directory and add this command to this file. You can now execute the StructureBenchmark test by running this script from the command line as follows (the command also shows the time taken by tests to run on a test machine):

```
C:\gwt\LoanServicingSystem>StructureBenchmark-hosted.cmd
..
Time: 114.469
OK (2 tests)
```

Successful execution of the test creates an XML report file named report-<number>.xml. This file stores details about the parameter value, the size of structure in the example, and the time taken by the test method to run in each case. For the test executed earlier, a report file named report-1199202146862.xml was created. Listing 7-14 shows the brief contents of this file.

Listing 7-14. *Partial Contents of the* report-1199202146862.xml *File Generated by Running Benchmark Tests*

```
<?xml version="1.0" encoding="UTF-8"?>
<gwt_benchmark_report date="Jan 1, 2008 9:12:26 PM" gwt_version="unknown">
  <category description="" name="">
    <benchmark class="com.apress.gwt.chapter3.client.StructureBenchmark"
      description="@gwt.benchmark.param size = sizeRange " name="testArrayList">
      <source_code>
  /**
   * @gwt.benchmark.param size = sizeRange
   */
  public void testArrayList(Integer size) {
    arrayList.clear();
    populateArrayList(size);
    for (int i = 1; i &lt; size.intValue(); i++) {
      arrayList.contains(new Integer(i));// new Integer(i));
    }
  }
      </source_code>
      <result agent="Mozilla/4.0 (compatible; MSIE 7.0; Windows NT 6.0; SLCC1;
          .NET CLR 2.0.50727; .NET CLR 3.0.04506; InfoPath.2)" host="127.0.0.1">
        <trial timing="1381.01953125">
          <variable name="size" value="10000"/>
        </trial>
```

```
         <trial timing="1421.734375">
           <variable name="size" value="10200"/>
         </trial>
         <trial timing="1478.03515625">
           <variable name="size" value="10400"/>
         </trial>
         <trial timing="1544.09765625">
           <variable name="size" value="10600"/>
           ...
           ...
       </benchmark>
    </category>
</gwt_benchmark_report>
```

Assuming the GWT directory is in your classpath, you should execute the benchmarkViewer.
cmd utility present in the GWT home directory as follows:

```
C:\gwt\chapter3>benchmarkViewer.cmd
```

Figures 7-7 and 7-8 show the result of executing the benchmarkViewer command.

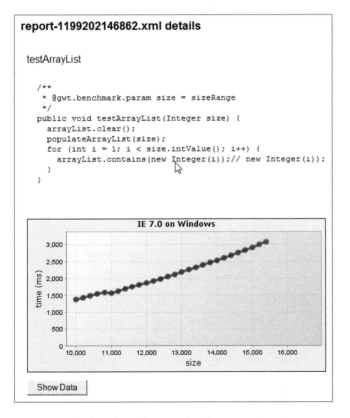

Figure 7-7. *The benchmark report for the* ArrayList *data structure*

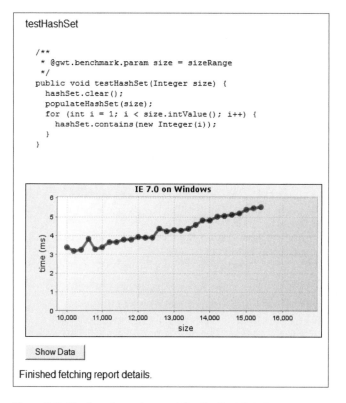

```
testHashSet

    /**
     * @gwt.benchmark.param size = sizeRange
     */
    public void testHashSet(Integer size) {
      hashSet.clear();
      populateHashSet(size);
      for (int i = 1; i < size.intValue(); i++) {
        hashSet.contains(new Integer(i));
      }
    }
```

Figure 7-8. *The benchmark report for the* HashSet *data structure*

The comparison clearly shows that the HashSet structure is much more efficient for the use case mentioned earlier. For data values from 10000 to 15000, the time taken when using HashSet is 3.2ms to 5.6ms, while in the case of ArrayList it is 1381ms to 3100ms. It's clear from the benchmark results that HashSet is a much more efficient choice for the example's requirement than ArrayList.

One thing to notice in the test class is that the time taken for the test method to run also includes the time to clear and populate the structure, as is highlighted in bold here:

```
public void testHashSet(Integer size) {
  hashSet.clear();
  populateHashSet(size);
  for (int i = 1; i < size.intValue(); i++) {
    hashSet.contains(new Integer(i));
  }
}
```

Along the lines of the setUp() and tearDown() methods exposed by Junit, GWT provides begin and end methods to separate the setup and teardown costs. To do this, simply name your methods begin[TestMethodName] and end[TestMethodName], and these methods will be executed before and after each test method in your test class. The time taken by these methods will not be included in the generated test reports. The code for the testHashSet(Integer) method listed earlier can be converted to the code shown in Listing 7-15 to avoid including setUp() and tearDown() costs from each test run.

Listing 7-15. *Separating the* setUp() *and* tearDown() *Costs from the* HashSet *Test Method*

```
/**
 * This method will be called before each run of testHashSet method.
 */
public void beginHashSet(Integer size) {
  populateHashSet(size);
}

public void testHashSet(Integer size) {
  for (int i = 1; i < size.intValue(); i++) {
    hashSet.contains(new Integer(i));
  }
}

/**
 * This method will be called after each run of testHashSet method.
 */
public void endHashSet(Integer size) {
  hashSet.clear();
}
```

Summary

In this chapter, you learned about testing GWT-based applications in detail. Testing is a fundamental part of any software development project and should not be left to the last stage of your system development.

The chapter discussed various aspects related to testing and also mentioned the tools and utilities available in the GWT framework for testing purposes. The chapter started with a discussion of junitCreator and then went on to discuss how to create the test structure without using it. Then the chapter dealt with testing asynchronous calls as well as using the benchmarking support available in the GWT framework to write benchmark tests for your code.

■■■

CHAPTER 8

Internationalizing Your Applications: A Modern-Day Reality

Over the past decade, we've seen an acceleration of companies expanding their businesses by attracting international markets through e-commerce. This requires the development of applications for customers who span multiple regions, languages, currencies, and even customs. If you want to adapt your applications to meet local and native requirements around the world, then this chapter is for you. It will help you understand what internationalization is and what support is available in GWT for internationalization. This includes a review of the various libraries and classes available in GWT specifically for internationalization. You will also learn how to create a complete internationalized application by going step by step over a simple example. After reading this chapter, you should be able to make your own internationalized applications using GWT.

What Is Internationalization?

We live in an international time, and applications need to reflect this. It's a reality that all developers must deal with. *Internationalization* is the process of designing your application to be compatible for different environments, particularly other regions or countries where the application needs to be run. For example, the most common requirement for localization is displaying a web application in the native language of the user. Other examples include supporting the local currency and the format of dates, time zones, numbers, and so on. Internationalization is an involved process and requires careful planning before the application is developed so you can avoid major rework afterward.

■Note The term *internationalization* is abbreviated as i18n, because there are 18 letters between the first *i* and the last *n*.

The common development practice followed for internationalization requires separating the actual usage of the data to be internationalized into properties files. The values in such properties files are eventually used when the application is executed. For example, a user with a locale set to English will be shown values from the properties file for English text. Similarly, the user with their locale set to French will see the values displayed from the properties file for the French language, and so on. An application that might require internationalization at some future time must be designed with careful planning to avoid rework later. Following such an approach allows you to support any new environment (region/locale) with ease in the future.

Internationalization in effect leads to separating the language and native data from the application source code and requires designing the application in a manner that can handle different languages and native data values.

Localization

On the other hand, *localization* is the process of translating the elements of an application for a specific locale. Localizing is the process of designing your application to behave in a locale-specific way, in other words, ensuring that your application changes as it is used in the different supported locales. This involves developing your application in a manner that allows it to reconfigure itself to display locale-specific text, dates, times, and so on.

It is important to understand the difference between internationalization and localization. According to Wikipedia, internationalization is the process of designing a software application so that it can be adapted to various languages and regions without engineering changes. Localization is the process of adapting software for a specific region or language by adding locale-specific components and translating text. Internationalization is done once per product, while localization is done once for each combination of product and locale.

■Note   The term *localization* is abbreviated as l10n, because there are ten letters between the first *l* and the last *n*.

Things to Remember While Developing an Internationalized Application

The process of internationalizing your application involves taking care of a few things:

- The most important thing for adding internationalization support to your applications is adequate planning. This involves designing the application from the ground up with internationalization in mind. Doing this one fundamental step correctly will save you tons of time in resetting and reconfiguring the application in the future. The application should not have any messages, dates, and numbers embedded in the source code, and all such instances of strings, numbers, dates, and so on, should be created as localizable elements by adding necessary hooks or lookup points.

- Make sure that all the characters required by the various locales are supported by the character set used by the application. It's an important decision to choose the right character set, keeping in mind the growing requirements of the application in the future.

- The application should be able to reconfigure itself to the various locale-specific requirements such as the direction of the text (from left to right, for example), the currency, and so on. This requires that the UI is built with flexibility so that it can reconfigure itself to such changes.

Understanding Character Encodings

Character encoding is an important concept in the internationalization of a web application. It is important that you choose the correct encoding to ensure that all relevant characters and languages to be supported by the application can be mapped using the chosen encoding.

The following are some concepts related to character encoding:

Character: The smallest component of a written language that has a semantic value is known as a character. Examples include digits and ideograms (Chinese characters).

Character set: A group of characters with no numerical value associated with them is known as the character set of that language. An example is Latin alphabets.

Coded character sets: These are character sets in which each character is associated with a scalar value. For example, ASCII and Unicode are two different coded character sets with ASCII having the uppercase letter *C* mapped to the scalar value of 67. A coded character set is meant to be encoded, in other words, converted into a digital representation so that the characters can be serialized in files, databases, or strings. This is done through a character encoding scheme or encoding. The encoding method maps each character value to a given sequence of bytes.

Important Character Sets

The following section lists a few of the most common character sets.

ASCII

American Standard Code for Information Interchange (ASCII) is a character encoding used to map English-language alphabets and character symbols to numbers. The standard ASCII character set is 7 bits and maps different letters and symbols in the number range of 0 to 127. (Computers use 8 bits as a storage unit, so the 8th bit is commonly used as a parity bit in standard ASCII). ASCII has been incorporated into the Unicode (explained next) character set as the first 128 symbols so that these characters are the same in both ASCII and Unicode.

Unicode

Unicode, also called Universal Character Set (UCS), is a 16-bit coded character set that was developed by the Unicode Consortium. Unicode contains most of the characters that are currently used in storing and exchanging data.

UTF-8

UTF-8 (also called 8-bit UCS/Unicode Transformation Format) is a multibyte 8-bit encoding in which each Unicode scalar value is mapped to a sequence of 1 to 4 bytes. One of the main advantages of UTF-8 is its compatibility with ASCII. If no extended characters are present, there is no difference between a character encoded in ASCII and the same character encoded in UTF-8. UTF-8 is most relevant for a web application.

In most situations, the encoding of characters in a character set is just an alternative representation of the underlying numerical or scalar values represented for the characters. For example, the character *ã* (a Latin small letter *a* with a tilde that is numerically represented as 227 in UTF-8) is encoded into 2 bytes: 0xC3 and 0xA3 in UTF-8.

Character Encoding and Web Applications

An important aspect of internationalizing a web application is this notion of character encoding. Character encoding is a mapping from a set of characters to sequences of code units. The preferred character encoding to use in the web environment is UTF-8. UTF-8 is an 8-bit character encoding supported by most browser versions. UTF-8 encodes all Unicode characters, which means no information is lost when communicating using the Java language because Java uses Unicode internally. Other types of encoding represent only a subset of the Unicode character set, which means that all languages might not be supported.

GWT's Internationalization Support

The module containing all the internationalization code provided by the GWT framework is named I18N and is explained in detail in the following sections.

The I18N Module

All the core classes and interfaces related to internationalization reside in the package named com.google.gwt.i18n. The internationalization types as defined in Table 8-1 (and shown in Figure 8-1) are included in the module com.google.gwt.i18n.I18N. Your module must inherit this module if you want to use any of the internationalization types provided by the framework in your application.

You can inherit the I18N module by using the <inherits> tag in your module's configuration file as follows:

```
<module>
  <!-- inherited modules, such as com.google.gwt.user.User -->
  <inherits name="com.google.gwt.i18n.I18N"/>
  <!-- other module settings -->
</module>
```

Table 8-1 defines the most important classes and interfaces provided by the GWT framework in this module.

Table 8-1. *Important Classes and Interfaces in the* I18N *Module*

Type	Description
Localizable	Useful for localizing algorithms encapsulated in a class
Constants	Useful for localizing typed constant values
Messages	Useful for localizing customizable messages
ConstantsWithLookup	Like Constants but with extra lookup flexibility for data-driven applications
Dictionary*	Useful when adding a GWT module to existing localized web pages

* Class

Figure 8-1 shows the hierarchy of these interfaces and classes.

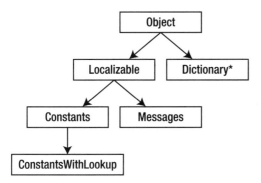

Figure 8-1. *Hierarchy of important classes and interfaces used for internationalization in GWT (* = Class)*

Internationalization Techniques Available in GWT

GWT offers a number of techniques to allow developers to internationalize their applications. These techniques can be classified into two broad categories: static and dynamic string internationalization.

Static String Internationalization

Static string internationalization refers to a method that relies on Java interfaces, properties files, and code generation to provide locale-aware messages and configuration settings. GWT provides the Constants, ConstantsWithLookup, and Messages interfaces for static string internationalization purposes, as listed in Table 8-2. (We will discuss these interfaces in detail later in the chapter.)

Table 8-2. *Interfaces Used for Static String Internationalization*

Interface Name	Description
Localizable	This is a marker interface and acts as the root of all interfaces used for static internationalization. An object of this type (that directly or indirectly extends or implements this interface) created using deferred binding allows values substitution based on locale.
Constants	This interface is useful for localizing constant values. (The values are bound to the application at compile time and as such do not allow dynamic remapping of properties files or constants based on different locales at runtime.)
Messages	Useful for localizing messages requiring arguments. (Like Constants, this also binds the values to the application at compile time and does not allow rebinding the values based on different locales at runtime.)
ConstantsWithLookup	This is just like Constants but with extra lookup flexibility for highly data-driven applications. This interface adds the ability to look up constants at runtime by referring to the key name as a string.

Dynamic String Internationalization

Dynamic string internationalization depends on the Dictionary class that looks up localized values defined in a module's host HTML page and does not require recompiling the application.

The Dictionary class allows your GWT application to use the strings supplied by the host HTML page. In this method, you simply put your strings in the body of your HTML page as simple JavaScript, and your GWT application can read and display these values to the end users. This method allows your GWT-based application to look up the key-value pairs at runtime and thus use them while rendering the UI to the user.

Since this value works by binding the key-value pairs from the host HTML page, this method does not recognize the locale-specific setting. Thus, it is up to the developer to configure the web server to correctly generate the correct localized strings while rendering a page to a user.

A major advantage this approach offers is that the application code does not require recompiling when the message values are changed or a set of new locales is added. This also leads to some problems. For example, since the compiler does not do any key checking, invalid keys cannot be caught beforehand. Table 8-3 lists the details of the Dictionary class.

Table 8-3. *Classes Used for Dynamic String Internationalization*

Class Name	Description
Dictionary	Useful when adding a GWT module to existing localized web pages. This technique allows the developer to add key-value pairs inside the application's host HTML page, and then the pairs can be looked up at runtime and used for displaying the values in the UI of the application.

With details about static and dynamic internationalization behind you, let's discuss in detail the Localizable interface, which serves as the base for all other interfaces defined in the internationalization hierarchy of GWT.

Exploring the Localizable Interface

This is a marker/tag interface that serves as the root for all types that are used in static internationalization. If you want to have locale-specific values substitution, then you should create an object of a type that directly or indirectly implements the Localizable interface. GWT's deferred binding and code generation using generators (as explained in Chapter 2) comes into play when this type object is instantiated using the GWT.create(...) method.

Understanding Locale-Specific Substitution of Values

An object of an interface or class, which directly or indirectly extends or implements the Localizable interface, must be instantiated by using the deferred binding approach (in other words, using the GWT.create(...) method). The initialized object gets values assigned from a properties file that is selected based on the value of the client property named locale.

For example, suppose you have an interface named MyConstants that extends the Localizable interface; then you would instantiate an object of this interface using the create() method in the GWT class, as shown here:

```
MyConstants myConstants = (MyConstants) GWT.create (MyConstants.class);
```

The localized instance assigned to the myConstants variable will be assigned an instance of an automatically generated subclass that is created using values from a properties file that is selected based on the set of rules mentioned in Table 8-4.

LL: Denotes the ISO language code.

CC: Denotes the ISO country code. (It is not necessary to have the country code specified, but if it is, then the language code must also be specified.)

Table 8-4. *Locale Value and the Corresponding Type and Properties File Being Used*

Locale Property Value	Type Used
Unspecified	The default type (MyConstants.properties)
LL	The type called type_LL (MyConstants_eu.properties if the language specified is English, or language code eu) or the default type if type_LL does not exist
LL_CC	The type called type_LL_CC if it exists; if not, then the type called type_LL; if not, then the default type (MyConstants_LL_CC.properties if it exists, otherwise MyConstants_LL.properties if it exists, and otherwise MyConstants.properties)

Setting and Using the Locale Value in Your Application

You can specify the locale of a module in two different ways; both require you to use the client property named locale.

First, you can use the <meta> tag in the host HTML page. Specifically, you can define the locale client property using the <meta> tag of your host HTML by using the following code (using gwt:property as the name so that it is recognized by GWT):

```
<meta name="gwt:property" content="locale=x_Y">
```

For example, the locale is set to en_US in the host HTML file shown here:

```
<html>
    <head>
        <meta name="gwt:module" content="com.apress.gwt.chapter8.UniversalApp ">
        <meta name="gwt:property" content="locale=en_US">
    </head>
    <body>
        <script src="gwt.js"></script>
    </body>
</html>
```

Note Using the <meta> tag requires that you define a different host HTML file for each locale.

Second, you can use part of the query string for rendering a page. Specifically, you can define the locale client property as part of the query string by entering a value for the property named locale. For example, the following hypothetical query string has the locale property set to en_US:

```
http://www.apress.com/accelerated-gwt.html?locale=en_US
```

Note In case the locale property is defined in both the <meta> tag and the query string, then the locale value specified in the query string will take precedence over the one specified in the <meta> tag.

GWT also requires that you mention each locale that you want your application to support in the module's XML file by extending the locale value. Suppose your application needs to support the French language; then you should extend the locale property in the module's XML file, as shown in bold in the following code snippet:

```
<module>
    <!-- Inherit the core Web Toolkit stuff.  -->
    <inherits name='com.google.gwt.user.User'/>
```

```
    <!-- Other modules and entry-point class declaration goes here -->

    <extend-property name="locale" values="fr"/>
</module>
```

Tool for Internationalizing Your GWT Applications

As mentioned in Chapter 1, the GWT framework provides the i18nCreator tool to get your internationalized application up and running quickly. This tool is explained next.

Understanding the I18nCreator Tool

This script generates internationalization scripts for doing static internationalization and also creates sample properties files for using with the application and scripts. The i18nCreator tool can also generate interfaces that extend either Constants or Messages as defined in Table 8-1 previously. This tool offers a command-line interface with several options:

```
i18nCreator [-eclipse projectName] [-out dir] [-overwrite] [-ignore]
    [-createMessages] interfaceName
```

The following list explains the options:

- -eclipse creates a debug launch config file for the named Eclipse project.

- -out is the directory where the output files will be written (default is the current directory).

- -overwrite overwrites any existing files.

- -ignore ignores any existing files (does not overwrite).

- -createMessages generates scripts for a Message interface rather than for the Constant interface.

- interfaceName is the fully qualified name of the interface that you want to create.

Before we get into the details of the other interfaces defined in the internationalization hierarchy, let's work through a simple example using the i18nCreator tool to see internationalization in action.

Creating Your First Internationalized Application

Let's go over a sample application to understand internationalization using GWT in detail. The application will show a button with some text on it. When the user clicks the button, the application will greet the user with a message: "Hello." I'll show how to develop the sample application in English and French, but you are free to create your own applications in as many languages as needed. The first step in developing the application is to create the project structure.

Creating the Project Structure

You should start by creating a project named `UniversalApp` inside a directory named `Chapter8` using the `projectCreator` and `applicationCreator` utilities explained in Chapter 1. The following code snippet shows the result of executing the `projectCreator` tool:

```
C:\gwt> projectCreator.cmd -eclipse chapter8 -out chapter8
Created directory chapter8\src
Created directory chapter8\test
Created file chapter8\.project
Created file chapter8\.classpath
```

Next you should create the sample application by using the `applicationCreator` tool, as shown here:

```
C:\gwt> applicationCreator -eclipse chapter8 -out chapter8 ➡
                com.apress.gwt.chapter8.client.UniversalApp

Created directory chapter8\src\com\apress\gwt\chapter8
Created directory chapter8\src\com\apress\gwt\chapter8\client
Created directory chapter8\src\com\apress\gwt\chapter8\public
Created file chapter8\src\com\apress\gwt\chapter8\UniversalApp.gwt.xml
Created file chapter8\src\com\apress\gwt\chapter8\public\UniversalApp.html
Created file chapter8\src\com\apress\gwt\chapter8\client\UniversalApp.java
Created file chapter8\UniversalApp.launch
Created file chapter8\UniversalApp-shell.cmd
Created file chapter8\UniversalApp-compile.cmd
```

Now you should use the `i18nCreator` tool. This tool will create the scripts and sample properties file for use in the application. The following code snippet shows the result of executing the `i18nCreator` tool:

```
C:\gwt> i18nCreator -eclipse chapter8 -out chapter8
                com.apress.gwt.chapter8.client.UniversalAppConstants
Created file chapter8\src\com\apress\gwt\chapter8\client\➡
    UniversalAppConstants.properties
Created file chapter8\UniversalAppConstants-i18n.launch
Created file chapter8\UniversalAppConstants-i18n.cmd
```

You should now open the project in Eclipse by importing it. The project structure should look like Figure 8-2.

The `i18nCreator` tool created a properties file named `UniversalAppConstants.properties` for the sample application. The properties files are of fundamental importance to internationalized applications because they store the text strings for the application in different languages.

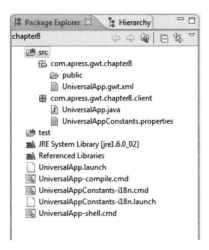

Figure 8-2. *Initial structure of the UniversalApp application in Eclipse*

Working with the Properties Files

The contents of the generated UniversalAppConstants.properties file are as follows:

```
#sample constant property to be translated in language specific versions of this➧
 property file
ClassName: UniversalAppConstants
```

Next, modify the UniversalAppConstants.properties file as follows:

```
#sample constant property to be translated in language specific versions of this➧
 property file
GreetingButtonText: Show Greeting
GreetingMessage: Hello
```

The UniversalAppConstants.properties file listed previously contains two constant mappings, with the keys being GreetingButtonText and GreetingMessage and the corresponding values being Show Greeting and Hello.

You should also create a corresponding French version of the UniversalAppConstants.properties file named UniversalAppConstants_fr.properties (following the naming convention mentioned in Table 8-4 previously). This file should be created in the com/google/gwt/chapter8/client package. The contents of this French version should be as follows:

```
#sample constant property to be translated in language specific versions of this➧
 property file
GreetingButtonText: Voir Salutation
GreetingMessage: Bonjour
```

Generating the Interface Corresponding to Property Files

You can use the shell file named `UniversalAppConstants-i18n.cmd` to create the mapping interface corresponding to the properties file. The contents of this shell file are as follows:

```
@java -cp "%~dp0\src;%~dp0\bin;C:/gwt/gwt-user.jar;C:/gwt/gwt-dev-windows.jar"
    com.google.gwt.i18n.tools.I18NSync -out "%~dp0\src"
    com.apress.gwt.chapter8.client.UniversalAppConstants
```

Running the `UniversalAppConstants-i18n.cmd` script file creates an interface that is named according to the properties file. In the sample example here, it is named `UniversalAppConstants` and is created in the `client` directory of the application. Go ahead and execute the shell file from Eclipse by double-clicking it or running it from the command line as follows:

```
C:\gwt\chapter8>UniversalAppConstants-i18n.cmd
```

The command returns with no output, but behind the scene it creates the interface that contains mappings from the properties file.

■**Note** You may have to refresh your Eclipse window for the newly created file to be visible in your project. (You can do this by pressing F5 from the Package Explorer window in Eclipse.)

Listing 8-1 shows the contents of this newly created `UniversalAppConstants.java` file.

Listing 8-1. *Contents of the Generated* `UniversalAppConstants` *Interface*

```
package com.apress.gwt.chapter8.client;

/**
 * Interface to represent the constants contained in resource  bundle:
 *     'C:/gwt/chapter8/src/com/apress/gwt/chapter8/client/➥
       UniversalAppConstants.properties'.
 */
public interface UniversalAppConstants
    extends com.google.gwt.i18n.client.Constants {

  /**
   * Translated "Show Greeting".
   *
   * @return translated "Show Greeting"
   * @gwt.key GreetingButtonText
   */
  String GreetingButtonText();
```

```
  /**
   * Translated "Hello".
   *
   * @return translated "Hello"
   * @gwt.key GreetingMessage
   */
  String GreetingMessage();
}
```

The generated interface contains convenient methods, which are named after each
property defined in the properties file and are mapped at compile time using the gwt.key
annotation. After creating an object, you can use these methods to retrieve the values corresponding to the key that a method represents. (If you can recall the PropertyFileReader
example from Chapter 2, you will realize the similarities between that example and what's
happening here. The biggest difference is that the generated code is using values from multiple properties files based on the specified locale.)

Adding Locale Values to a Module's XML File

As mentioned previously, GWT requires that you mention each locale that you want your
application to support in the module's XML file by extending the locale value. Since the
UniversalApp application needs to support the French language, modify the module's XML
file (UniversalApp.gwt.xml), and extend the locale property as shown in bold in the following code snippet:

```
<module>
    <!-- Inherit the core Web Toolkit stuff.                -->
    <inherits name='com.google.gwt.user.User'/>

    <!-- Specify the app entry-point class.                 -->
    <entry-point class='com.apress.gwt.chapter8.client.UniversalApp'/>

    <extend-property name="locale" values="fr"/>
</module>
```

GWT uses deferred binding (as explained in Chapter 2) for internationalization. The
generator class for internationalization is named LocalizableGenerator and is defined in the
com.google.gwt.i18n.rebind package. This generator takes an interface of type Localizable,
and it generates different versions of classes to map keys in the properties files to methods in
your interface. A different class is produced for every value of the locale property set in the
module's XML file. Based on the current locale, an instance of the appropriate class is created
by the binding mechanism.

Setting Up the Host HTML File

Next you should change the default host HTML file (UniversalApp.html in the com.apress.
gwt.chapter8.public folder) to look similar to code shown in Listing 8-2.

Listing 8-2. *Contents of the Modified Host HTML File Named* UniversalApp.html

```html
<html>
  <head>
    <title>Wrapper HTML for UniversalApp</title>
    <style>
      body,td,a,div,.p{font-family:arial,sans-serif}
      div,td{color:#000000}
    </style>
    <script language='javascript'
        src='com.apress.gwt.chapter8.UniversalApp.nocache.js'></script>
  </head>

  <body>
    <h2>UniversalApp</h2>
    <table align=center>
      <tr>
        <td id="slot1"></td>
        <td id="slot2"></td>
      </tr>
    </table>
  </body>
</html>
```

Setting the Module's Entry-Point Class

The only thing left now is for the application to use this interface and the values from the properties file in the code. You should modify the entry-point class named UniversalApp in the com.apress.gwt.chapter8.client package to look like the code in Listing 8-3.

Listing 8-3. UniversalApp *Class with the* onModuleLoad() *Method Using the* UniversalAppConstants *Interface to Access the Corresponding Properties File*

```java
package com.apress.gwt.chapter8.client;

import com.google.gwt.core.client.EntryPoint;
import com.google.gwt.core.client.GWT;
import com.google.gwt.user.client.ui.Button;
import com.google.gwt.user.client.ui.ClickListener;
import com.google.gwt.user.client.ui.Label;
import com.google.gwt.user.client.ui.RootPanel;
import com.google.gwt.user.client.ui.Widget;

/**
 * Entry-point class for the UniversalApp application
 *
 * @author Vipul Gupta (vipulgupta.vg@gmail.com)
 *
 */
```

```java
public class UniversalApp implements EntryPoint {

  /**
   * This is the entry-point method.
   */
  public void onModuleLoad() {
    final UniversalAppConstants appConstants = (UniversalAppConstants) GWT
        .create(UniversalAppConstants.class);
    final Button button = new Button(appConstants.GreetingButtonText());
    final Label label = new Label();

    button.addClickListener(new ClickListener() {
      boolean toggleLabel = true;

      public void onClick(Widget sender) {
        if (toggleLabel) {
          label.setText(appConstants.GreetingMessage());
          toggleLabel = false;
        } else {
          label.setText("");
          toggleLabel = true;
        }
      }
    });
    RootPanel.get("slot1").add(button);
    RootPanel.get("slot2").add(label);
  }
}
```

The code in Listing 8-3 creates an object for the UniversalAppConstants interface using the deferred binding mechanism (by using the GWT.create(...) method to create object). The UniversalAppConstants interface exposes different methods for each property defined in the properties file, and these methods are used to get the localized values of the properties.

Running the Application

You can execute the application at this point by using the UniversalApp-shell.cmd script, either by double-clicking this file in Eclipse or by running it from the command line, as shown here:

```
C:\gwt\chapter8>UniversalApp-shell.cmd
```

Figure 8-3 and Figure 8-4 show the result of executing UniversalApp-shell.cmd. By default, the application maps to property values in the UniversalAppConstants.properties file (following the rules in Table 8-4) and gets English values based on the properties.

Figure 8-3. *The UniversalApp application when it is started*

When the Show Greeting button is clicked, the application displays the greeting, as shown in Figure 8-4.

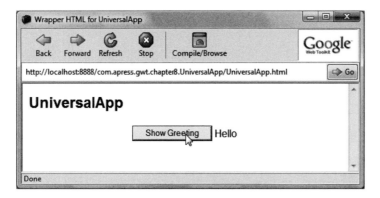

Figure 8-4. *The UniversalApp application when the Show Greeting button is clicked*

Now let's see how the French version of the application can be executed. If you recall, it was mentioned earlier in the chapter that one way of using the locale value in your application is as part of the query string. The French version of the properties file was named according to the rules specified in Table 8-4, and hence you can use the locale value in the query string to get the French version of your application going. You should now modify the query string in Figure 8-4 by appending it with the locale value set to fr (the ISO code for French), as shown here in bold:

```
http://localhost:8888/com.apress.gwt.chapter8.UniversalApp/➥
    UniversalApp.html?locale=fr
```

Now click the Go/Refresh button to get the application going. Figure 8-5 shows the result of executing the application in French mode.

Figure 8-5. *French version of the UniversalApp application when it is started*

When the Voir Salutation ("Show Greeting" in French) button is clicked, the application displays the greeting, as shown in Figure 8-6.

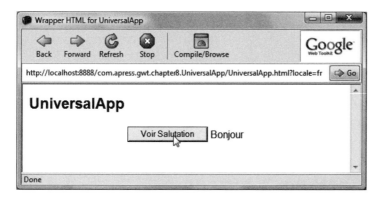

Figure 8-6. *French version of the UniversalApp application when the Voir Salutation button is clicked*

You can see the flexibility provided by the properties files by modifying the UniversalAppConstants.properties file and changing the value of the GreetingMessage property from Hello to Hello Reader, as shown here in bold:

```
#sample constant property to be translated in language specific versions of this➡
 property file
GreetingButtonTexl: Show Greeting
GreetingMessage: Hello Reader
```

■**Note** The values in the properties file accept values with spaces and tabs but not multiline values.

Now run the application again by executing the UniversalApp-shell.cmd script, either by double-clicking the file in Eclipse or by running it from the command line. When the application is loaded, click the Show Greeting button. You will notice the application getting loaded with the new message, as shown in Figure 8-7.

Figure 8-7. *UniversalApp after the value in the properties file is changed*

Using the i18NCreator command as i18nCreator -eclipse chapter8 com.apress.gwt. chapter8.client.UniversalAppConstants creates UniversalAppConstants-i18n.cmd, which when executed generates an interface from the properties file. The generated interface extends the Constants interface in the i18n package in the GWT framework. As the name of the interface suggests, constants are fixed values, and their values cannot be changed at run-time. Let's look at the Constants interface in detail.

Exploring the Constants Interface

Like Localizable, the Constants interface is also a marker/tag interface, and it allows the compile-time binding of the values mentioned in the properties files. The Constants interface extends the Localizable interface, and thus the objects of this type have the ability to understand the locale-specific substitution of values explained earlier. You've already learned how to use the i18nCreator tool with the Constants interface. Now I'll explain the details of working with the Constants interface manually.

Example of Using the Constants Interface

You should start by creating an interface that extends the Constants interface. You should also create properties files corresponding to the name of the interface and create them in the same package.

For example, say you have created an interface named MyConstants in the com.apress. gwt.chapter8.client package. Then your properties files should also be named after the interface such as com/apress/gwt/chapter8/client/MyConstants.properties, and so on, with locale added to the name, as explained in Table 8-4 previously.

The code in Listing 8-4 gives an example of creating the MyConstants interface with methods to access different properties in the properties files.

Listing 8-4. *Using the* Constants *Interface to Access Properties Mentioned in Properties Files*

```
package com.apress.gwt.chapter8.client;

import com.google.gwt.i18n.client.Constants;

/**
 * Interface to represent Constants in an application
 *
 * @author Vipul Gupta (vipulgupta.vg@gmail.com)
 *
 */
public interface MyConstants extends Constants {
  /**
   * @return the localized name of the book
   */
  String chapterDescription();

  /**
   * @return the localized name of the chapter
   */
  String chapterName();
}
```

The compiler looks for the properties files that contain properties with the same names as the method names in the interface during compilation. The compiler also checks the values of the properties for return type compatibility during the compilation step. Sample properties files for the MyConstants interface are defined in the com/apress/gwt/chapter8/client folder as follows:

- English version (MyConstants.properties):

    ```
    chapterDescription = This chapter explains Internationalization
    chapterName = Internationalization
    ```

- French version (MyConstants_fr.properties):

    ```
    chapterDescription = Ce chapitre explique Internationalisation
    chapterName = Internationalisation
    ```

It is not necessary for your method to have the same names as the property names in the properties files. GWT does provide a document-based property (gwt.key), which can be used to map a property with any name to a method with a different name. An example to demonstrate this is as follows:

```
package com.apress.gwt.chapter8.client;

import com.google.gwt.i18n.client.Constants;

/**
 * Interface to represent Constants in an application
 *
 * @author Vipul Gupta (vipulgupta.vg@gmail.com)
 *
 */
public interface MyConstants extends Constants {
  /**
   * @gwt.key chapterDescription
   * @return the localized name of the book
   */
  String description();

  /**
   * @return the localized name of the chapter
   */
  String chapterName();
}
```

Before you use the MyConstants interface, it is important that you understand the format of method declaration in the Constants interface.

Format of Methods in the Interface Extending the Constants Interface

The methods in your interface (which extends the Constants interface) must follow this format:

```
returnType nameOfMethod()
```

The return types of the methods follow the rules declared in Table 8-5.

Table 8-5. *Valid Options for Return Types of Methods of Type* Constants

Return Type of Method (Interpreted and Checked by Compiler During Compilation Step)	Description
String	Simple string value
String[]	Comma-separated array of strings (\\, used to escape commas)
int	int value
float	float value
double	double value

Return Type of Method (Interpreted and Checked by Compiler During Compilation Step)	Description
Boolean	boolean value ("true" or "false")
Map	A map created by reading the comma-separated list of property names that act as keys into the map; the values of these property names act as corresponding values of the corresponding keys in the map

Creating an Entry-Point Class to Access the Interface

Next you should use the MyConstants interface to access the values in your properties file by modifying the onModuleLoad() method in the entry-point class (in the UniversalApp application), as shown in Listing 8-5.

Listing 8-5. *Modified Entry-Point Class of UniversalApp, Demonstrating the Custom* Constants *Interface to Access Properties from the Properties Files*

```
package com.apress.gwt.chapter8.client;

import com.google.gwt.core.client.EntryPoint;
import com.google.gwt.core.client.GWT;
import com.google.gwt.user.client.ui.Button;
import com.google.gwt.user.client.ui.ClickListener;
import com.google.gwt.user.client.ui.Label;
import com.google.gwt.user.client.ui.RootPanel;
import com.google.gwt.user.client.ui.Widget;

/**
 * Entry-point class for the UniversalApp application
 *
 * @author Vipul Gupta (vipulgupta.vg@gmail.com)
 *
 */
public class UniversalApp implements EntryPoint {

  /**
   * This is the entry-point method.
   */
  public void onModuleLoad() {
    MyConstants myConstants = (MyConstants)GWT.create (MyConstants.class);
    String chapterDescription = myConstants.description();
    String chapterName = myConstants. chapterName();
    RootPanel.get("slot1").add(new Button(chapterDescription));
    RootPanel.get("slot2").add(new Label(chapterName));
  }
}
```

Now it's time to run the application by executing the `UniversalApp-shell.cmd` script, either by double-clicking the file in Eclipse or by running the script from the command line. When the application is loaded, the messages corresponding to the chapter description and name will be displayed on the screen. You can execute the French version of the application by appending the `locale` parameter to the URL, as explained previously in the chapter.

Exploring the Messages Interface

Messages displayed using the `Constants` interface have fixed values, but sometimes you'll want to display customized messages and still have the flexibility to localize these messages based on `locale`. GWT provides a mechanism to localize and display customized messages by using the `Messages` interface (which is a marker/tag interface that extends the `Localizable` interface and hence the other properties of it). The messages are defined using a specified template and follow the rules of the template. Before you create an interface (which extends the `Messages` interface), it is important to understand the format of the method prototype to be followed in such an interface.

Format of Methods in the Interface Extending the Messages Interface

The methods in the interface that extend the `Messages` interface must follow these rules:

```
// The parameters are optional and can be of any type.
//  The parameters are converted into strings by the JRE at runtime.
String methodName(parameters)
```

Now let's work through a simple example of using the `Messages` interface. Let's start by creating a custom interface for the application.

Creating a Custom Interface

Similar to how you used the `Constants` interface explained earlier, you can use the `Messages` interface by defining an interface that extends the `Messages` interface. Each method in the interface must match the name of the property defined in the properties file or have a corresponding `gwt.key` annotation, as explained earlier with the `Constants` interface. Listing 8-6 shows how to use the `Messages` interface.

Listing 8-6. *Using the* Messages *Interface to Create an Interface to Access Customized Properties*

```
package com.apress.gwt.chapter8.client;

import com.google.gwt.i18n.client.Messages;

/**
 * Interface to represent Greeting Messages in an application
 *
```

```
 * @author Vipul Gupta (vipulgupta.vg@gmail.com)
 *
 */
public interface GreetingMessages extends Messages {
  /**
   * @param username name of the individual
   * @return a birthday message greeting the individual
   */
  String birthdayMessage(String name);

  /**
   * @param name1 name of one member of the couple
   * @param name2 name of second member of the couple
   * @return anniversary message greeting the couple
   */
  String anniversaryMessage(String name1, String name2);
}
```

Next you should set up the properties files corresponding to this interface.

Working with the Properties Files

In the GreetingMessage example, the compiler will look for properties with the names birthdayMessage and anniversaryMessage. The values of these properties should be format-ted as messages taking one and two arguments, respectively. A sample properties file (GreetingMessages.properties in the com/apress/gwt/chapter8/client folder) for the interface is as follows:

```
#sample constant property to be translated in language specific versions of this➥
 property file
birthdayMessage = Happy Birthday {0}
anniversaryMessage = Happy Anniversary {0} & {1}
```

■Note The compiler checks at compile time to ensure that the messages in the properties files have the required number of parameters as in the methods in the interface. {0} is mapped to the first parameter passed to the method, {1} to the first, and so on. This is important to remember because the location of parameters might change in messages in different languages, but their mapping to parameters passed to the method remains the same.

For example, the message ({1},{2}) in one language could be localized as ({2},{1}) in another. However, in both cases, {1} maps to the first, and {2} maps to the second parameter passed to the method corresponding to the property.

Creating an Entry-Point Class to Access the Interface

You can use the MyConstants interface to access the values in the properties file by modifying the onModuleLoad() method in the entry-point class (in the UniversalApp application), as listed in Listing 8-7.

Listing 8-7. *Using the* Messages *Interface to Access Properties Mentioned in Properties Files*

```
package com.apress.gwt.chapter8.client;

import com.google.gwt.core.client.EntryPoint;
import com.google.gwt.core.client.GWT;
import com.google.gwt.user.client.ui.Label;
import com.google.gwt.user.client.ui.RootPanel;

/**
 * Entry-point classes define <code>onModuleLoad()</code>.
 *
 * @author Vipul Gupta (vipulgupta.vg@gmail.com)
 *
 */
public class UniversalApp implements EntryPoint {

  /**
   * This is the entry-point method.
   */
  public void onModuleLoad() {
    GreetingMessages messages = (GreetingMessages) GWT
        .create(GreetingMessages.class);

    Label birthdayLabel = new Label(messages.birthdayMessage("Apress"));
    // Greet birthday to a user
    RootPanel.get("slot1").add(birthdayLabel);

    Label anniversaryLabel = new Label(messages.anniversaryMessage("Vipul", "Ria"));
    // Greet anniversary to a couple
    RootPanel.get("slot1").add(anniversaryLabel);

  }
}
```

With the entry-point class all set up, it's time to run the application.

Running the Application

You can run the application by executing the `UniversalApp-shell.cmd` script. You can do this either by double-clicking the file in Eclipse or by running it from the command line. When the application is loaded, the birthday and anniversary messages, customized based on the values passed in the code, are displayed on the screen, as shown in Figure 8-8. You can try a localized version of this application by following the French version examples for the `Constants` interface discussed previously in the chapter.

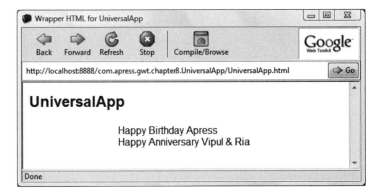

Figure 8-8. *UniversalApp displaying customized messages using the* Messages *interface*

You learned about using the `Messages` interface and using it to customize the messages at runtime in this section, and you developed a simple application by writing an interface that extended from the `Messages` interface. You can use the `i18nCreator` tool to automate this task. When run with the `-createMessages` flag, the `i18nCreator` tool generates the script to create an interface that extends `Messages` and that can be used for customizing the text loaded from the properties file.

Creating the Messages Interface Using i18nCreator

You saw the `i18nCreator` tool in action earlier in the chapter to create scripts and a sample properties file for the `Constants` interface. You can do the same for the `Messages` interface by using the `-createMessages` flag with the `i18nCreator` tool. The following code snippet shows the result of executing the `i18nCreator` tool:

```
C:\gwt\chapter8>i18nCreator -eclipse chapter8 -createMessages ➡
    com.apress.gwt.chapter8.client.UniversalAppMessages
Created file C:\gwt\chapter8\src\com\apress\gwt\chapter8\client\UniversalAppMess
ages.properties
Created file C:\gwt\chapter8\UniversalAppMessages-i18n.launch
Created file C:\gwt\chapter8\UniversalAppMessages-i18n.cmd
```

Figure 8-9 shows the application structure after running the `i18nCreator` tool with the `-createMessages` flag.

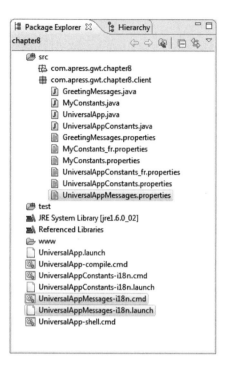

Figure 8-9. *Application structure after running the* `i18nCreator` *tool with the* `-createMessages` *flag*

Just like the `Constants` example earlier in the chapter, you can add properties with corresponding values in the properties file and then use the `UniversalAppMessages-i18n.cmd` script to create the corresponding interface for use.

GWT also provides a different version of the `Constants` interface called `ConstantsWithLookup` with some additional features; it is explained next.

Exploring the ConstantsWithLookup Interface

The `ConstantsWithLookup` interface extends from the `Constants` interface and works the same way as the `Constants` interface. It provides additional lookup methods to retrieve the constant values at runtime with the key string.

The differentiating factor between `Constants` and `ConstantsWithLookup` is that the latter does not do any static code reduction (static code reduction removes any unused constants accessor methods and forces all defined constants to be included in the compiled JavaScript file). If this added lookup-by-name functionality is not explicitly needed by your application, then you should extend your property interfaces from the `Constants` interface rather than `ConstantsWithLookup`. This will allow the compiler to remove unused accessor methods from the compiled JavaScript code. Table 8-6 lists the methods in the `ConstantsWithLookup` interface.

Table 8-6. *Methods in* ConstantsWithLookup

Method Name	Description
getBoolean(String)	Allows looking up a boolean value by method name
getDouble(String)	Allows looking up a double value by method name
getFloat(String)	Allows looking up a float value by method name
getInt(String)	Allows looking up an int value by method name
getMap(String)	Allows looking up a Map by method name
getString(String)	Allows looking up a String value by method name
getStringArray(String)	Allows looking up a String[] value by method name

A method called on an object of type ConstantsWithLookup will throw an exception in the following cases:

- The called method does not exist in your interface type.

- The cast of the returned value using any of the lookup methods shown in Table 8-6 is invalid (such as a String to an int).

If you have an interface defined in your application as shown in Listing 8-8, then you can create an instance of UniversalLookupConstants as follows:

```
final UniversalLookupConstants appConstants = (UniversalLookupConstants)
    GWT.create(UniversalLookupConstants.class);
```

Listing 8-8. *Using the* ConstantsWithLookup *Interface to Map Properties in Properties Files*

```
package com.apress.gwt.chapter8.client;

import com.google.gwt.i18n.client.ConstantsWithLookup;

/**
 *
 * @author Vipul Gupta (vipulgupta.vg@gmail.com)
 *
 */
public interface UniversalLookupConstants extends ConstantsWithLookup {

  String name();

  double salary();

  String address();
}
```

After creating the instance as mentioned previously, you can retrieve the constant values from your properties files using one of the two ways (by using the method defined in the interface or by using the lookup method) shown in Table 8-7.

Table 8-7. *Different Ways to Retrieve Property Values from an Object of Type* ConstantsWithLookup

Interface Method	Lookup Method
appConstants.name();	appConstants.getString("name");
appConstants.salary();	appConstants.getDouble("salary");
appConstants.address();	appConstants.getString("address");

Making a method call such as appConstants.getDouble("address") would throw a runtime exception because the address() method in the interface returns a String and not a double. Keep this in mind while using the ConstantsWithLookup interface and add code to catch exceptions appropriately.

The GWT framework also provides a way to pass parameters to the application by embedding them into the host HTML page. This is discussed in detail in the following section.

Embedding Data into Your Host HTML Pages

You can use the host HTML page to pass parameters to the application by using <meta> tags and passing variable names and their values as content to the tag. This functionality makes it easy to integrate GWT into your existing applications without requiring major rework or changes. A sample host HTML page with the locale parameter value embedded into the page (in bold) by using the <meta> tag is as follows:

```
<html>
    <head>
        <title>Wrapper HTML for UniversalApp</title>
        <style>
            body,td,a,div,.p{font-family:arial,sans-serif}
            div,td{color:#000000}
            a:link,.w,.w a:link{color:#0000cc}
            a:visited{color:#551a8b}
            a:active{color:#ff0000}
        </style>

        <!-- Properties can be specified using the meta tag here -- >
        <meta name='gwt.property' content='locale=en_fr'>

        <script language='javascript'
                    src='com.apress.gwt.chapter8.UniversalApp.nocache.js'></script>
    </head>
    <body>
        <h1>UniversalApp</h1>
```

```
    <table align=center>
        <tr>
            <td id="slot1"></td><td id="slot2"></td>
        </tr>
    </table>
    </body>
</html>
```

Examining and Using the Dictionary Class

With the Dictionary class, you can look up key-value string pairs defined in the module's host HTML page rather than values compiled in your application's code. The string-value pairs must be defined as a JavaScript object in the context of the host HTML page. For example, say the following JavaScript object is defined in the host HTML page of your application:

```
var  BookDetails = {
    name: "Accelerated GWT",
    year: "2008",
    publisher: "apress"
};
```

The Dictionary class provides a set of methods to retrieve the keys and values from the JavaScript object, as listed in Table 8-8.

Table 8-8. *Methods in the* Dictionary *Class*

Method Name	Description
get(String keyName)	Returns the value associated with the given key
getDictionary(String keyName)	Returns the dictionary associated with the given name
keySet()	Returns the set of keys associated with the dictionary
values()	Returns the set of values associated with the dictionary

You can now use the Dictionary class to access values from the embedded JavaScript object at runtime and display them to the user of the application. It is important to understand that the Dictionary object basically looks up these mappings for use without reference to the locale. The following code shows how a Label can be populated with values from the JavaScript object:

```
Label bookLabel = new Label();
public void displayBookDetails (Label bookLabel) {
  Dictionary bookDetails = Dictionary.getDictionary("BookDetails");
  String bookName = bookDetails.get("name");
  String publishYear = bookDetails.get("year");
  String publisherName = bookDetails.get("publisher");
  bookLabel.setText(bookName +  " was published in " + publishYear
      + " by " + publisherName);
}
```

■Note The code for the `displayBookDetails()` method discussed previously assumes the presence of an object named `BookDetails` with corresponding keys named `name`, `year`, and `publisher` in the object. These values are resolved only at runtime, and thus there is a high probability of error in case of key name mismatch or nonavailability of certain keys. Therefore, it is important that you follow the proper process for this in your development project.

Localizing Dates, Times, Numbers, and Currencies

GWT also provides a set of classes that are useful for localizing the dates, times, numbers, and currencies used in your application. Table 8-9 lists these classes.

Table 8-9. *Classes Used for Localizing Dates, Times, Numbers, and Currency in GWT*

Class Name	Description
DateTimeFormat	Used for parsing and formatting dates and time using the locale
NumberFormat	Used for parsing and formatting numbers using the locale

Examining the NumberFormat Class

The `NumberFormat` class formats and parses numbers using patterns specific to the current locale. It provides support for a large number of patterns such as currency symbols, decimal formats, percentages, scientific notation, and so on. Table 8-10 lists some of the important methods available in this class.

Table 8-10. *Important Methods in the* NumberFormat *Class*

Method Name	Description
getCurrencyFormat()*	Provides the standard currency format for the default locale
getDecimalFormat()*	Provides the standard decimal format for the default locale
getPercentFormat()*	Provides the standard percent format for the default locale
getScientificFormat()*	Provides the standard scientific format for the default locale
getFormat(String pattern)*	Gets a NumberFormat instance for the default locale using the specified pattern and the default currencyCode
String format (double number)	Formats a double to produce a string
String getPattern()	Returns the pattern used by this number format

* *Static and returns a* NumberFormat

The following code sample demonstrates how to use NumberFormat to format a number in the corresponding currency format:

```
NumberFormat formatter = NumberFormat.getCurrencyFormat();
formatter.format(82374234.234);
```

The output of the previous code in the English and French locales is as follows:

en: $82,374,234.23

fr: 82 374 234,23 €

If instead you used the getPercentFormat() to get the percentage formatter, as follows:

```
NumberFormat formatter = NumberFormat.getPercentFormat();
formatter.format(82374234.234);
```

then the output in English and French locales would be as follows:

en: 8,237,423,423%

fr: 8 237 423 423 %

With an understanding of the NumberFormat class, the only thing left for you to examine is the DateTimeFormat class, which, as the name suggests, is used to format dates and times as per the locale.

Examining the DateTimeFormat Class

The DateTimeFormat class formats and parses dates and times using patterns specific to the current locale. Just like NumberFormat discussed earlier, the DateTimeFormat class provides methods to format input in different ways such as the full date, full date time, long date, medium time, and so on. The following code sample demonstrates how to use DateTimeFormat to format a given string representing the date and time:

```
DateTimeFormat formatter = DateTimeFormat.getMediumTimeFormat();
Formatter.format(formatter.parse("3 may  2007 9:01 pm"));
```

The output of the previous code in the English and French locales is as follows:

en: 9:01:00 PM

fr: 21:01:00

If instead you used getFullDateTimeFormat() to get the text percentage formatter, as follows:

```
DateTimeFormat formatter = DateTimeFormat.getFullDateTimeFormat();
Formatter.format(formatter.parse("3 may  2007 9:01 pm"));
```

then the output in the English and French locales would be as follows:

en: Thursday, May 3, 2007 9:01:00 PM GMT+05:30

fr: jeudi 3 mai 2007 21 h 01 GMT+05:30

Summary

This concludes our discussion of internationalization using the GWT framework. The chapter started with an introduction to internationalization followed by details about some of the important character sets. The chapter also explained in detail some of the internationalization support offered by the GWT framework, specifically the i18n module and the various interfaces and classes.

You also learned about static and dynamic string internationalization before moving into details about the Localizable interface and a discussion of the locale-specific substitution of values in your application. This was followed by a discussion of the different ways to set and use the locale values in an application. The chapter demonstrated a complete internationalized application that was created using the i18nCreator tool.

The chapter ended with details about embedding data into your host HTML pages and the support offered by GWT in localizing dates, times, numbers, and currencies in your applications. With all this information, you should now be able to make your own internationalized applications using GWT with ease.

■ ■ ■

CHAPTER 9

Some Important, Not-to-Be-Missed Techniques

The History Mechanism, Deployment, Server-Side Sessions, Bundling ImageBundles, and Creating Reusable Modules

This chapter will discuss various techniques that are necessary to complete your understanding of the GWT framework. I'll start with a discussion of the GWT history mechanism, including the `History` class, and explain how you can add history support to a GWT application.

Then I'll discuss the steps needed to deploy a GWT-based application on an application server. You have been concentrating throughout the book on using and understanding the various components offered by GWT and testing them in the hosted browser, but eventually an application needs to be deployed on an application server.

Next you will learn about server-side sessions and how you can use and leverage them in your GWT-based applications to maintain data for users across multiple requests.

`ImageBundles` are used to bundle a set of images in your application into a single image. But what if your application has multiple `ImageBundles` and all of these bundles are required in the application? You can use an `ImageBundle` to bundle all these bundles as well. You will learn how to do that in this chapter.

I'll also introduce you to the `<super-source>` tag and explain how this tag can help you extend or modify the JRE emulation library used by the GWT framework.

Finally, the chapter will discuss how to package your modules so that you can reuse them across multiple applications.

Understanding the History Mechanism

One common problem with Ajax-based web applications is the inability of applications to respond correctly when users click the browser's Back and Forward buttons. The developers of the GWT framework attacked this problem from the beginning and included support for handling these events by providing hooks into the browser's history mechanism and working with the history stack. The framework supports managing history both programmatically and via user actions related to clicking hyperlinks.

To understand the problem being discussed, you should start the BookStore application you developed in Chapter 6 and click the Computer category. You will see a list of books in the Computer category, as shown in Figure 9-1.

Figure 9-1. *BookStore application created in Chapter 6 showing the list of books*

Next, click the Back button in the hosted mode's browser window. You will notice that nothing happens in response to that event. To make the user's experience better, the application should return to the previous page, that is, to the start page of the BookStore application, which displays the list of book categories in the store. (You can close the application now. Going forward, I'll discuss the steps that are needed to add history support to this application.)

The most important class for adding history support to your application is History, which is located in the com.google.gwt.user.client package. This class allows the framework to interact with the browser's history stack. GWT maintains the history of the browser as tokens (which are strings defined by the developer of the application), and these tokens have the state of the application mapped to them by the developer. Based on the token, you put the application in the corresponding state.

History Class

The History class forms the backbone of the history mechanism and is explained in this section. All the methods in the History class are static and are listed in Table 9-1.

Table 9-1. *Methods in the* History *Class*

Method Name	Description
addHistoryListener(...)	Adds a listener to be informed of changes to the browser's history
removeHistoryListener(...)	Removes a history listener
forward()	Programmatic equivalent of the user clicking the browser's Forward button
back()	Programmatic equivalent of the user clicking the browser's Back button
onHistoryChanged()	Executed when the history stack changes
getToken()	Gets the current history token
newItem(String)	Adds a new browser history entry

When the application starts up, the history stack starts as empty, and based on the user's event of clicking the Back/Forward button or the developer programmatically invoking the newItem(String) method, a new token is added to the history stack. Whenever a history token is added to the history stack, the onHistoryChanged(String token) method in the HistoryListener object is executed. Based on the token received, you are free to do whatever needs to be done with the application to bring it to the state reflected by the token.

Steps to Add History Support

The following are the steps you should follow to add history support to an application. (The BookStore application you developed in Chapter 6 is used as an example to explain these steps in later sections.)

1. Add a type of HistoryListener to your application by implementing the HistoryListener interface, and add the HistoryListener object to the History class.

   For example, in the BookStore application, you can introduce this type by implementing the HistoryListener interface in the module's entry-point class named BookStore.

2. Next, add history tokens in response to user events in the history stack. These tokens should be representative of the current state of the application, and based on the token, the application should be able to return to the current state.

3. Add an iframe to the host HTML page of the application to hook up the history mechanism in your application.

Adding History Support to an Application

This section will walk you through the steps to add history support to the BookStore application you had developed in Chapter 6, which will help solidify your understanding of how the history mechanism works. The BookStore application has two types of screens: the main category screen and the books display screen. The goal of this example is to provide users with the ability to move back and forward between these screens.

The application starts with an empty history stack. When a category label is clicked, you should insert a token named after the category. This reflects which types of books the user wants to see. Every time a token is inserted into the history stack, the onHistoryChanged(...) method of the HistoryListener is called. So instead of directly showing the books display screen using the showWidget(...) method of the DeckPanel, you should move the logic to show the books display panel to the onHistoryChanged(...) method. This also helps you handle situations where a user has bookmarked a page with a specific token. So when the application starts, the history initialization logic checks to see whether any token was passed as part of the URI of the application. If a token actually is passed, then you should explicitly add the token to the history stack, which in turn calls the onHistoryChanged(...) method, and the token gets handled; otherwise, you should just show the main category panel.

So, the flow basically moves as follows: The user sees the categories of books and clicks a category. When that category is chosen, you insert a token named after that category into the history stack. You'll add a history token named category to the history stack when the user clicks one of the categories and moves forward to the books display page.

In this example, you'll modify the onHistoryChanged(...) method to respond to tokens by adding the logic to show the books display screen corresponding to a specific category when a token with a category name is encountered. In all the other cases—that is, when a token other than a category name is encountered—your code should show the main category page.

So, let's now modify the BookStore application as explained previously. The changes are restricted to two files: the main module's entry-point class named BookStore.java and the main module's HTML file named BookStore.html. Listing 9-1 shows the revised BookStore class; the changes are highlighted in bold and explained inline.

Listing 9-1. BookStore *Class with Changes in Bold to Highlight the Addition of History Support to the BookStore Application*

```
package com.apress.gwt.chapter6.client;

import java.util.ArrayList;

import com.google.gwt.core.client.EntryPoint;
import com.google.gwt.core.client.GWT;
import com.google.gwt.user.client.History;
import com.google.gwt.user.client.HistoryListener;
import com.google.gwt.user.client.Window;
import com.google.gwt.user.client.rpc.AsyncCallback;
import com.google.gwt.user.client.ui.Button;
import com.google.gwt.user.client.ui.CheckBox;
import com.google.gwt.user.client.ui.ClickListener;
import com.google.gwt.user.client.ui.DeckPanel;
import com.google.gwt.user.client.ui.FlexTable;
```

```java
import com.google.gwt.user.client.ui.Grid;
import com.google.gwt.user.client.ui.Label;
import com.google.gwt.user.client.ui.Panel;
import com.google.gwt.user.client.ui.RootPanel;
import com.google.gwt.user.client.ui.VerticalPanel;
import com.google.gwt.user.client.ui.Widget;

/**
 * @author Vipul Gupta (vipulgupta.vg@gmail.com)
 */
public class BookStore implements EntryPoint, ClickListener, HistoryListener {

  DeckPanel mainPanel;
  VerticalPanel booksPanel;
  ArrayList booksBeingDisplayed;
  FlexTable table;

  // We have assumed a standard username for our application. In a production
  // environment, this would be assigned based on the logged-in user.
  String userName = "VG";

  // We create an array of the various category names in the system. The
  // array is useful to figure out if a token belongs to a category in the system
  private static ArrayList booksCategoryNames = new ArrayList();
  static {
    booksCategoryNames.add("Computer");
    booksCategoryNames.add("Fiction");
    booksCategoryNames.add("Horror");
    booksCategoryNames.add("Romance");
  }

  private int CATEGORY_PANEL_INDEX = 0;
  private int BOOKS_PANEL_INDEX = 1;

  public void onModuleLoad() {
    mainPanel = new DeckPanel();
    booksPanel = new VerticalPanel();
    booksBeingDisplayed = new ArrayList();
    table = new FlexTable();

    mainPanel.add(createCategoryPanel());
    mainPanel.add(booksPanel);
    RootPanel.get("slot1").add(mainPanel);

    // We remove the code for showing the main category panel from here and move
    // it to initHistory() method.
    initHistory();
  }
```

```
/*
 * This method initializes the History mechanism in the application. It first
 * checks to see if any token is passed in the URI used to refer to the
 * application. If a token is passed then it is added to the history stack by
 * using History.newItem(...) method, which internally calls the
 * onHistoryChanged(...) method of the HistoryListener. If no token is
 * passed then this method displays the category panel.
 */
private void initHistory() {
  History.addHistoryListener(this);

  // Check if any tokens are passed in the startup URI
  String historyToken = History.getToken();
  if (historyToken.length() == 0) {
    mainPanel.showWidget(CATEGORY_PANEL_INDEX);
  } else {
    History.newItem(historyToken);
  }
}

/**
 * Create the category panel and add the various categories to it.
 */
private Panel createCategoryPanel() {
  VerticalPanel categoryPanel = new VerticalPanel();
  Label categoryHeading = new Label("Books Categories");
  categoryHeading.addStyleName("heading");

  Grid grid = new Grid(5, 1);
  grid.setWidget(0, 0, categoryHeading);
  grid.setWidget(1, 0, addCategories("Computer"));
  grid.setWidget(2, 0, addCategories("Fiction"));
  grid.setWidget(3, 0, addCategories("Horror"));
  grid.setWidget(4, 0, addCategories("Romance"));

  categoryPanel.add(grid);
  return categoryPanel;
}

/**
 * Utility method to add a category label having a click listener registered to it.
 */
private Widget addCategories(final String categoryName) {

  Label categoryLabel = new Label(categoryName);
  categoryLabel.addClickListener(new ClickListener() {

    public void onClick(Widget sender) {
```

```
      // Instead of creating a books panel directly, we delegate the
      // responsibility
      // of creating and showing the panel to the history mechanism. We just add
      // a token corresponding to the category chosen by the user in the history
      // stack. This internally calls the onHistoryChanged(...) method, which
      // handles the creation and display of the books panel accordingly.
      History.newItem(categoryName);
    }
  });
  return categoryLabel;
}


/**
 * Utility method to create the books panel. The method first removes the existing
 * books panel from the deck and then creates a new panel and adds and shows
 * the same. The method calls the helper getBooks(...) method to retrieve the
 * books belonging to a specified category.
 */
private void createBooksPanel(String categoryName) {

  mainPanel.remove(booksPanel);
  booksPanel = new VerticalPanel();
  table = new FlexTable();

  mainPanel.add(booksPanel);
  mainPanel.showWidget(BOOKS_PANEL_INDEX);

  Label bookCategoryHeading = new Label(categoryName + " Books");
  bookCategoryHeading.addStyleName("book-category-heading");
  booksPanel.add(bookCategoryHeading);

  getBooks(categoryName);
}


/**
 * The getBooks() method just makes a call to the wrapper getListOfBooks(...)
 * method in the BookUtil class. The getListOfBooks(...) method internally
 * makes the actual RPC call to the server.
 */
private void getBooks(String categoryName) {
  BookUtil.getListOfBooks(categoryName, this);
}


/**
 * Asynchronous callback object class to handle the servers
 * response to getBooks(...) method call.
 */
```

```java
public class BookListUpdaterCallback implements AsyncCallback {

  public void onFailure(Throwable caught) {
    GWT.log("Error in retrieving books list.", caught);
    Window.alert("Error in retrieving books list. Try again later.");
  }

  public void onSuccess(Object result) {
    booksBeingDisplayed = (ArrayList) result;
    displayBooks((ArrayList) result);
  }
}

/**
 * Asynchronous callback object class to handle the servers
 * response to storeOrder (...) method call.
 */
public class StoreOrderCallback implements AsyncCallback {
  public void onFailure(Throwable caught) {
    GWT.log("Error in storing order.", caught);
    Window.alert("Error in storing order. Try again later.");
  }

  public void onSuccess(Object result) {
    showSuccessMessage((String) result);
  }
}

/*
 * Implementation of ClickListeners onClick(...) method to handle the button
 * click event. We just accumulate the list of all books selected by the user
 * and send the same to the server to store it accordingly.
 */
public void onClick(Widget sender) {
  ArrayList selectedList = new ArrayList();
  for (int i = 0; i < booksBeingDisplayed.size(); i++) {
    if (((CheckBox) table.getWidget(i + 1, 0)).isChecked()) {
      selectedList.add(booksBeingDisplayed.get(i));
    }
  }
  BookUtil.storeOrder(selectedList, userName, this);
}

/**
 * Utility method to display the list of books returned by the server and
 * belonging to a specific category to the user.
 */
```

```
private void displayBooks(ArrayList booksList) {
  Label nameHeading = new Label("Name");
  Label authorHeading = new Label("Author");

  nameHeading.addStyleName("heading");
  authorHeading.addStyleName("heading");

  int rowNum = 0;

  table.setWidget(rowNum, 1, nameHeading);
  table.setWidget(rowNum, 2, authorHeading);

  Book book = null;
  Label name = null;
  Label author = null;
  CheckBox selectBook = null;

  for (int i = 0; i < booksList.size(); i++) {
    rowNum++;
    book = (Book) booksList.get(i);
    name = new Label(book.getName());
    author = new Label(book.getAuthor());
    selectBook = new CheckBox();
    table.setWidget(rowNum, 0, selectBook);
    table.setWidget(rowNum, 1, name);
    table.setWidget(rowNum, 2, author);
  }

  Button button = new Button("Order books");
  button.addClickListener(this);

  table.getFlexCellFormatter().setColSpan(++rowNum, 0, 2);
  table.setWidget(rowNum, 0, button);
  booksPanel.add(table);
}

/**
 * Simple utility method to display a message as an alert to the user. In the
 * BookStore application we use this method to show the message returned
 * by the server and affirming the confirmation of books ordered by the user.
 */
private void showSuccessMessage(String message) {
  Window.alert("[Server] : " + message);
}
```

```
    /**
     * Implementation of the only method in HistoryListener interface.
     * The method checks if the tokens value is one of the books category name.
     * If it is, then the method creates and displays the bookPanel by making a call
     * to createBooksPanel(...) method. If the tokens value is not from the list of
     * categories name, then this method displays the main category selection page.
     */
    public void onHistoryChanged(String historyToken) {
      if (booksCategoryNames.contains(historyToken)) {
        createBooksPanel(historyToken);
        return;
      }
      mainPanel.showWidget(CATEGORY_PANEL_INDEX);
    }
}
```

With the changes to the BookStore class out of the way, you should now add an iframe
to the host HTML page of the application. Listing 9-2 shows the host HTML page of the
BookStore application, modified to include the iframe that is needed to include history
support in the application.

Listing 9-2. *The Host HTML File* (BookStore.html) *of the BookStore Application with the iframe
Element (in Bold)*

```
<html>
  <head>
    <script language='javascript'
        src='com.apress.gwt.chapter6.BookStore.nocache.js'>
    </script>
  </head>

  <body>

    <!-- OPTIONAL: include this if you want history support -->
    <iframe src="javascript:''" id="__gwt_historyFrame"
        style="width:0;height:0;border:0">
    </iframe>

    <center><h2>BookStore</h2></center>
    <table align=center>
      <tr>
        <td id="slot1"></td>
      </tr>
    </table>
  </body>
</html>
```

■Note GWT uses an iframe element to store and retrieve history. Failure to include the iframe will result in errors.

Now that you've made all the required changes, the next logical step is to run the application and see the history support in the BookStore application in action. Figure 9-2 shows the state of application when it starts up.

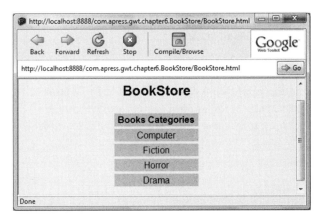

Figure 9-2. *BookStore application displaying the category screen at the time of startup*

Now click the Computer category to get the list of books belonging to that category. Figure 9-3 shows the state of application after the Computer category is clicked. (Notice the changed URL, with the history token prefixed to the original URL.) Instead of directly mapping to the displayBooks page, the redirect to booksDisplay is done because of event handling in response to changes in the history stack.

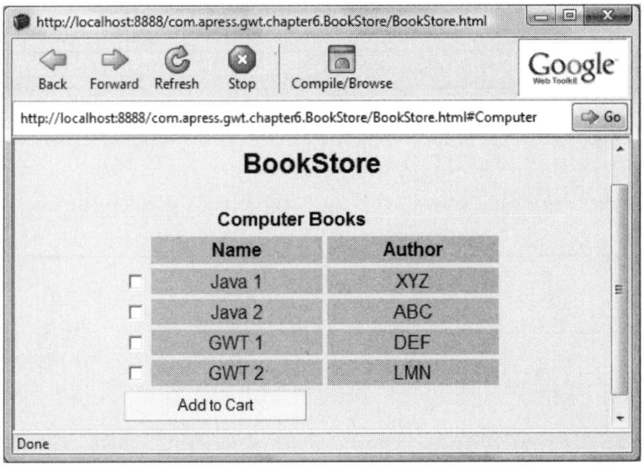

Figure 9-3. *BookStore application displaying the books display screen when the computer category is clicked*

You should now click the Back and Forward buttons to see the history mechanism in action. By clicking the Back button, the application will return to its previous stage, that is, to the category page shown in Figure 9-2. After this, you should click the Forward button, and the application will again come back to the books display screen for the Computer category of books.

You should notice that the application displays the Computer category screen, but it does not store the state of any check boxes (selected or not) before you click the Back button. This is solely because the code written in the example does not do that. You can do that in your applications by passing the state of the check boxes to the application when the Back button is clicked and creating a token that represents that state. Later whenever that token is encountered again, the state of the UI should be set up again.

■**Note** You should notice the URL of the application in Figure 9-3. When the user clicks the Computer category, the URL changes from `http://localhost:8888/com.apress.gwt.chapter6.BookStore/BookStore.html` to `http://localhost:8888/com.apress.gwt.chapter6.BookStore/BookStore.html#Computer`.

The Hyperlink Widget and Its Integration with the History Mechanism

GWT provides a widget named `Hyperlink` in the `com.google.gwt.user.client.ui` package and serves as an internal hyperlink. That is, the `Hyperlink` widget provided by the GWT widget library lets you create links within the application. The `Hyperlink` widget also helps in mapping history tokens by adding a token to the history stack whenever a hyperlink is clicked. The `Hyperlink` class provides constructors that associate a history token to the `Hyperlink` class. Table 9-2 describes these constructors.

Table 9-2. *Methods in the* Hyperlink *Class*

Constructor	Description
Hyperlink(String text, boolean asHTML, String targetHistoryToken)	Creates a hyperlink with its text and target history token specified. (If this constructor is used with the asHTML value set to true, then the text is treated as HTML content.)
Hyperlink(String text, String targetHistoryToken)	Creates a hyperlink with its text and target history token specified.

Let's create a `Hyperlink` widget using the following code snippet:

```
Hyperlink displayLink = new Hyperlink("Display Books", "displayBooks");
```

When the previously mentioned code snippet is executed, a `Hyperlink` widget is created. When added to the UI, it is displayed as shown in Figure 9-4.

Display Books

Figure 9-4. *An internal hyperlink using the GWT's* `Hyperlink` *class*

When the user clicks a hyperlink, the `onHistoryChanged(...)` method of the `HistoryListener` is passed the token associated with the `Hyperlink` widget. In the previous example, when the user clicks the Display Books hyperlink (as shown in Figure 9-4), the `displayBooks` token is passed to the `onHistoryChanged(...)` method. The token is also suffixed to the URL of the browser; that is, the URI of the application in the browser will have `#displayBooks` appended to it.

■**Note** `Hyperlink` widgets, as mentioned previously, are used to create internal links. GWT does *not* have a special widget or method to create external links. However, you can use the `HTML` widget to create an external link. For example, suppose you want to create an external link to `http://apress.com`. You can create this external link by using the `HTML` widget as follows:

```
HTML apressLink = new HTML("<a href=\"http://apress.com\">Apress</a>");
```

Deploying a GWT-Based Application

You have developed a number of applications in the book and have also tested them in a hosted-mode browser throughout that time. A hosted-mode browser helps in testing and debugging the application quickly, but eventually you have to deploy your application to a web server so that users can access and use it.

The following sections will discuss how you can deploy a GWT-based application to a web server. I will use LoanServicingSystem application that you developed throughout the book as the example while discussing the various steps needed to deploy a GWT-based application on the Tomcat web server. Let's start with a discussion of the directory structure.

Default Directory Structure of a Web Application

To start with, you should understand the default directory structure that any web-based application should follow. All web applications follow a standardized directory structure, as shown here:

```
/App_Name -- Root of the web application
/App_Name/WEB-INF/web.xml   -- Deployment descriptor of the application
/App_Name/WEB-INF/classes -- All the Java class files go here
/App_Name/WEB-INF/lib   -- All the library (JAR) files go here
```

Steps for Deploying a GWT Application on a Web Server

The directory structure as listed previously is used to deploy a GWT-based application as well and will be used throughout the discussion in this section. The steps you need to follow to deploy an application on a web server are as follows:

1. You should start by compiling the application. Let's run `LoanServicingSystem-compile.cmd` to compile the LoanServicingSystem application. The result of running the command is as follows:

```
C:\gwt\LoanServicingSystem>LoanServicingSystem-compile.cmd
Output will be written into
   C:\gwt\LoanServicingSystem\www\com.apress.gwt.chapter3.LoanServicingSystem
Compilation succeeded
```

Listing 9-3 shows the contents of the `C:\gwt\LoanServicingSystem\www\com.apress.gwt.chapter3.LoanServicingSystem` folder where the compiler has generated files for the application.

Listing 9-3. *Contents of the LoanServicingSystem Application After Compilation*

```
121576CECBD637D8E20DCF1B1E1EF872.cache.html
121576CECBD637D8E20DCF1B1E1EF872.cache.js
121576CECBD637D8E20DCF1B1E1EF872.cache.xml
224FA6F497CF1936A2A2D9D1D424CA26.cache.html
224FA6F497CF1936A2A2D9D1D424CA26.cache.js
224FA6F497CF1936A2A2D9D1D424CA26.cache.xml
4DD4DF89FF2D870FA442F54558A9C46F.cache.html
4DD4DF89FF2D870FA442F54558A9C46F.cache.js
4DD4DF89FF2D870FA442F54558A9C46F.cache.xml
66A811725296358A5DBAA9D0557C3F09.cache.html
66A811725296358A5DBAA9D0557C3F09.cache.js
66A811725296358A5DBAA9D0557C3F09.cache.xml
clear.cache.gif
com.apress.gwt.chapter3.LoanServicingSystem-xs.nocache.js
com.apress.gwt.chapter3.LoanServicingSystem.nocache.js
D9D6D4F760F88DE4A02369952CACCB42.gwt.rpc
E4144FB897A8CF603FB1CCE9B56970CA.cache.html
E4144FB897A8CF603FB1CCE9B56970CA.cache.js
E4144FB897A8CF603FB1CCE9B56970CA.cache.xml
gwt.js
history.html
hosted.html
LoanServicingSystem.css
LoanServicingSystem.html
```

The compiler creates a lot of files during the compilation step, and some of these are intermediate files that are not needed after the compilation step ends. You should remove these files before deploying the application on the web server.

2. Delete unnecessary files from the compiler output. Chapter 2 of the book mentioned the <Hash>.cache.xml files generated by the compiler. These files list the various choices made by the compiler while generating the optimized JavaScript code for specific browsers. As such, these files are not needed when the application is deployed and should be removed. Also, the history.html file is needed only if your application has added support for history management. Since the LoanServicingSystem does not support history management, you should remove this file as well.

3. Create the directory structure for deploying the application.

   You should create a directory named LoanServicingSystem (the discussion assumes you create it in the C: drive of your machine). After that, you should copy all the files from Listing 9-3 (after deleting the .cache.xml and history.html files mentioned in step 2) to this directory.

4. Create the web application's structure inside the deployment directory. You should create the structure as follows for packaging the application for deployment:

```
C:\LoanServicingSystem
C:\LoanServicingSystem\WEB-INF\
C:\LoanServicingSystem\WEB-INF\lib
C:\LoanServicingSystem\WEB-INF\classes
```

5. Copy the required library files to the lib folder of the web application's directory structure.

   You should copy the library file named gwt-servlet.jar from the gwt distribution folder (C:\gwt) to the C:\LoanServicingSystem\WEB-INF\lib folder.

6. Copy the Java class files to the classes folder of the web application's directory structure.

   Assuming you have kept the Eclipse property of Build Automatically enabled (as mentioned in Chapter 1), you should copy all the files and folders under C:\gwt\LoanServicingSystem\bin to the C:\LoanServicingSystem\WEB-INF\classes folder.

7. Next create a deployment descriptor, and include the servlet mappings for your GWT application in it.

   You should create a file named web.xml in the C:\LoanServicingSystem\WEB-INF folder. Then you should add the servlet mapping for the LoanRequestServiceImpl to it. Listing 9-4 shows the contents of the C:\LoanServicingSystem\WEB-INF\ web.xml file.

Listing 9-4. *Contents of the Deployment Descriptor File for the LoanServicingSystem Application*

```xml
<?xml version="1.0" encoding="ISO-8859-1"?>

<web-app xmlns="http://java.sun.com/xml/ns/j2ee"
    xmlns:xsi="http://www.w3.org/2001/XMLSchema-instance"
    xsi:schemaLocation="http://java.sun.com/xml/ns/j2ee
    http://java.sun.com/xml/ns/j2ee/web-app_2_5.xsd" version="2.5">

    <servlet>
        <servlet-name>LoanServicingSystem</servlet-name>
        <servlet-class>
            com.apress.gwt.chapter3.server.LoanRequestServiceImpl
        </servlet-class>
    </servlet>
    <servlet-mapping>
        <servlet-name>LoanServicingSystem</servlet-name>
        <url-pattern>/LoanRequestService</url-pattern>
    </servlet-mapping>
</web-app>
```

■**Note** I'll be using the Tomcat web server for deploying the application. If you don't have a copy of Tomcat, then you can download one from `http://tomcat.apache.org`. Even though I will be using the Tomcat web server, the steps mentioned here to deploy the application remain the same, whatever application server you may use.

---

8. Deploy the application on the Tomcat web server. (The root directory of the Tomcat web server is referred to as TOMCAT_HOME from now on.)

   Move the directory that you created to the TOMCAT_HOME\webapps directory. Specifically, you should move C:\LoanServicingSystem to the TOMCAT_HOME\webapps folder. With this step, you have successfully deployed the LoanServicingSystem application on the Tomcat web server. Congratulations!

9. Finally, you should now run the Tomcat web server and test the application in action. Once the server has started, you can use the following URL in a browser window to see the application in action:

   `http://localhost:8080/LoanServicingSystem/LoanServicingSystem.html`

Figure 9-5 displays the application running in a browser.

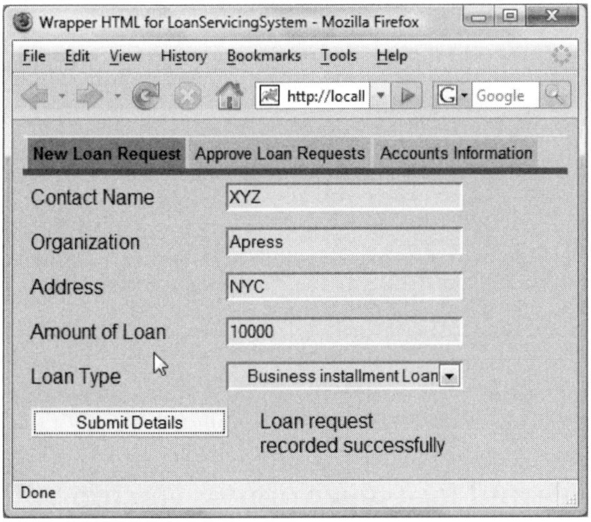

Figure 9-5. *LoanServicingSystem application running on the Tomcat web server*

Maintaining Server Sessions with a GWT Application

A number of web applications rely on server-side sessions to record information from multiple requests made by the same user. This becomes necessary because the HTTP protocol does not provide any facility to store data related to a single user across different requests. Typically, this is useful in situations where the user works across multiple requests to finish a single transaction such as an e-commerce site where the user can put things he likes in a cart as he browses the site across multiple pages (requests).

For example, let's consider the BookStore application discussed previously. Typically such an application allows the user to select books from different categories and order them together. So, as the user selects some books from a category, these books can be put into a cart that is represented by a session on the server side, and in the end the user can see all the books in the cart and order them together. Your application may even provide for finishing the transaction later, in other words, using the session across multiple logins by a user by persisting the session using a storage mechanism when the user logs out. This allows the user to leave the transaction midway and continue it from the same point in a later login.

You may recall from Chapter 4 that the implementation of every remote service on the server in GWT has to extend from RemoteServiceServlet. RemoteServiceServlet provides a getThreadLocalRequest() method that returns the javax.servlet.http.HttpServletRequest object corresponding to the current call and can be used to get access to the session. Table 9-3 lists some of the important methods related to managing sessions from the RemoteServiceServlet class.

Table 9-3. *Some Important Methods from the* RemoteServiceServlet *Class Relevant to Maintaining Sessions*

Method Name	Description
getThreadLocalRequest()	Returns the javax.servlet.http.HttpServletRequest object for the current call.
getThreadLocalResponse()	Returns the javax.servlet.http.HttpServletResponse object for the current call.
onBeforeRequestDeserialized(...)	If you want to examine the serialized version of the request payload before it is deserialized into objects, then you should override this method.

In the next section, you'll learn how to use sessions in the context of GWT by extending the BookStore application and allowing users to store books in session on the server.

Modifying the RemoteService and Its Asynchronous Version

You should start by adding a new method named addToCart(...) to the remote service. This method adds a list of books selected by the user into the session and returns all the books (including the new ones passed as parameters to the method) from the session to the caller method. Listing 9-5 shows the relevant part of the remote service, BookStoreService, with this new method added in bold.

Listing 9-5. *The New Method Added to the Service Interface of the BookStore Application*

```
public interface BookStoreService extends RemoteService {

  ...
  ...

  /**
   * The annotation specifies that the parameter named 'books' is a List
   * that will only contain com.apress.gwt.chapter6.client.Book objects.
   *
   * @gwt.typeArgs books <com.apress.gwt.chapter6.client.Book>
   * @gwt.typeArgs <com.apress.gwt.chapter6.client.Book>
   *
   */
  public List addToCart(List books);
}
```

Listing 9-6 shows the corresponding async service interface with this new method added (in bold).

Listing 9-6. *The New Method Added to the Async Interface of the BookStore Application*

```
public interface BookStoreServiceAsync extends RemoteService {
  ...

  public void addToCart(List books, AsyncCallback callback);
}
```

Introducing the Callback Class Corresponding to the New Service Method

You also need to add a new AsyncCallback object to handle the response to this new RPC call. You can add a new inner class named AddToCartCallback inside the BookStore class. The text of the click button in the UI is changed to say "Add to cart" instead of "Order books." You also need to change the onClick(...) method of the button to call the corresponding addToCart(...) wrapper method defined in the BookUtil class. Listing 9-7 shows all the changes in the BookStore class in bold.

Listing 9-7. *The New Callback Class (Corresponding to the Method Added to the Service Interface) and Other Modifications in the Entry-Point Class of the BookStore Application*

```
public class BookStore implements EntryPoint, ClickListener, HistoryListener {
  ...

  public class AddToCartCallback implements AsyncCallback {
    public void onFailure(Throwable caught) {
      GWT.log("Error in adding books to cart.", caught);
      Window.alert("Error in adding books to cart. Try again later.");
    }

    public void onSuccess(Object result) {
      ArrayList list = (ArrayList) result;
      StringBuffer buffer = new StringBuffer();
      for (int i = 0; i < list.size(); i++) {
        buffer.append("[" + ((Book) list.get(i)).name + "] ");
      }
      Window.alert("Cart contains " + buffer.toString());
    }
  }

  public void onClick(Widget sender) {
    ArrayList selectedList = new ArrayList();
    for (int i = 0; i < booksBeingDisplayed.size(); i++) {
      if (((CheckBox) table.getWidget(i + 1, 0)).isChecked()) {
        selectedList.add(booksBeingDisplayed.get(i));
      }
    }
    BookUtil.addToCart(selectedList, this);
  }

  private void displayBooks(ArrayList booksList) {
    Label nameHeading = new Label("Name");
    Label authorHeading = new Label("Author");

    nameHeading.addStyleName("heading");
    authorHeading.addStyleName("heading");
```

```
int rowNum = 0;

// table.setWidget(rowNum, 0, select);
table.setWidget(rowNum, 1, nameHeading);
table.setWidget(rowNum, 2, authorHeading);

for (int i = 0; i < booksList.size(); i++) {
  rowNum++;
  Book book = (Book) booksList.get(i);
  Label name = new Label(book.getName());
  Label author = new Label(book.getAuthor());
  CheckBox selectBook = new CheckBox();
  table.setWidget(rowNum, 0, selectBook);
  table.setWidget(rowNum, 1, name);
  table.setWidget(rowNum, 2, author);
}

Button button = new Button("Add to Cart");
button.addClickListener(this);

table.getFlexCellFormatter().setColSpan(++rowNum, 0, 2);
table.setWidget(rowNum, 0, button);
booksPanel.add(table);
  }
}
```

Adding the Server-Side Implementation for the New Service Method

You also need to add the server-side implementation for this new method. The implementation of this method just gets the HttpSession from the request and adds the list of books selected by the user into a Set, which is stored in the session. (We're using the Set as the underlying data structure so that a book is stored only one time in the cart on the server.) Listing 9-8 shows the changes in the remote service implementation on the server side in bold.

Listing 9-8. *The New Method Being Added and Other Modifications Being Made in the Server-Side Implementation of* BookStoreService

```
package com.apress.gwt.chapter6.server;

import java.util.ArrayList;
import java.util.List;
import java.util.TreeSet;

import javax.servlet.http.HttpServletRequest;
import javax.servlet.http.HttpSession;

import com.apress.gwt.chapter6.client.Book;
import com.apress.gwt.chapter6.client.BookStoreService;
import com.google.gwt.user.server.rpc.RemoteServiceServlet;
```

```java
/**
 * @author Vipul Gupta (vipulgupta.vg@gmail.com)
 */
public class BookStoreServiceImpl extends RemoteServiceServlet implements
    BookStoreService {
  ......................................
  private static final String BOOKS_ATTRIBUTE_NAME = "books";
  ......................................
  private static ArrayList<Book> booksInStore = new ArrayList<Book>();
  static {
    ...
    booksInStore.add(new Book("Alien World", "PQR", "Fiction"));
    booksInStore.add(new Book("Time Travel", "GHI", "Fiction"));
  }

...

  @SuppressWarnings("unchecked")
  public List addToCart(List books) {

    HttpServletRequest request = this.getThreadLocalRequest();
    HttpSession session = request.getSession();
    TreeSet<Book> cart = (TreeSet<Book>) session
        .getAttribute(BOOKS_ATTRIBUTE_NAME);
    if (cart == null) {
      cart = new TreeSet<Book>(books);
    }
    cart.addAll(books);
    session.setAttribute(BOOKS_ATTRIBUTE_NAME, cart);
    return new ArrayList(cart);
  }
}
```

Modifying the Util Class to Support the New Method

You also need to add a wrapper method around the RPC call in the BookUtil class, as shown in Listing 9-9.

Listing 9-9. *The Addition of the New Wrapper Method in the* BookUtil *Class*

```java
public class BookUtil {
  ......................................

  public static void addToCart(List books, BookStore bookStore) {
    serviceInstance.addToCart(books, bookStore.new AddToCartCallback());
  }
}
```

Tweaking the Domain Object for Use

Since the application is using a TreeSet on the server side (to keep copies of unique books in a sorted order), the application requires that you implement the Comparable interface in the Book object. The implementation in this book will differentiate between books based on their names (in an actual production system this should be based on unique IDs for books). Listing 9-10 shows the changes in the Book object in bold.

Listing 9-10. *The Modifications in the* Book *Class to Make Its Instances Comparable (Done by Implementing the* Comparable *Interface)*

```
public class Book implements Serializable, Comparable {

  ...
  public int compareTo(Object param) {
    return this.name.compareTo(((Book)param).name);
  }
}
```

Running the Application

It's now time for you to run the BookStore application and observe the cart (implemented using sessions) in action. Figures 9-6 to 9-10 show the application at different stages.

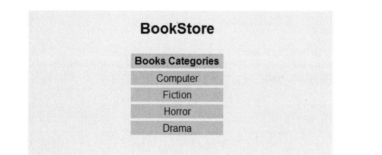

Figure 9-6. *Initial state of the BookStore application*

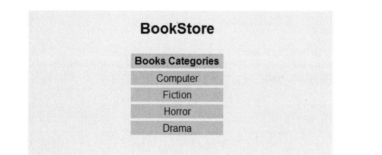

Figure 9-7. *BookStore application displaying computer books along with the user selections*

Figure 9-8. *BookStore application displaying contents of the cart returned by the server after the user clicks the Add to Cart button*

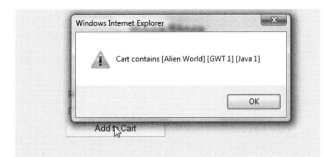

Figure 9-9. *BookStore application displaying list of books in the Fiction category (you can press the Back button in the browser window, and then select the Fiction category to get to this screen)*

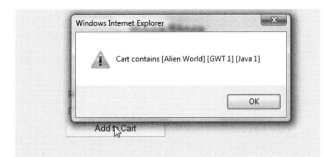

Figure 9-10. *BookStore application displaying contents of the cart returned by the server after the user clicks the Add to Cart button. Notice the addition of the book selected by the user from the Fiction category to the list representing the user's cart.*

Creating an ImageBundle of Bundles

In Chapter 5 you learned about ImageBundle and how it's useful in grouping a large number of images into a single image comprising all the required images. By grouping images into a single image, the application becomes more responsive and faster. This is because the browser has to make only a single HTTP call to load all the images represented by the bundle.

But what if your application has images of different categories grouped together into separate bundles? Can ImageBundle help you in optimizing further?

The answer to this question is yes. Since each ImageBundle is itself an image behind the scenes, you can use the ImageBundle again to bundle all the ImageBundles in your application into one single bundle.

Let's look at some code to understand how an ImageBundle of bundles can be created. This section will show how to extend the AdvancedWidgets application developed in Chapter 5. The AdvancedWidgets application created an ImageBundle represented by the FlowerImages interface, as shown in Listing 9-11.

Listing 9-11. FlowerImages *Interface Representing the* ImageBundle *for the Flower Gallery*

```
package com.apress.gwt.chapter5.client.images;

import com.google.gwt.user.client.ui.AbstractImagePrototype;
import com.google.gwt.user.client.ui.ImageBundle;

/**
 * @author Vipul Gupta (vipulgupta.vg@gmail.com)
 */
public interface FlowerImages extends ImageBundle {

  /**
   * The metadata tag contains no '/' characters, so pink.jpg
   * must be located in the same package as FlowerImages.
   *
   * @gwt.resource pink.jpg
   */
  public AbstractImagePrototype getPinkThumbnail ();

  public AbstractImagePrototype red();

  public AbstractImagePrototype yellow();

  public AbstractImagePrototype white();
}
```

Let's assume the application needs a set of icons to be used at various places and these icons are also grouped together into an ImageBundle represented by the interface named IconImages, as shown in Listing 9-12.

Listing 9-12. IconImages *Interface Representing the* ImageBundle *for Icons to Be Used in the Flower Gallery*

```
package com.apress.gwt.chapter5.client.images;

import com.google.gwt.user.client.ui.AbstractImagePrototype;
import com.google.gwt.user.client.ui.ImageBundle;

/**
 * @author Vipul Gupta (vipulgupta.vg@gmail.com)
 */
public interface IconImages extends ImageBundle {

  /**
   * @gwt.resource icon_left.jpg
   */
  public AbstractImagePrototype getLeftIcon();

  /**
   * @gwt.resource icon_top.jpg
   */
  public AbstractImagePrototype getTopIcon();

  /**
   * @gwt.resource icon_right.jpg
   */
  public AbstractImagePrototype getRightIcon();
}
```

To group the previously mentioned two bundles into a single ImageBundle, you need to create a new type that represents both these bundles. You do this by creating an interface named GalleryImages that extends both these interfaces, as shown in Listing 9-13.

Listing 9-13. GalleryImages *Interface Representing the* ImageBundle *for Icons and Flowers to Be Used in the Flower Gallery*

```
package com.apress.gwt.chapter5.client.images;

/**
 * @author Vipul Gupta (vipulgupta.vg@gmail.com)
 */
public interface GalleryImages extends FlowerImages, IconImages {

}
```

You can use the same process you used for the FlowerImages bundle in order to create instances of type GalleryImages. Specifically, you create an object of type GalleryImages using the GWT.create(...) method so that it can pass through the generator registered for ImageBundle, that is, ImageBundleGenerator. The following is the snippet for creating an object of GalleryImages with the help of ImageBundleGenerator by using the GWT.create(...) method:

```
final GalleryImages images = (GalleryImages) GWT.create(GalleryImages.class);
```

After creating an object of GalleryImages as shown earlier, the respective methods declared in the two different interfaces that GalleryImages extends from can be used from this instance to retrieve the respective images. For example, you can retrieve the right icon and the pink thumbnail by using the following code:

```
Image rightIcon = images. getRightIcon().createImage();
Image pinkThumbnailImage = images.getPinkThumbnail().createImage();
```

Understanding and Using the <super-source> Tag

If you recall the module file structure from Chapter 1, you'll remember that the module XML file has a <source> tag that helps you declare the location of the source folder for the client code. This tag was not referenced after Chapter 1 because all the examples in the book used the default configuration of <source path="client">, which means the source for the client code will be in a subpackage called client under the package where the project's module XML file is defined. For example, if your application's module file is com/apress/gwt/example/ Sample.gwt.xml, then the source code for the client will be in the package com.apress.gwt. example.client.

However, sometimes you might want to add some classes so that the package for those classes does not match the underlying directory structure in the file system. For example, suppose the application uses an object of type java.util.BitSet at the server end and wants to pass the BitSet object to the client for processing. This scenario will not work in a GWT application because the GWT emulation library does not include java.util.BitSet and because the compiler will complain about this if you try to use it in the client code. But GWT provides a way around this. If you have a concrete implementation of java.util.BitSet (which uses only the classes supported by GWT's JRE emulation library) and want to use it in the client code, then you can add this implementation to your application as follows:

1. Add the class under a specific package in your application. For example, you can place your custom implementation of the java.util.BitSet class under a specific folder in the project such as com/apress/gwt/example/custom/java/util/BitSet.java. (It is important to note that the package declaration for the BitSet.java file should be set to java.util.)

2. Next you should use the <super-source> tag and add it to the module's configuration XML. For the java.util.BitSet example mentioned previously, you need to add the <super-source path="custom"/> line to the project's module configuration file.

The <super-source path="custom"/> tag signals to the compiler that it should treat any files in the com.apress.gwt.example.custom package to be at the root package of the classpath.

If you think about this carefully, you will realize that by using the `<super-source>` tag, you can add your own custom implementation of the JRE library and extend/modify the emulated library as per your application's needs.

Packaging a GWT Module for Reuse

There will always be situations where you create a tool or functionality and find that it's applicable to multiple applications. This situation provides an opportunity to put the modular application structure in GWT to good use. GWT applications are themselves recognized as modules, and you have been working with external modules by including at least the most basic module in all your applications since the beginning of the book.

This fundamental module is `com.google.gwt.user.User`, and you have been including it in all the applications that have been discussed in this book by using the `inherits` tag in the application's module XML file. The following code snippet shows the core `User` module being included in your application:

```
<module>
    <!-- Inherit the core Web Toolkit.              -->
    <inherits name='com.google.gwt.user.User'/>

    <!-- Specify the app entry-point class.         -->
    <entry-point class='com.apress.gwt.news.client.NewsClient'/>
</module>
```

Similar to the `User` module provided by the GWT framework, you can also package your modules to be reused and include them in multiple applications. In this section, I will go over the steps you need to follow to package your application as a reusable module.

But before I go over the steps, it's important to know that packaging a module for reuse requires that the *source code for the Java files is included with their compiled class files*. This requirement of bundling the source code is applicable only for the code from the *client* package, because the GWT compiler needs access to the source to convert the Java code into its JavaScript equivalent. For any standard project created by using the `applicationCreator` utility, the class files are stored by Eclipse in the `bin` folder inside the project's root folder. You can copy the contents of the `bin` folder in the `src` folder at the time of packaging, or you can configure the Eclipse IDE to create class files directly in the `src` folder.

■**Note** You can configure Eclipse to compile the Java files directly into the `src` folder as follows: Start by right-clicking your Eclipse project in the Package Explorer window of Eclipse, and then choose Build Path followed by Configure Build Path. The properties pop-up window will be displayed. You should choose the Source tab in this pop-up window. On the bottom of the Source tab, you'll see an option for choosing the default output folder. Click the Browse button, and choose your project's `src` folder. Then click OK in the Choose Folder pop-up window, followed by clicking OK in the properties pop-up window.

Steps to Package an Application as a Reusable Module

This section will discuss the various steps you need to follow to package an application as a reusable module. The PropertyFileReader application from Chapter 2 is a good candidate of functionality that could be reused in multiple applications, so this section will use it as the example to be packaged and converted into a reusable module. The steps for creating a reusable module from the PropertyFileReader application are as follows:

1. Start by creating a temporary folder named `PropertyFileReader`. I created this folder in the root folder (`C:\`) of my system (the fully qualified path of the folder being `C:\PropertyFileReader`).

2. Copy the contents of the `src` folder from the PropertyFileReader application (`C:\gwt\Generator\src`) to the `PropertyFileReader` folder created in step 1. The reusable module only needs the configuration XML file named `PropertyFileReader.gwt.xml`, the marker interface file named `PropertiesReader.java`, and the generator class named `PropertyReaderGenerator.java`. (As mentioned previously, the module only needs to include the source of the client code; therefore, you can even skip copying the `PropertyReaderGenerator` file.) You should delete rest of the files from the copied folder.

   You should also modify the module XML file, `PropertyFileReader.gwt.xml`, by removing the entry-point property from it. The modified XML file is as follows:

   ```
   <module>
       <!-- Inherit the core Web Toolkit stuff. -->
       <inherits name='com.google.gwt.user.User'/>

       <generate-with
       class="com.apress.gwt.chapter2.rebind.PropertyReaderGenerator">
           <when-type-assignable
               class="com.apress.gwt.chapter2.client.PropertiesReader"/>
       </generate-with>

   </module>
   ```

3. Next copy the class files corresponding to the previously mentioned Java files from the `bin` (`C:\gwt\Generator\bin`) folder to the `PropertyFileReader` folder created in step 1.

   The `PropertyFileReader` (the temporary folder created in step1) folder after steps 2 and 3 should look as follows:

   ```
   C:\PropertyFileReader
   C:\PropertyFileReader\com
   C:\PropertyFileReader\com\apress
   C:\PropertyFileReader\com\apress\gwt
   C:\PropertyFileReader\com\apress\gwt\chapter2\PropertyFileReader.gwt.xml
   C:\PropertyFileReader\com\apress\gwt\chapter2\client\PropertiesReader.java
   C:\PropertyFileReader\com\apress\gwt\chapter2\client\PropertiesReader.class
   C:\PropertyFileReader\com\apress\gwt\chapter2\rebind\PropertyReaderGenerator.class
   ```

4. The last step needed to make your module easily distributable is to package the
PropertyFileReader folder as a JAR file. I used jar (the Java archive tool) available in
the Java JDK to package the module as a JAR file. The command I used to package the
folder into JAR file along with the command's output is as follows:

```
C:\PropertyFileReader>jar -cvf PropertyFileReader.jar .
added manifest
adding: com/(in = 0) (out= 0)(stored 0%)
adding: com/apress/(in = 0) (out= 0)(stored 0%)
adding: com/apress/gwt/(in = 0) (out= 0)(stored 0%)
adding: com/apress/gwt/chapter2/(in = 0) (out= 0)(stored 0%)
adding: com/apress/gwt/chapter2/client/(in = 0) (out= 0)(stored 0%)
adding: com/apress/gwt/chapter2/client/PropertiesReader.class(in = 144) ➥
    (out= 120)(deflated 16%)
adding: com/apress/gwt/chapter2/client/PropertiesReader.java(in = 143) ➥
    (out= 124)(deflated 13%)
adding: com/apress/gwt/chapter2/PropertyFileReader.gwt.xml(in = 451) ➥
    (out= 232)(deflated 48%)
adding: com/apress/gwt/chapter2/rebind/(in = 0) (out= 0)(stored 0%)
adding: com/apress/gwt/chapter2/rebind/PropertyReaderGenerator.class➥
    (in = 6796) (out= 2929)(deflated 56%)
```

With this, the PropertyFileReader module is ready to be used and included in any GWT
application.

Using the New Module in a Sample Application

Let's create a simple application to use the PropertyFileReader module. Start by creating
a project named ModuleChecker with the entry-point class as com.apress.gwt.chapter9.
client.ModuleChecker using the projectCreator and applicationCreator utilities explained
in Chapter 1. After this, open this project in Eclipse.

Next, create a new interface named BookPropertiesReader in the com.apress.gwt.
chapter9.client package, and copy the contents of com.apress.gwt.chapter2.client.
BookPropertiesReader interface from the PropertyFileReader application from Chapter 2
to it. You should also create a folder named res (to store resource files at the project's root;
C:\gwt\ModuleChecker\res in my case) and copy the book.properties file from the res folder
in the PropertyFileReader application (from Chapter 2) to it.

Now you should modify the ModuleChecker.gwt.xml file and add the PropertyFileReader
module to it. This is shown in bold in the following snippet:

```
<module>
    <!-- Inherit the core Web Toolkit stuff. -->
    <inherits name='com.google.gwt.user.User'/>

    <inherits name='com.apress.gwt.chapter2.PropertyFileReader'/>

    <!-- Specify the app entry-point class. -->
    <entry-point class='com.apress.gwt.chapter9.client.ModuleChecker'/>
</module>
```

You should also modify the onModuleLoad() method of the entry-point class, ModuleChecker.java, to look as follows:

```
public void onModuleLoad() {
  BookPropertiesReader reader = (BookPropertiesReader) GWT
      .create(BookPropertiesReader.class);
  RootPanel.get("slot1").add(new Label(reader.year()));
  RootPanel.get("slot1").add(new Label(reader.getBookName()));
  RootPanel.get("slot1").add(new Label(reader.publisher()));
  RootPanel.get("slot1").add(new Label(reader.getAuthorName()));
}
```

Now create a folder named lib inside the ModuleChecker application, and copy the PropertyFileReader.jar you had created previously to it.

Before the application can be executed, you need to include the PropertyFileReader module and res folder in the classpath of the application. The changes to ModuleChecker-shell.cmd are shown in bold in the following code snippet:

```
@java -cp "%~dp0\src;%~dp0\bin;C:/gwt/gwt-user.jar;C:/gwt/gwt-dev-windows.jar;➥
%~dp0/lib/PropertyFileReader.jar;%~dp0/res"
        com.google.gwt.dev.GWTShell -out "%~dp0\www" %*
        com.apress.gwt.chapter9.ModuleChecker/ModuleChecker.html
```

■**Note** The command listed previously from the ModuleChecker-shell.cmd script is a single command, but individual elements of it have been broken into multiple lines to fit the width of this page. You can just type the same command on a single line and see the hosted browser load with your application.

With all this done, the application can now be executed by running ModuleChecker-shell.cmd from the command line as follows. (You should ensure that the project is built properly before executing the ModuleChecker-shell.cmd script.)

```
C:\gwt\ModuleChecker>ModuleChecker-shell.cmd
```

When the previously mentioned command is executed, the application will launch in hosted mode, and the values from the book.properties property file will be displayed. With this, you have successfully packaged and reused a GWT module. Just like the example mentioned in this section, you can package your reusable components into modules and use them in multiple applications with ease.

Summary

This chapter covered the essential techniques that are required for using the GWT framework for your real-world applications, including deploying applications to a web server and packaging the applications as modules for reuse. The chapter started with a discussion of the history mechanism and explained how you can use the history support provided by the GWT framework. With GWT, adding history support to Ajax applications becomes a simple task, and the chapter demonstrated this by adding history support to the BookStore application you developed in Chapter 6. As part of the history mechanism discussion, the chapter also explained the Hyperlink widget and how it is linked with the history mechanism offered by GWT.

In addition, the chapter discussed maintaining server-side sessions while using a GWT-based application. The chapter explained this by extending the BookStore application started in Chapter 6 by adding session support to it.

Finally, the chapter discussed how to use an ImageBundle to bundle multiple image bundles. By bundling multiple ImageBundles, you optimize your applications a step further because they can make a single request to download the bundle of all bundles.

■ ■ ■

CHAPTER 10

Peeking Into the Upcoming GWT 1.5 Release

This book was written with GWT 1.4.61, the most recent version on the download site as of this writing. But such is the nature of open source frameworks that I have been writing about a moving target.

This chapter will discuss some of the major changes that are expected in the 1.5 release of the framework. It will also explain how you can download and set up the initial milestone release of version 1.5. You will also learn how to compile and modify some of the major applications developed in this book so you can take advantages of the features introduced by the upcoming 1.5 release. During the process of porting the applications onto the new release, you will learn about some of the better ways to perform the same tasks you learned about in the book.

Understanding the Major Changes in Version 1.5

The most important and notable change in the upcoming 1.5 release is the support for Java 1.5 language constructs and syntax for the client code of your GWT applications. Until now, all the code you have written for the client part of the application in this book conformed to Java 1.4 language constructs and syntax. This meant you were not allowed to use generics, enums, nice `for` loops, static imports, annotations, and so on, in the client code of your applications. The upcoming release 1.5 adds support for the entire Java 1.5 language constructs and syntax to the GWT compiler.

What does this mean for you as a GWT application developer? This addition allows you to write the same type-safe code in the client part of your GWT applications (using generics) as you have likely become used to writing in real-world Java-based applications (and, I hope by this stage of the book, the server-side code for your GWT-based applications). For example, rather than using the `gwt.typeArgs` annotation, you can use generics for the RPC code. You can also rely on autoboxing, the `for` loops introduced in Java 1.5, annotations, and so on, to write much cleaner, easier-to-read, and more robust code for your applications.

Setting Up Your Environment for Using Version 1.5

As of this writing, milestone 2 of the 1.5 release has already been released by the GWT team. You can download this milestone release from `http://code.google.com/p/google-web-toolkit/downloads/list?can=4&q=version:1.5` (refer to the following note as well). I downloaded the file named `gwt-windows-0.0.2415.zip` (for the Windows platform) and unzipped it at `C:\gwt15` on my machine. Figure 10-1 shows the contents of this directory.

Name	Size
doc	
samples	
about.html	3 KB
about.txt	1 KB
applicationCreator.cmd	1 KB
benchmarkViewer.cmd	1 KB
COPYING	13 KB
COPYING.html	16 KB
gwt-benchmark-viewer.jar	3,435 KB
gwt-dev-windows.jar	9,646 KB
gwt-ll.dll	13 KB
gwt-module.dtd	6 KB
gwt-servlet.jar	513 KB
gwt-user.jar	2,146 KB
i18nCreator.cmd	1 KB
index.html	6 KB
junitCreator.cmd	1 KB
projectCreator.cmd	1 KB
release_notes.html	53 KB
swt-win32-3235.dll	352 KB

Figure 10-1. *List of files after extracting the* gwt-windows-0.0.2415.zip *file in the* C:\gwt15 *folder*

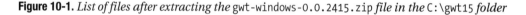

■Note In general, open source libraries go through several initial milestone releases, which gives the user of these libraries a chance to give feedback to the developers before the final release is made. The link mentioned previously for milestone 2 of the 1.5 release may change in the future, so you should either check the `http://code.google.com/webtoolkit/download.html` link for the latest releases of the framework or make a quick search on any popular search engine for *GWT 1.5 release* so you can download the latest release of the framework for your application development.

Being open source, the GWT framework gives you the opportunity to download and peek into the changes being made in the code base of the framework, before an official release containing the changes is made. You can download and build the latest source code of the GWT framework locally by using the instructions at `http://code.google.com/webtoolkit/makinggwtbetter.html`. However, since the framework is actively under development, you might encounter broken features in the code you built from the trunk. If that is the case, you should report it using the link on the page and/or wait for the code in the trunk to be fixed. To avoid such situations, it is advisable to stick to the major releases of the framework that are fully tested against the supported features for your production applications.

Testing the New Release

Recall the NewsClient application you developed in Chapter 1. We tried modifying the newEntries array (by using generics to specify the type of objects for the ArrayList) in the NewsClient class in the "What Version of the Java Language Does the GWT Support?" section in Chapter 2. When executed against the 1.4.61 release, the application failed to start with messages stating that Java 5.0 constructs are not available for the client code. Let's run this example against the new release of the framework.

I started by creating a project named NewsClient15 in the C:\gwt15 folder using the projectCreator and applicationCreator utilities as follows:

```
C:\gwt15>projectCreator.cmd -eclipse NewsClient15 -out NewsClient15
Created directory NewsClient15\src
Created directory NewsClient15\test
Created file NewsClient15\.project
Created file NewsClient15\.classpath


C:\gwt15>applicationCreator.cmd -out NewsClient15 -eclipse NewsClient15 ➥
    com.apress.gwt.news.client.NewsClient
Created directory NewsClient15\src\com\apress\gwt\news
Created directory NewsClient15\src\com\apress\gwt\news\client
Created directory NewsClient15\src\com\apress\gwt\news\public
Created file NewsClient15\src\com\apress\gwt\news\NewsClient.gwt.xml
Created file NewsClient15\src\com\apress\gwt\news\public\NewsClient.html
Created file NewsClient15\src\com\apress\gwt\news\client\NewsClient.java
Created file NewsClient15\NewsClient.launch
Created file NewsClient15\NewsClient-shell.cmd
Created file NewsClient15\NewsClient-compile.cmd
```

I opened the NewsClient15 project in Eclipse and modified the entry-point class named NewsClient (com.apress.gwt.news.client.NewsClient) to resemble Listing 10-1. (These changes resemble the changes we tried in the "What Version of the Java Language Does the GWT Support?" section in Chapter 2.) Notice the use of generics (shown in bold) to specify the types of objects that the ArrayList can contain.

Listing 10-1. *Contents of the Entry-Point Class for the NewsClient Application Using the New Version of the GWT Library*

```
package com.apress.gwt.news.client;

import java.util.ArrayList;

import com.google.gwt.core.client.EntryPoint;
import com.google.gwt.user.client.Random;
import com.google.gwt.user.client.Timer;
import com.google.gwt.user.client.ui.Label;
import com.google.gwt.user.client.ui.RootPanel;
```

```java
/**
 * @author Vipul Gupta (vipulgupta.vg@gmail.com)
 */
public class NewsClient implements EntryPoint {

  private static final ArrayList<String> newsEntries = new ArrayList<String>();
  static {
    newsEntries.add("News Entry 1");
    newsEntries.add("Another News Entry");
    newsEntries.add("Yet another news entry");
    newsEntries.add("One Final news entry");
  }

  public void onModuleLoad() {

    final Label label = new Label();

    // Create a new timer that keeps changing the news text
    Timer t = new Timer() {
      public void run() {
        label.setText(getNewsEntry());
      }
    };
    // Schedule the timer to run every 2 seconds.
    t.scheduleRepeating(2000);
    RootPanel.get().add(label);
  }

  private String getNewsEntry() {
    return newsEntries.get(Random.nextInt(newsEntries.size()));
  }
}
```

You should now execute the application in hosted mode by using NewsClient-shell.cmd as follows:

```
C:\gwt15\NewsClient15>NewsClient-shell.cmd
```

You should see the hosted browser being loaded and the application running without any errors, just as you observed in Figure 2-1 and Figure 2-2 in Chapter 2.

This example demonstrated that the GWT framework now supports the Java 5.0 language constructs for the client code by using generics in the NewsClient application. Let's understand the other changes in the upcoming 1.5 release in the context of the BookStore and LoanServicingSystem applications you developed in this book.

Using Version 1.5 of the GWT Framework

To understand how things are affected by the new release in your existing applications, I'll take the code of the BookStore, LoanServicingSystem, and AdvancedWidgets applications developed in the book and run it across the 1.5 milestone release of the framework. I'll start by showing how to set up the BookStore example to run against the 1.5 release.

Setting Up and Running the BookStore Example on the New Version of the Library

Start by copying the `C:\gwt\bookstore` folder to the `C:\gwt15` folder. Delete all the generated files from the `C:\gwt15\bookstore` folder so that the contents of this folder look like Figure 10-2.

Name	Size
src	
test	
BookStore.launch	2 KB
.project	1 KB
.classpath	1 KB
BookStore-shell.cmd	1 KB
BookStore-compile.cmd	1 KB

Figure 10-2. *Contents of the* `C:\gwt15\bookstore` *folder*

Modify the `.classpath`, `BookStore.launch`, `BookStore-compile.cmd`, and `BookStore-shell.cmd` files, and change the reference to the libraries in these files from the `c:\gwt` folder to the `c:\gwt15` folder. For example, the original `BookStore-shell.cmd` file looks like this:

```
@java -cp "%~dp0\src;%~dp0\bin;C:/gwt/gwt-user.jar;C:/gwt/gwt-dev-windows.jar"
   com.google.gwt.dev.GWTShell -out "%~dp0\www" %*
   com.apress.gwt.chapter6.BookStore/BookStore.html
```

The modified `BookStore-shell.cmd` file (with changes in bold) looks like this:

```
@java -cp "%~dp0\src;%~dp0\bin;C:/gwt15/gwt-user.jar;C:/gwt15/gwt-dev-windows.jar"
   com.google.gwt.dev.GWTShell -out "%~dp0\www" %*
   com.apress.gwt.chapter6.BookStore/BookStore.html
```

■**Note** The changes in these four files are required because these files were created using the `projectCreator` and `applicationCreator` utilities in the `C:\gwt` (representing version 1.4.61) folder. If you started by creating these applications using the utilities in the `C:\gwt15` folder (representing the upcoming GWT 1.5 release), then these files should have been correctly created with the path of libraries in the `gwt15` folder.

With the library paths in all these files configured properly, you should open the project in Eclipse by importing it. (Ensure that the old bookstore project is deleted from your Eclipse workspace, because Eclipse does not allow adding multiple projects with the same name. If you delete the existing project from Eclipse, make sure you select the Do Not Delete Contents option to avoid deleting the source code of your project.)

Once the project is opened in Eclipse, run the BookStore application (assuming that, as mentioned in Chapter 1, the Build Automatically setting of your Eclipse IDE is enabled) by double-clicking the BookStore-shell.cmd script. The application will start up in a hosted window, as shown in Figure 10-3 and Figure 10-4.

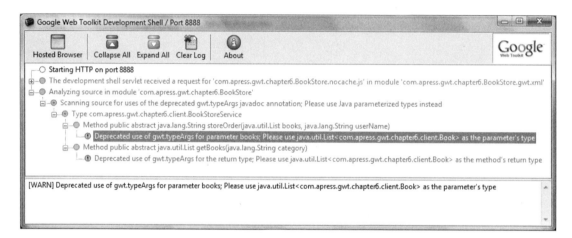

Figure 10-3. *Embedded web server window that shows the application log and error stack trace*

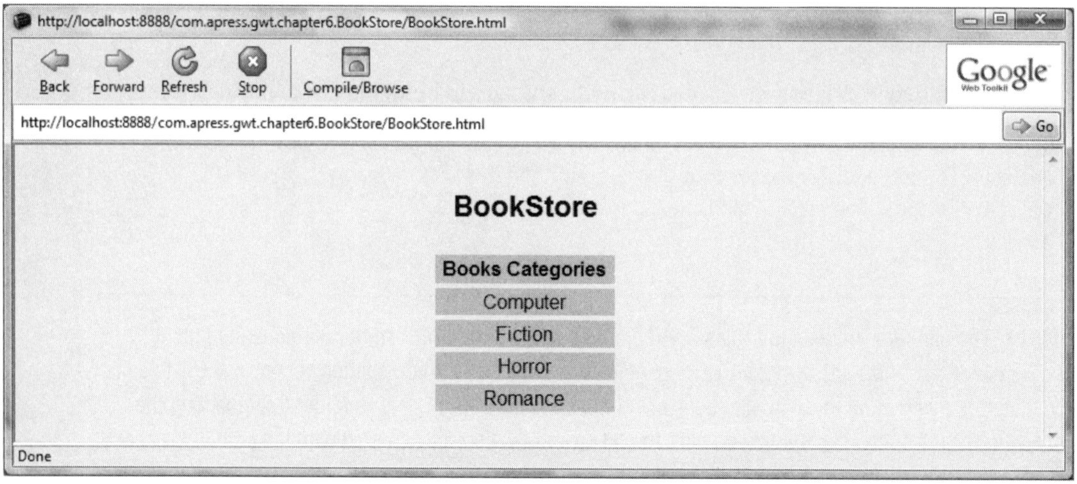

Figure 10-4. *BookStore application displaying the different categories of books available*

Type-Safe Collections by Using Generics

The point to notice in Figure 10-3 is the warning message in the stack trace stating the following:

```
Method public abstract java.lang.String storeOrder(java.util.List books,
    java.lang.String userName)
Deprecated use of gwt.typeArgs for parameter books; Please use
    java.util.List<com.apress.gwt.chapter6.client.Book> as the parameter's type

Method public abstract java.util.List getBooks(java.lang.String category)
Deprecated use of gwt.typeArgs for the return type; Please use
    java.util.List<com.apress.gwt.chapter6.client.Book> as the method's return type
```

The compiler has started throwing a warning message stating that the gwt.typeArgs parameter tag you learned in Chapter 6, which is used for specifying the objects in collections used in your client code, is now deprecated and you should use generics to specify the type of the objects that will be used in the collection classes. You should go ahead and change the BookStoreService class to do exactly this. Listing 10-2 shows the modified BookStoreService class (with changes from the original class in bold).

Listing 10-2. *Modified* BookStoreService *Interface Using Generics to Specify the Objects Contained in Collection Classes Rather the* gwt.typeArgs *Parameter Tag*

```
package com.apress.gwt.chapter6.client;

import java.util.List;

import com.google.gwt.user.client.rpc.RemoteService;

/**
 * @author Vipul Gupta (vipulgupta.vg@gmail.com)
 */
public interface BookStoreService extends RemoteService {

  public List<Book> getBooks(String category);

  public String storeOrder(List<Book> books, String userName);

  public List<Book> addToCart(List<Book> books);
}
```

After making this change, restart the application by using the BookStore-shell.cmd script as explained earlier. The application will execute without any warnings on this run in the embedded web server window that shows the application log and stack trace. Even though there will be *no* further warnings in the embedded web server window of the GWT framework, you would still see some warnings by the Java compiler related to the type safety of collection classes and the AsyncCallback objects used in your application's code. You should modify the BookStoreServiceAsync, BookUtil, and BookStoreServiceImpl classes and add the type of objects used in the lists (Book object in this application) in these classes to ensure type safety. I will explain the new type-safe AsyncCallback object and how to use it next.

The Type-Safe AsyncCallback Object

Even after modifying the List classes (by adding generics to them) in the BookStoreServiceAsync interface, the Java compiler would still throw some warnings related to the AsyncCallback object. The warnings would state that references to the generic type AsyncCallback<T> should be parameterized. This is because the AsyncCallback object has also been made type safe, and you should specify the return type of the RPC method as the type to the corresponding callback object. In other words, the AsyncCallback object should be parameterized with the return type of the RPC call as follows:

AsyncCallback<Return type of the RPC call>

This return type also gets mapped to the parameter of the onSuccess(...) method of the AsyncCallback object, which is defined to handle the response of the RPC call. For example, Listing 10-3 and Listing 10-4 show the StoreOrderCallback class (defined in the com.apress.gwt.chapter6.client.BookStore class) in the BookStore application in its original and modified forms.

Listing 10-3. *Original Version of the* StoreOrderCallback *Class*

```
public class StoreOrderCallback implements AsyncCallback {
    public void onFailure(Throwable caught) {
      GWT.log("Error in storing order.", caught);
      Window.alert("Error in storing order. Try again later.");
    }

    public void onSuccess(Object result) {
      showSuccessMessage((String) result);
    }
}
```

Listing 10-4. *Modified Version of the* StoreOrderCallback *Class (with Changes in Bold)*

```
public class StoreOrderCallback implements AsyncCallback<String> {
    public void onFailure(Throwable caught) {
      GWT.log("Error in storing order.", caught);
      Window.alert("Error in storing order. Try again later.");
    }

    public void onSuccess(String result) {
      showSuccessMessage(result);
    }
}
```

The modified BookListUpdaterCallback class and related changes in the BookStore class are as follows:

```
public class BookStore implements EntryPoint, ClickListener, HistoryListener {
  ...
  private List<Book> booksBeingDisplayed;
  ...
  public class BookListUpdaterCallback implements AsyncCallback<List<Book>> {

    public void onFailure(Throwable caught) {
      GWT.log("Error in retrieving books list.", caught);
      Window.alert("Error in retrieving books list. Try again later.");
    }

    public void onSuccess(List<Book> result) {
      booksBeingDisplayed = result;
      displayBooks(result);
    }
  }
  ...
  private void displayBooks(List<Book> booksList) {
    ...
  }
}
```

Just like the BookListUpdaterCallback, you should also modify the AddToCartCallback
class. Next you should modify the async service interface for the BookStore application.
Listing 10-5 shows the modified BookStoreServiceAsync interface (with changes from
the original class in bold).

Listing 10-5. *Modified* BookStoreServiceAsync *Interface Using Generics to Specify the Objects
Contained in Collection Classes and the Return Type of the RPC Call in the* AsyncCallback *Objects*

```
package com.apress.gwt.chapter6.client;

import java.util.List;

import com.google.gwt.user.client.rpc.AsyncCallback;
import com.google.gwt.user.client.rpc.RemoteService;

/**
 * @author Vipul Gupta (vipulgupta.vg@gmail.com)
 */
public interface BookStoreServiceAsync extends RemoteService {

  public void getBooks(String category, AsyncCallback<List<Book>> callback);

  public void storeOrder(List<Book> books, String userName,
      AsyncCallback<String> callback);

  public void addToCart(List<Book> books, AsyncCallback<List<Book>> callback);
}
```

You should modify the rest of the classes along similar lines and use generics to specify the types of all objects used in the BookStore application. This will make the application more type-safe and less prone to error.

Now let's migrate the LoanServicingSystem application to work with this new library and observe any issues created by the newer version of the framework.

Setting Up the LoanServicingSystem Example on the New Library

Follow the same steps as you did for the BookStore application previously to set up the LoanServicingSystem application using the GWT 1.5 libraries. The only thing to remember for this application is that you should also keep the test folder and all the corresponding test scripts (such as TestLoanServicingSystem-hosted.cmd), and change the path of the GWT library in all these test scripts as well. The new library has introduced some changes in the benchmark-related classes. I'll explain these changes in the context of the LoanServicingSystem application.

New Package for the Benchmark Classes

As soon as you open the LoanServicingSystem project (with modifications to map it to the new library) in Eclipse, you will see some errors in the test folder, specifically in the StructureBenchmark class. A close investigation will reveal that the IDE is throwing errors in finding the Benchmark, IntRange, and Operator classes used in this test. The reason for these errors is that the benchmarking classes have been moved from the com.google.gwt.junit.client package to the com.google.gwt.benchmarks.client package. Fixing the imports at the top of this file to use the new package for these files will remove the compile errors from the project.

The New Annotations for Benchmark Tests

Next go to the command line and start the benchmark tests using the StructureBenchmark-hosted. cmd script as follows:

```
C:\gwt15\LoanServicingSystem>StructureBenchmark-hosted.cmd
```

```
.Rebinding com.apress.gwt.chapter3.client.StructureBenchmark
  Invoking <generate-with
    class='com.google.gwt.benchmarks.rebind.BenchmarkGenerator'/>
      Scanning Benchmarks for deprecated annotations; please see
       com.google.gwt.benchmarks.client.Benchmark for more information
          [WARN] Deprecated use of gwt.benchmark.param at class
            com.apress.gwt.chapter3.client.StructureBenchmark in public void
            testArrayList(java.lang.Integer size); please use the ➥
new Benchmark JDK 1.5
            annotations in com.google.gwt.benchmark.client
          [WARN] Deprecated use of gwt.benchmark.param at class
            com.apress.gwt.chapter3.client.StructureBenchmark in public void
            testHashSet(java.lang.Integer size); please use the new Benchmark JDK 1.5
            annotations in com.google.gwt.benchmark.client
```

```
.
Time: 122.922
```

```
OK (2 tests)
```

Notice the warnings introduced by the compiler about the gwt.benchmark.param parameter tag when it tried to compile and execute the StructureBenchmark class. Chapter 7 explained the @gwt.benchmark.param parameter tag, which is used in the accompanying Javadoc of the method for specifying the name of the parameter that covers the range of values across which the tests would be run. The new 1.5 release has introduced a few Java annotations that can be used for simplifying your development needs.

Instead of the gwt.benchmark.param parameter tag, you use the @RangeField annotation (defined in the com.google.gwt.benchmarks.client package) for the function parameter. Similar to the gwt.benchmark.param parameter tag, this annotation will specify the name of the variable that contains the range across which the tests need to be run. The original version of the testHashSet(...) method is as follows:

```
/**
 * @gwt.benchmark.param size = sizeRange
 */
public void testHashSet(Integer size) {
    ...
}
```

The modified version of the testHashSet(...) method is as follows:

```
public void testHashSet(@RangeField("sizeRange") Integer size) {
    ...
}
```

You should also modify the testArrayList(...) method in a similar manner as well. After you've modified these two methods by using the @RangeField annotation, you should execute the application again as follows to confirm that no further warnings are thrown by the compiler:

```
C:\gwt15\LoanServicingSystem>StructureBenchmark-hosted.cmd
..
Time: 51.174
```

```
OK (2 tests)
```

The tests run with no further warnings. A number of other annotations related to the benchmark test are introduced by the new version of the library. All these annotations are defined in the com.google.gwt.benchmarks.client package and are as follows:

@IterationTimeLimit: This annotation specifies a custom time limit for the maximum amount of time for which each iteration of your benchmark test method is allowed to run. If this limit is exceeded by a particular iteration, then the test is stopped, and the iteration skips to the next set of values in the range. (A value of 0 signifies that all values in the range will be exhaustively tested without any upper bound on the amount of time to be used for each iteration of your test.)

@RangeField: This annotation specifies a field containing the entire range of values for a parameter to a method. The field must belong to the same class in which this annotation is used. The field must be either an Iterable, Enum, or array whose type matches the parameter being annotated.

@RangeEnum: This is similar to the @RangeField annotation; this annotation specifies an Enum class that contains the entire range of values for a parameter to a method.

@Setup: This annotation specifies a setup method that will be executed before the annotated test method. Setup methods are automatically executed by the benchmarking framework before their matching test methods, and the time taken by these methods is excluded from the final benchmark reports. (Chapter 7 mentioned begin[TestMethodName] and end[TestMethodName], which were used for the same purpose of specifying the setup and teardown logic. The @Setup annotation gives you the flexibility to name your setup and teardown methods without any restrictions whatsoever.)

@Teardown: This annotation specifies a teardown method that will be executed after the annotated test method. Teardown methods are automatically executed by the benchmarking framework after their matching test methods, and the time taken by these methods is excluded from the final benchmark reports.

Listing 10-6 shows the modified StructureBenchmark class, demonstrating the use of some of these annotations.

Listing 10-6. *Modified* StructureBenchmark *Class Demonstrating the Use of Some of the New Annotations (in Bold)*

```
package com.apress.gwt.chapter3.client;

import java.util.ArrayList;
import java.util.HashSet;

import com.google.gwt.benchmarks.client.Benchmark;
import com.google.gwt.benchmarks.client.IntRange;
import com.google.gwt.benchmarks.client.IterationTimeLimit;
import com.google.gwt.benchmarks.client.Operator;
import com.google.gwt.benchmarks.client.RangeField;
import com.google.gwt.benchmarks.client.Setup;
/**
 * @author Vipul Gupta (vipulgupta.vg@gmail.com)
 */
public class StructureBenchmark extends Benchmark {

  public HashSet<Integer> hashSet = new HashSet<Integer>();
  public ArrayList<Integer> arrayList = new ArrayList<Integer>();
```

```
final IntRange sizeRange = new IntRange(10000, 15500, Operator.ADD, 200);

/**
 * Must refer to a valid module that sources this class.
 */
public String getModuleName() {
  return "com.apress.gwt.chapter3.LoanServicingSystem";
}

/**
 * Populates the ArrayList with integers 0 <= x <= size
 *
 * @param size Upper limit of the integers to add in the structure
 */
public void populateArrayList(Integer size) {
  arrayList.clear();
  for (int i = 0; i <= size.intValue(); i++)
    arrayList.add(i);
}

/**
 * Populates the HashSet with integers 0 <= x <= size
 *
 * @param size Upper limit of the integers to add in the structure
 */
public void populateHashSet(Integer size) {
  hashSet.clear();
  for (int i = 0; i <= size.intValue(); i++)
    hashSet.add(i);
}

/**
 * JUnit requires a method that takes no arguments. It is not used for
 * Benchmarking.
 */
public void testArrayList() {
}

@Setup("populateArrayList")
@IterationTimeLimit(1000)
public void testArrayList(@RangeField("sizeRange") Integer size) {
  for (int i = 1; i < size.intValue(); i++) {
    arrayList.contains(i);
  }
}
```

```
  public void testHashSet() {
  }

  @Setup("populateHashSet")
  @IterationTimeLimit(1000)
  public void testHashSet(@RangeField("sizeRange") Integer size) {
    for (int i = 1; i < size.intValue(); i++) {
      hashSet.contains(i);
    }
  }
}
```

Setting Up the AdvancedWidgets (ImageGallery) Example on the New Library

Follow the same steps as you did for the BookStore and LoanServicingSystem applications previously to set up the AdvancedWidgets application using the GWT 1.5 libraries. The new library has introduced a new annotation for using an ImageBundle. In the next section, you'll use this annotation in the context of the AdvancedWidgets application.

The New Resource Annotation for ImageBundle

Once the project is opened in Eclipse, run the AdvancedWidgets application (assuming that, as mentioned in Chapter 1, the Build Automatically setting of your Eclipse IDE is enabled) by double-clicking the AdvancedWidgets-shell.cmd script. The application will start up in the hosted window and will throw some warnings in the corresponding log window as follows:

```
Rebinding com.apress.gwt.chapter5.client.images.GalleryImages
    Invoking <generate-with ➥
      class='com.google.gwt.user.rebind.ui.ImageBundleGenerator'/>
        Analyzing method 'getPinkThumbnail' beginning on line 8 of ➥
          C:\gwt15\AdvancedWidgets\src\com\apress\gwt\chapter5\client\➥
          images\FlowerImages.java
            Use of @gwt.resource in javadoc is deprecated; use the ➥
              annotation ImageBundle.@Resource instead
```

The compiler has started throwing a warning message stating that the gwt.resource parameter that you learned in Chapter 5, which is used for specifying the resource corresponding to a method in your ImageBundle, is now deprecated and you should use the new ImageBundle.@Resource annotation to specify the resource that should be used for a specific method in the ImageBundle. Go ahead and change the FlowerImages interface to do exactly this. Listing 10-7 and Listing 10-8 show the original and modified FlowerImages interface.

Listing 10-7. *Original Version of the* FlowerImages *Interface*

```
package com.apress.gwt.chapter5.client.images;

import com.google.gwt.user.client.ui.AbstractImagePrototype;
import com.google.gwt.user.client.ui.ImageBundle;

/**
 * Interface representing the ImageBundle for the AdvancedWidgets application.
 *
 * @author Vipul Gupta (vipulgupta.vg@gmail.com)
 */
public interface FlowerImages extends ImageBundle {

  /**
   * The metadata tag contains no '/' characters, so pink.jpg
   * must be located in the same package as FlowerImages.
   *
   * @gwt.resource pink.jpg
   */
  public AbstractImagePrototype getPinkThumbnail();

  public AbstractImagePrototype red();
  public AbstractImagePrototype yellow();
  public AbstractImagePrototype white();
}
```

Listing 10-8. *Modified Version of the* FlowerImages *Interface (with the Use of the New Annotation in Bold)*

```
package com.apress.gwt.chapter5.client.images;

import com.google.gwt.user.client.ui.AbstractImagePrototype;
import com.google.gwt.user.client.ui.ImageBundle;

/**
 * Interface representing the ImageBundle for the AdvancedWidgets application.
 *
 * @author Vipul Gupta (vipulgupta.vg@gmail.com)
 */
public interface FlowerImages extends ImageBundle {

  /**
   * If the path is unqualified (that is, if it contains no slashes), then it is
   * sought in the package enclosing the image bundle to which the annotation is
   * attached. If the path is qualified, then it is expected that the string can
   * be passed verbatim to ClassLoader.getResource()
   */
```

```
@ Resource("pink.jpg")
public AbstractImagePrototype getPinkThumbnail();

public AbstractImagePrototype red();
public AbstractImagePrototype yellow();
public AbstractImagePrototype white();
}
```

Just like Listing 10-8, you should also modify the IconImages interface (created in Chapter 9) in the com.apress.gwt.chapter5.client.images package to use the @Resource annotation. Once all these changes are made, you should run the application again to confirm that no further warnings are thrown by the compiler.

Exploring the Output Structure of Compilation with the New Release

Let's compare the output generated when we compile the LoanServicingSystem application using the two different versions of the library.

Using the 1.4.61 version of the GWT library, you get the following output:

```
C:\gwt\LoanServicingSystem>LoanServicingSystem-compile.cmd
Output will be written into ➡
    C:\gwt\LoanServicingSystem\www\com.apress.gwt.chapter3.LoanServicingSystem
Copying all files found on public path
Compilation succeeded
```

Using the 1.5 version of the GWT library, you get the following output:

```
C:\gwt15\LoanServicingSystem>LoanServicingSystem-compile.cmd
Compiling module com.apress.gwt.chapter3.LoanServicingSystem
Compilation succeeded
Linking compilation into ➡
    C:\gwt15\LoanServicingSystem\www\com.apress.gwt.chapter3.LoanServicingSystem
```

Notice the statement about the linking compilation in the output generated by the newer version. I will discuss this in just a moment, but let's first deploy and test the application on the Tomcat web server, as you did in Chapter 9.

Recall the "Deploying a GWT-Based Application" section from Chapter 9 where you learned the steps for structuring your application for deployment on an external web server. Steps 1 and 2 of that section mentioned that you need to pick up the contents of the C:\gwt\ LoanServicingSystem\www\com.apress.gwt.chapter3.LoanServicingSystem folder and clean up the intermittent compiler-generated files that are not required for deployment purposes. The 1.5 release actually does this cleaning-up job for you by putting the intermittent compiler-generated output files in a separate folder. The output of the compilation step with the new release goes into the following folders:

C:\gwt15\LoanServicingSystem\www\com.apress.gwt.chapter3.LoanServicingSystem: The standard project output goes here. You need to use the contents of this folder for deployment purposes.

`C:\gwt15\.gwt-tmp\compiler\com.apress.gwt.chapter3.LoanServicingSystem`: The intermittent output generated by the compiler goes into two separate folders here. The files in this folder are *not* required to be used for deployment purposes. The two subfolders of this folder are as follows:

- `compilations`: This folder stores the JavaScript compilations created by the compiler. These files are used to generate the final output files in the `C:\gwt15\LoanServicingSystem\www\com.apress.gwt.chapter3.LoanServicingSystem` folder.

- `generated`: As the name suggests, this folder stores the files generated by the compiler for the application. For example, the `.rpc` files (for Serializable types) and the `.png` files (for ImageBundle) are created in this folder.

The only thing you need to do differently for deploying the application generated by the 1.5 version of the library is to ignore step 2 from the "Deploying a GWT-Based Application" section in Chapter 9; in addition, for step 3, you should copy the files created in the `C:\gwt15\LoanServicingSystem\www\com.apress.gwt.chapter3.LoanServicingSystem` folder as explained previously in this section. You should try this exercise to see your application running as smoothly as it was with the 1.4.61 library.

Now I'll discuss the linkers mentioned in the compilation output in the GWT 1.5 library. Recall from Chapter 2 that the GWT compiler also creates an `xs.nocache.js` file that is the cross-site bootstrap file and other scripts for the cross-site version of the application. However, having both the standard and cross-site output in every deployment is not required because in most cases you would generally deploy either the standard or the cross-site version of the application. The new library allows you to create different outputs for different requirements by using corresponding linkers for them. Linkers basically create a different set of output for different requirements.

By default, the standard linker (abbreviated `std` in the library) is used. If you want to create a cross-site (abbreviated `xs` in the GWT library) style of output for your applications, then you can use the newly introduced `<add-linker>` tag in the module's XML file and add the `xs` linker to the module. The modified module XML file for the LoanServicingSystem application (`LoanServicingSystem.gwt.xml`), with the `add-linker` property in bold, is as follows:

```
<module>
    <!-- Inherit the core Web Toolkit stuff.  -->
    <inherits name='com.google.gwt.user.User'/>

    <inherits name="com.google.gwt.http.HTTP"/>

    <add-linker name="xs"/>

    <!-- Specify the app entry point class.              -->
    <entry-point class='com.apress.gwt.chapter3.client.LoanServicingSystem'/>

    <stylesheet src="LoanServicingSystem.css" />

    <servlet path="/LoanRequestService"
        class="com.apress.gwt.chapter3.server.LoanRequestServiceImpl"/>
</module>
```

If you compile the application again (after adding the xs linker in the module's XML file) by using the LoanServicingSystem-compile.cmd script, then the compiler output would be as follows:

```
C:\gwt15\LoanServicingSystem>LoanServicingSystem-compile.cmd
Compiling module com.apress.gwt.chapter3.LoanServicingSystem
Compilation succeeded
Linking compilation into➥
    C:\gwt15\LoanServicingSystem\www\com.apress.gwt.chapter3.LoanServicingSystem
```

With the cross-site linker added to the application, the compiler created the cross-site version of the application in the same folder as was done for the standard linker. One thing to notice in the output of the cross-site linker is that instead of creating an xs.nocache.js file (in version 1.4.61), the bootstrap file of the cross-site version of the application also has the extension of nocache.js. In effect, the compiler now creates only one version of the application, the standard or the cross-site, based on the linker added into your application. You should go ahead and compile the application in both standard and cross-site modes and observe the changes in the output.

■**Note** If you have a GWT application that is hosted on a server different from the one on which it is embedded, then the same-origin policy (explained in Chapter 2) will restrict referencing the .nocache.js file in your <script> tag. This is where the cross-site version of the application comes to the rescue. You can use the module's xs.nocache.js file (or the nocache.js file generated by the cross-site linker in 1.5 version of the framework) to overcome this problem. For example, if you host your application on http://apress.com but want to use it from http://books.apress.com, then the cross-site version of the bootstrap file (xs.nocache.js in 1.4.61 or nocache.js created by cross site linker in 1.5) needs to be used on the page on http://books.apress.com.

Summary

This chapter examined some of the changes in the upcoming 1.5 release of the GWT framework. The main focus of the 1.5 release is the support for Java 5.0 language syntax and constructs for the client code of the application, and I gave a demonstration of how to use these constructs in the client code. The addition of the Java 5.0 language constructs and syntax gives developers of the GWT framework the opportunity to make the client-side code more type-safe. Generics have been added to a large number of classes to achieve this. This chapter also explained the changes you need to make in the RPC code and AsyncCallback classes, which are required to make use of these new features introduced by the GWT framework. The newer version of the library also added Java annotations for declaring certain functionalities. The newly added Java annotations for benchmark tests were explained as part of this chapter. The chapter finished with a brief summary of the changes made in the output structure and how you can use linkers to create different outputs for different requirements in the compile step.

Index

■Symbols

@IterationTimeLimit annotation, 275
@RangeEnum annotation, 276
@RangeField annotation, 275–276
@Resource annotation, 278, 280
@Setup annotation, 276
@Teardown annotation, 276
<add-linker> tag, 281
<inherits> tag, 259
<meta> tag, setting locale client property using, 208, 228
<source> tag, 258
<super-source> tag, 258–259

■A

AbstractImagePrototype, 120
adapter classes, 108, 109
add method (TabPanel class), 118
ADD method (Operator class), 191
addCheckPoint method (GWTTestCase class), 176
addHistoryListener method (History class), 235
<add-linker> tag, 281
addMouseListeners method, 126
addStyleDependentName method (UIObject class), 62
addStyleName method (UIObject class), 61–62
addXXXListener method (FocusWidget class), 64
AdvancedWidgets example. *See* ImageBundles
annotations in Java 1.5 library, 275–276, 278, 280
Ant build files, creating, 7–8
applicationCreator utility, 8, 11, 259, 269
applications
    bootstrap process, 52–54
    building, 9, 127, 129, 246–247
    creating, 6–9, 11, 16–22, 136–146
    cross-site/standard, 281–282
    deploying, 245–248, 280–281
    directory structure, 245, 247
    modules. *See* modules
    naming, 270
    optimization. *See* ImageBundles
    running, 6, 9–11, 22–24, 51, 127, 215–218, 225
    structure, standard, 7
    widgets, adding, 114–115
applyTo method (AbstractImagePrototype class), 120
arithmetic classes, 29
array classes, 30
ASCII character set, 203–204
AsyncCallback class, 91–93, 95–96, 185, 187–188, 251, 272–274
asynchronous code, testing, 175, 176, 184–189
asynchronous communication, 89–90
asynchronous interface, creating, 91, 94–95, 140–143, 149–150
autocompile, 9

■B

back method (History class), 235
begin methods in benchmark testing, 198, 276
Benchmark class, 189–191
benchmark testing
    annotations in Java 1.5 library, 275–276, 278, 280
    begin/end methods, 198, 276
    benefits, 191
    classes, 6, 189–191, 274–275
    described, 189
    example, 192–194, 196–198
    process, 189–190
    setup methods, 276
    teardown methods, 276
    time limits, 275
benchmarkViewer tool, 6, 190
binding, deferred, 35–36, 52

bookstore example
  asynchronous interface, 149–150
  controller class, 150
  creating, 147
  CSS style sheet, 158
  described, 147
  domain objects, creating, 147
  entry-point class, 151, 156
  history support, 234, 236, 242–245
  HTML file, 159
  running, 160–161, 254–255
  server sessions, 250–254
  server-side implementation, 156
  service interface, 148–149
  version 1.5 feature alterations, 269–274
  XML file, 158
bootstrap process, 52–54
branch method, 37
browsers
  deferred binding for, 35
  embedded web, 28
  GWT support, 3
  web server communication, 34
  windows dimensions, properties for
    getting, 35
Build Automatically options, 247
button events, 106
button widgets, 59–60, 66, 105, 110–111
ButtonBase class, 64

C

.cache.html files, 52, 54
.cache.js files, 54
.cache.xml files, 53–54, 247
callback functions, 89, 91–92, 95–96, 141, 143.
    See also AsyncCallback class
cancel method (Timer class), 20
catchExceptions method (GWTTestCase
    class), 176
CellPanel class, 72–76
center widgets, 72
ChangeListener, 107
character sets, 203–204
characters, defined, 203
CharSequence interface, 29
check boxes, storing state in history, 244
CheckBox widgets, 66, 110, 131
class file storage, 259
class libraries, 28–30, 31, 134

classes
  adding outside directory structure,
    258–259
  declaring method in, 41–42
  from java packages, 28–30
clearCheckpoints method (GWTTestCase
    class), 176
click events, receiving, 64
ClickListener, 107
client packages, 11
Cloneable interface, 29
coded character sets, defined, 203
collection classes, 30, 146
commit method, 37
Commons FileUpload library, 134
Comparable interface, 29
compilers
  GWTCompiler, 9, 100, 223, 280–281
  Java-to-JavaScript, 27–28
compiling projects, 9, 127, 129, 246–247
Composite class, 79–80
composites, 79, 80, 86–87. *See also* TabPanel
    widgets
Constants interface (I18N module), 205–206,
    218–221, 226
ConstantsWithLookup interface (I18N
    module), 205–206, 226–228
container widgets, 79, 80, 86–87. *See also*
    TabPanel widgets
controller classes, 142–143, 150
country code, ISO, 207
createImage method
    (AbstractImagePrototype class), 120
cross-site applications, linking, 281–282
CSS, styling UIObject classes, 61–62, 85,
    110–116, 158
CSS Style classes, 158
currency localization, 230–231
custom serializable objects, 135, 162,
    163–165

D

data type classes, 29
date classes, 30
date localization, 230–231
DateTimeFormat class, 230–231
dead code elimination, 28
debugging, 3, 28
decode method (URL class), 167

deferred binding, 35–36, 52
delayTestFinish method (GWTTestCase
      class), 176, 185–186, 188, 191
dependent style rules for widgets, 62–63
deploying applications, 245–248, 280–281
deserialize method (Serializer objects), 165
development tools
      GWTCompiler, 9, 100, 223, 280–281
      embedded web browser, 27–28
DialogBox widgets, 110–112
Dictionary class (I18N module), 205–206,
      229–230
directory structure, web-based applications,
      245, 247
DockPanel widgets, 72, 75–76, 116
dynamic class loading, 34–35
dynamic string internationalization, 206

E

Eclipse property of Build Automatically, 247
Eclipse window, refreshing, 212
encode method (URL class), 167
encodeComponent method (URL class), 167
encoding, character, 203–204
end methods in benchmark testing, 198, 276
entry-point class, 12–13, 16, 18–19, 49–50,
      151, 156
error classes, 29
error events, 106
escape method, 36
escaped string content, 36
Event class, 106
EventListener, 107
eventObject class, 30
events, 64, 105–108, 126
exception classes, 29–30
extend-property property, 15

F

fail method, 188
files, uploading, 131, 134
FileUpload widgets, 131
final fields, 136
finishTest method (GWTTestCase class), 176,
      185–186, 191
FirstApplication-compile.cmd, 11
FirstApplication-shell.cmd, 9–11
FlexTable widgets, 76–78, 110, 126
flower images example, 121–124, 126–129

FlowPanels, 78–79
focus events, 106
FocusListener, 107–108
FocusWidget class, 64
format method (NumberFormat class), 230
FormPanels, 130–131, 134
forms, 130. *See also* FormPanels
forward method (History class), 235
Frame widgets, 110
framework components
      class libraries, 28–30, 31, 134
      compilers, 9, 100, 223, 280–281
      embedded web browser, 27–28
      testing, 171–172, 175, 184–185, 190, 193

G

gen flag, GWTCompiler, 100
generate method (generator class), 36
generator class
      autogenerate example, 39–44, 49–52
      creating objects via, 36
      described, 36
      methods, 36
      remote service objects, 100–101, 103
      for RPC-related code, 146
GeneratorContext interface, 37
generics, 271–274
GET HTTP request, 166
get method (Dictionary class), 229
get method (RootPanel class), 72
get methods (ConstantsWithLookup
      interface), 227–228
get methods (NumberFormat class), 230–231
getBodyElement method (RootPanel class),
      72
getCheckpoints method (GWTTestCase
      class), 176
getDictionary method (Dictionary class), 229
getField method, 38
getFields method, 38
getHTML method (ButtonBase class), 64
getHTML method (AbstractImagePrototype
      class), 120
getMetaData method, 38
getMetaDataTags method, 38
getMethods method, 38
getModuleBaseURL method, 126
getModuleName method (GWTTestCase
      class), 175–176, 178, 184

getName method (HasName interface), 131
getPackage method (JClassType), 38
getPackage method (TypeOracle), 38
getParent method (Widget class), 63
getPattern method (NumberFormat class), 230
getPropertyOracle method, 37
getPropertyValue method, 38
getSubtypes method, 38
getTestResults method (GWTTestCase class), 176
getText method (ButtonBase class), 64
getThreadLocalRequest method (RemoteServiceServlet class), 249–250
getThreadLocalResponse method (RemoteServiceServlet class), 250
getToken method (History class), 235
getType method, 38
getTypeOracle method, 37
Google Web Toolkit (GWT)
    advantages, 1, 3
    described, 1, 3
    files for, 6
    modes, 4–6, 28, 99, 174
    setting up, 4, 8
    version, 31
Google Web Toolkit (GWT) 1.5 release
    annotations, 275–276, 278, 280
    AsyncCallback objects, 272–274
    compilation output, 280–281
    download location, 266
    generics, 271–274
    ImageBundle changes, 278–280
    Java 1.5 support, 265, 267–275
Grid widgets, 76–77, 110, 126
GWT. See Google Web Toolkit
gwt directory, 8
gwt-benchmark-viewer.jar file, 6
GWTCompiler, 9, 100, 223, 280–281
GWT.create method, 35–36, 40–41
gwt-dev-linux.jar file, 6, 23
gwt-dev-windows.jar file, 6, 23, 43
gwt.js files, 54
gwt.key property, 42, 219–220, 222
gwt.rpc files, 54
gwt-servlet.jar file, 6, 247
GWTShell class, 6, 11, 22–23
GWTTestCase class, 175–176, 178, 185, 189
gwt-user.jar file, 6, 23

H

HashMaps, 161–162
HasName interface, 131
Hidden widgets, 131
history, GWT application, 54
History class, 235
history support, 15–16, 234–236, 242–244
history.html files, 54, 247
HistoryListener class, 235, 245
HorizontalPanels, 72–73
host HTML file, 99
hosted mode, 4–6, 9–11, 22–24, 28, 99, 174
HTML elements, CSS style classes, 110
HTML files, 15–16, 21–22, 51, 159
HTML widgets, 110, 245
HTMLTable widgets, 76–78, 110–111
HTTP requests, server communication via, 166–167
HyperLink widgets, 110, 244–245

I

i18n (internationalization). See internationalization
I18N module, 204–208, 213, 218–221, 222–224, 226–228
i18nCreator utility, 9, 209–211, 218, 225–226
iframe element for history support, 235, 242–243
image gallery ImageBundle example, 121–124, 126–129
Image widgets, 110
ImageBundleGenerator, 119–120
ImageBundles
    advantages, 119–120, 256
    creating, 120, 257
    described, 119–120
    example, 121–124, 126–129
    of ImageBundles, 256–258
    process, 129–130
    uses, 233
    version 1.5 library features, 278–280
images, naming, 120
inherits property, 14
<inherits> tag, 259
initWidget method (Composite class), 79–80
input box widgets, 59–60
instantiate method (Serializer objects), 164
internationalization
    character encoding, 203–204
    compiler effects, 223

Constants interface, 205–206, 218–221, 226
ConstantsWithLookup interface, 205–206, 226–228
creating application with, 209–215
dates/times/numbers/currency, 230–231
described, 201–202
development practices, 202–204
Dictionary class, 205–206, 229–230
dynamic string, 206
entry-point class, 214–215, 221, 224
extend-property property, 15
GWT support, 204–205
HTML file, 213–214, 228–230
Localizable interface, 205–208
localization compared, 202
mapping interface, 212–213
Messages interface, 205–206, 222–224
properties files, 210–211, 213, 217
running application, 215–218, 222, 225
static string, 205–206
tools for, 9, 209–211, 218, 225–226
XML file, 208, 213
IntRange class, 191, 274
isAttached method (Widget class), 63
isEnabled method (FocusWidget class), 64
isLoggable method, 37
IsSerializable interface, 30, 54, 136, 148, 162
isVisible method (UIObject class), 61
Iterable class, 190
@IterationTimeLimit annotation, 275
iterator interfaces, 30
iterator method (IntRange class), 191

■J
JAR files, adding to classpath, 181–182
Java class files, 247
Java classes, supported, 27
Java language
    annotations, 275–276, 278, 280
    binding in, 35
    support, current version, 31, 33
    version 1.5 features, 265, 267–275
Java source code, bundling, 259
Java Virtual Machine (JVM), 28
JavaScript language, characteristics, 35
java.util.Properties class, 39
javax.servlet.http.HttpServletRequest, 249
JClassType class, 38
JRE emulation library, 28–30

JUnit testing framework, 171–172, 175, 184–185, 190, 193
junitCreator utility, 9, 172–174, 189
JVM (Java Virtual Machine), 28

■K
keyboard events, 64, 106
KeyboardListener, 107–108
KEYEVENTS, 105
keySet method (Dictionary class), 229
KitchenSink sample application, 70

■L
l10n (localization), 202. See also internationalization
Label widgets, 61, 66, 110. See also text label widgets
language code, ISO, 207
laying out, 70, 72–79
linking, cross-site/standard application, 281–282
links, internal/external, 110, 244–245
ListBox widgets, 69–70, 110, 131
listener interfaces, 30
listener objects, 106–108. See also adapter classes
load events, 106
LoadListener, 107
loan request/servicing system example
    composites, 80
    cross-site linking, 281
    custom serialization, 162, 164–165
    deploying, 246–248
    entry-point class, 85
    host HTML file, 84
    HTTP communication, 167
    listener use, 107–108
    running, 86, 248–249
    server communication, 136–146
    style sheets, including, 113–114
    TabPanel use, 116–119
    testing, 172–175, 177–184, 186, 189
    version 1.5 feature alterations, 274–275
locale client property, 207–208, 213, 216, 222
Localizable interface (I18N module), 205–208, 213
localization, 202. See also internationalization
log method, 37

■M

MenuBar widgets, 110
Messages interface (I18N module), 205–206, 222–224
<meta> tag, setting locale client property using, 208, 228
method calls inlining, 28
mock callback objects, use in testing, 187–189
modes, GWT, 4–6, 28, 99, 174
module configuration files, 97
moduleName.gwt.xml file, 11–12
modules
    adding to applications, 15–18
    described, 11–12
    file contents/structure, 11–12
    inheriting, 14
    reuse, 259, 260–262
    tags, 12–15
mouse events, 64, 105–106, 126
mouseEnter method, 124
mouseLeave method, 124
MouseListener, 107–109, 126
MouseListenerAdapter, 109
MULTIPLY method (Operator class), 191

■N

new command, 36
newItem method (History class), 235
news-serving client example, 17–24, 31–33, 267–268
nextBoolean method, Random, 21
nextDouble method, Random, 21
nextInt method, Random, 21
.nocache.js files, 54, 282
notify method, unavailability, 29
notifyAll method, unavailability, 29
NumberFormat class, 230–231
numbers, localization, 230
numeric classes, 29

■O

objects
    creating new, 36
    serializable, 54, 135–136, 148, 162, 163–165
onAttach method (Widget class), 63
onBeforeRequestDeserialized method (RemoteServiceServlet class), 250
onBeforeTabSelected method (Widget class), 107

onBrowserEvent method (Widget class), 63, 107
onCellClicked method (Widget class), 107
onChange method (Widget class), 107
onClick method (Widget class), 107
onDetach method (Widget class), 63
onError method (Widget class), 107
onFailure method (AsyncCallback class), 92, 188
onFocus method (Widget class), 107
onHistoryChanged method (History class), 235–236
onHistoryChanged method (HistoryListener class), 245
onKeyDown method (Widget class), 107
onKeyPress method (Widget class), 107
onKeyUp method (Widget class), 107
onLoad method (Widget class), 63, 107
onLostFocus method (Widget class), 107
onModuleLoad method (Entry-point classes), 12, 16, 18, 20
onMouseDown method (Widget class), 107
onMouseEnter method (Widget class), 107
onMouseLeave method (Widget class), 107
onMouseMove method (Widget class), 107
onMouseUp method (Widget class), 107
onPopupClosed method (Widget class), 107
onScroll method (Widget class), 107
onSuccess method (AsyncCallback class), 92–93, 187–188
onTabSelected method (Widget class), 107
onTreeItemSelected method (Widget class), 107
onTreeItemStateChanged method (Widget class), 107
onUnload method (Widget class), 63
open source libraries, releases, 266
Operator class, 191, 274
optimization, application. *See* ImageBundles

■P

packaging modules for reuse, 259, 260–262
panels, 70, 71, 72–79, 112, 116–119
PasswordTextBox widgets, 69, 110, 131
PopupListener, 107
POST HTTP request, 166
primary style rules for widgets, 61–63
projectCreator utility, 7–8, 269
projects. *See* applications
properties files, 39, 210–211, 213, 217, 219, 222–223, 226–228

PropertyFileReader example, 39–44, 49–52, 260–262
PropertyOracle interface, 38
public packages, 11
public property, 14
PushButton widgets, 67, 110

■Q–R

query string, setting locale client property using, 208

RadioButton widgets, 67, 110, 131
Random class, 21
@RangeEnum annotation, 276
@RangeField annotation, 275–276
read data methods (SerializationStreamReader interface), 163
reflection, 34–36
remote method invocation (RMI), 89. *See also* remote procedure calls
remote procedure calls (RPCs)
  asynchronous communication, 89–90
  controller classes, 142–143, 150
  creating application with, 136–146
  creating asynchronous interface, 91, 94–95, 140–143, 149–150
  creating service interface, 90–91, 94–95, 140, 143, 148–149
  example implementation, 93–97, 99–100
  making, 92–93, 97
  same origin policy restrictions, 34
  server-side implementation, 144–146
  testing, 14
  uses, 89, 135
remote service. *See* server sessions
RemoteService interface, 90, 100–101, 103
RemoteServiceServlet class, 249–250
removeFromParent method (Widget class), 63
removeHistoryListener method (History class), 235
removeStyleDependentName method (UIObject class), 62
removeStyleName method (UIObject class), 62
removeXXXListener method (FocusWidget class), 64
REPORT_PATH field (Benchmark class), 191
RequestBuilder class, 166–167

@Resource annotation, 278, 280
résumé upload service example, 131, 134
reuse, module, 259, 260–262
RichTextArea widget, 70
RMI (remote method invocation), 89. *See also* remote procedure calls
RootPanel class, 21, 72
RPCs. *See* remote procedure calls
run method (GWTTestCase class), 176
run method (Timer class), 20
runTest method (GWTTestCase class), 176

■S

same origin policy, 32–34, 282
same site policy, 32–34, 282
schedule method (Timer class), 20
scheduleRepeating method (Timer class), 20
script property, 15
ScrollListener, 107
selection list widgets, 59–60
sendRequest method (RequestBuilder class), 166
Serializable classes, 136
Serializable objects, 54, 135–136, 148, 162, 163–165
serialization, 135. *See also* remote procedure calls
SerializationStreamReader interface, 163
SerializationStreamWriter interface, 162
serialize method (Serializer objects), 164–165
server communication, 166–167. *See also* remote procedure calls
server packages, 11
server sessions, 249–255
server-side implementation of service interface, 142–143, 150
ServiceDefTarget interface, 188
ServiceInterfaceProxyGenerator class, 146. *See also* generator class
servlet property, 14–15
setElement method (UIObject class), 60–61
setElement method (Widget class), 63
setEnabled method (FocusWidget class), 64
setHeader method (RequestBuilder class), 166
setHTML method (ButtonBase class), 64
setName method (HasName interface), 131
setPassword method (RequestBuilder class), 166
setSize method (UIObject class), 61

setStyleName method (UIObject class),
    61–62
setStylePrimaryName method (UIObject
    class), 62
setText method (ButtonBase class), 64
setTimeoutMillis method (RequestBuilder
    class), 166
@Setup annotation, 276
setup costs, execution, 190, 198–199
setup method (TestCase class), 190
setUser method (RequestBuilder class), 166
setVisibleCount method (ListBox class), 70
single origin policy, 32–34, 282
source objects, 106
source property, 14
<source> tag, 258
StackPanel, 112
standard applications, linking, 281–282
static string internationalization, 205–206
std (standard linker), 281
stepping function (Operator class), 191
string interning, 28
string-handling classes, 29
stylesheet property, 15
styling UIObject classes, 61–62, 85, 110–116,
    158
<super-source> tag, 258–259
synchronized keyword, 29
synchronous communication, 89
synchronous interface, creating, 90–91,
    94–95, 140, 143, 148–149
system classes, 29

■T
TabBar widgets, 110, 114–116
tabbed pages, 112, 116–119
TableListener, 107
TabListener, 107, 116
TabPanel widgets, 112, 116–119
tags, module file, 12–15
@Teardown annotation, 276
teardown costs, execution, 190, 198–199
teardown methods, 190, 276
TestCase class (JUnit), 190
testing. See also benchmark testing;
    GWTTestCase class
  asynchronous code, 175, 176, 184–189
  benefits, 171
  JUnit testing framework, 171–172, 175,
    184–185, 190, 193
  manual set up, 178–179
  mock callback object use, 187–189
  open source frameworks, 171
  remote procedure calls, 14
  running from command line, 179, 184, 196
  running from Eclipse, 179–183
  strategies, 171
  test cases, 171
  unit, 171, 174–175, 177–179
  user interface code, 175
  utilities, 9, 172–174, 189
text label widgets, 59–60
TextArea widgets, 68–69, 110, 131
TextBox widgets, 68, 110, 131
TextBoxBase class, 65
time classes, 30
time limits in benchmark testing, 275
Timer class, 20, 184–186
times, localization, 230–231
ToggleButton widgets, 68
Tomcat web server, 248
transient fields, 136
Tree widgets, 110
TreeItem widgets, 110
TreeListener, 107
TreeLogger interface, 37
TreeLogger.Type enum, 37
tryCreate method, 37
typeArgs annotation, 146
TypeOracle class, 38

■U
UCS (Universal Character Set), 203–204
UCS/Unicode Transformation Format, 204
UIObject class, 60–63
undefined events, 106
Unicode character set, 203–204
unit testing, 171, 174–175, 177–179
Universal Character Set (UCS), 203–204
URL class, 166–167
URLs, 23, 33, 126
user interface code, testing, 175
User module, 259
user-interface widgets. See widgets
UTF-8 character set, 204

■V
values method (Dictionary class), 229
VerticalPanels, 72, 74